THE POLITICS
OF INTERNATIONAL
CREDIT

J. ANDREW SPINDLER

THE POLITICS
OF INTERNATIONAL
CREDIT

*Private Finance and Foreign Policy
in Germany and Japan*

THE BROOKINGS INSTITUTION
Washington, D.C.

Copyright © 1984 by

THE BROOKINGS INSTITUTION

1775 Massachusetts Ave. N.W., Washington, D.C. 20036

Library of Congress Cataloging in Publication data:

Spindler, J. Andrew (James Andrew), 1950–
  The politics of international credit.

  Includes bibliographical references and index.
  1. Banks and banking, International. 2. Loans,
Foreign. 3. Banks and banking, West German. 4. Banks
and banking, Japanese. 5. Banks and banking, American.
6. Germany (West)—Foreign relations. 7. Japan—Foreign
relations—1945– . 8. United States—Foreign relations—1981– . I. Title.
HG3881.S65 1984   332.1′5   83-73394
ISBN 0-8157-8070-2
ISBN 0-8157-8069-9 (pbk.)

1 2 3 4 5 6 7 8 9

Str, 20.00/12.00/6/13/84

THE BROOKINGS INSTITUTION is an independent organization devoted to nonpartisan research, education, and publication in economics, government, foreign policy, and the social sciences generally. Its principal purposes are to aid in the development of sound public policies and to promote public understanding of issues of national importance.

The Institution was founded on December 8, 1927, to merge the activities of the Institute for Government Research, founded in 1916, the Institute of Economics, founded in 1922, and the Robert Brookings Graduate School of Economics and Government, founded in 1924.

The Board of Trustees is responsible for the general administration of the Institution, while the immediate direction of the policies, program, and staff is vested in the President, assisted by an advisory committee of the officers and staff. The by-laws of the Institution state: "It is the function of the Trustees to make possible the conduct of scientific research, and publication, under the most favorable conditions, and to safeguard the independence of the research staff in the pursuit of their studies and in the publication of the results of such studies. It is not a part of their function to determine, control, or influence the conduct of particular investigations or the conclusions reached."

The President bears final responsibility for the decision to publish a manuscript as a Brookings book. In reaching his judgment on the competence, accuracy, and objectivity of each study, the President is advised by the director of the appropriate research program and weighs the views of a panel of expert outside readers who report to him in confidence on the quality of the work. Publication of a work signifies that it is deemed a competent treatment worthy of public consideration but does not imply endorsement of conclusions or recommendations.

The Institution maintains its position of neutrality on issues of public policy in order to safeguard the intellectual freedom of the staff. Hence interpretations or conclusions in Brookings publications should be understood to be solely those of the authors and should not be attributed to the Institution, to its trustees, officers, or other staff members, or to the organizations that support its research.

Foreword

THROUGHOUT the 1970s and early 1980s, the role of commercial banks
in international finance expanded greatly, reflecting the growth of
international trade, the emergence of newly industrializing countries
eager to acquire export markets and foreign capital, and the need to
recycle petrodollars after the oil price increases of 1973–74 and 1979–
80. These developments presented banks with unprecedented opportunities and risks. By the early 1980s, the Eurodollar market, in which
commercial banks are the principal intermediaries, had swelled to more
than $2 billion. At the same time, commercial bank loans to developing
countries outside of OPEC approached $250 billion.

As banks expand their international business dealings, they both
influence and are influenced by the domestic and the foreign policies of
the countries where they are headquartered. Governments differ in their
attitudes toward leading commercial banks. They also differ in their
capacity and willingness to influence the international allocation of credit
by their banks. In this study J. Andrew Spindler focuses on the links
between private finance and foreign policy. He deals mainly with the
Federal Republic of Germany and Japan, though he is also concerned
with the United States. One of his principal aims is to compare the links
between commercial banking and foreign policy in Germany and Japan
with those in the United States. He argues that the United States cannot
and should not attempt to copy German and Japanese patterns, but
rather that U.S. officials, public and private, can learn much from
Germany and Japan about the relation between banking and foreign
policy.

When he wrote this book, Spindler was a business fellow in the

Brookings Foreign Policy Studies program, on leave from the International Department of the Continental Illinois National Bank of Chicago. He became a vice-president of that bank in 1982 and a special director of its newly formed Credit Risk Evaluation Division in 1983. Throughout his research, Spindler drew on his previous experience in international banking, particularly in Asia-Pacific markets, where he first noted marked differences in the relations between the Japanese, European, and American commercial banks and their respective home governments.

Numerous bankers, government officials, and others in Germany, Japan, and the United States provided invaluable assistance through interviews. While observing their preference for anonymity, Spindler remains deeply grateful for the critical insights and information that they provided. Efforts were made to record their opinions accurately, and footnotes indicate those instances where the text depends on interview material. Without the help they so generously provided, he could not have written many of the cases illustrating German and Japanese practices.

The author thanks John D. Steinbruner, director of the Brookings Foreign Policy Studies program, for his steadfast guidance and support throughout the project. He is also grateful to Leo C. deGrijs, executive vice-president at Continental, for facilitating his business fellow arrangement with Brookings. Alfred F. Miossi, also executive vice-president at Continental, provided constant encouragement.

Spindler also records his appreciation to those who read all or part of the manuscript at various stages and offered valuable comments. Among those deserving special thanks are Robert G. Gilpin, Jr., Richard P. Mattione, Susan D. Oliver, Jonathan D. Aronson, Helmut von der Bey, Pierre Ferrand, Eric W. Hayden, Richard H. Henry, Werner Jentsch, Peter J. Katzenstein, Peter B. Kenen, Michael Kreile, R. David Luft, Eiichi Matsumoto, Rüdiger Sass, Judith A. Thompson, and Joseph A. Yager. Others who offered important help and support included Stephen W. Dizard, Stephan M. Haggard, Ed. A. Hewett, Jan R. Liss, John A. McAdams, Kenneth A. Oye, Alex J. Pollock, William L. Staples, and Maureen S. Steinbruner.

Kanako Yamashita and William G. Miossi served as summer research assistants on the project. Ann M. Ziegler processed countless revisions of the manuscript cheerfully and thoroughly. Nancy D. Davidson edited the manuscript, Alan G. Hoden verified it, Nancy Snyder was the proofreader, and Florence Robinson was the indexer.

The study was funded in part by grants from the Ford Foundation and the German Marshall Fund of the United States. Brookings acknowledges with gratitude the generosity of the Continental Illinois Bank in allowing the author to spend time at Brookings in order to write this book.

The opinions expressed in this book are those of the author alone, and should not be ascribed to the Continental Illinois Bank, to the Ford Foundation, to the German Marshall Fund, to those who were interviewed or asked to comment on the manuscript, or to the trustees, officers, or other staff members of the Brookings Institution.

BRUCE K. MACLAURY
President

November 1983
Washington, D.C.

Contents

Tables

Figure

CHAPTER ONE

Banks and Governments

THE international activities of commercial banks and the foreign policy concerns of their home governments have become increasingly intertwined in recent years. This has resulted largely from an increase in emphasis by most industrial states on the economic components of their foreign policies and from the simultaneous rapid expansion of international banking.

Some of the most far-reaching effects of this mutual involvement drew wide attention during 1982–83 when a record number of developing and Eastern bloc countries, including several of the largest borrowers in international financial markets, sought to reschedule at least $50 billion in commercial bank loans.[1] The governments and leading banks of industrial countries were forced to deal with the political and financial consequences of this imbroglio, which stemmed from lending programs that the banks had pursued in a context of official acquiescence, if not encouragement. The overlap between the concerns of commercial banks and their home governments' foreign policy machinery predates this critical period in international finance, however. Similarly, the scope of that overlap reaches far beyond the banks' problem loans to developing countries.

Particularly since 1973, official policymakers in industrial countries have seen economic and commercial interests encroach on the domain of "high politics" in unprecedented ways. At the same time, both the

1. "The International Banking Markets in 1982," *Bank of England Quarterly Bulletin,* vol. 23 (March 1983), p. 45. Other estimates of the amount of commercial debt that these countries sought to restructure during 1982–83 run as high as $100 billion. See, for example, M. S. Mendelsohn, "Lessons Learned: 'Brutal' Mexican Action May Be Model for Countries Which Can't Service Debt," *American Banker,* July 27, 1983.

changing nature and magnitude of the role of large banks in the world economy have led to their involvement in commercial relationships with far-reaching political ramifications. Recent examples of such relationships have included American banks' multibillion-dollar financial dealings with Iran at the time of the seizure of American hostages in November 1979; an estimated $15 billion in outstanding commercial bank claims on Poland when martial law was imposed there in December 1981; and a staggering $64 billion in foreign bank loans to Mexico when a major economic and financial crisis overtook that country late in the summer of 1982. In addition to coping with these political involvements, banks have faced an increasing array of commercial decisions fraught with political significance, ranging from whether or not to lend in South Africa or Taiwan to what role to play in promoting domestic exports or assisting third world nations on the verge of insolvency. This study, undertaken in light of the growing entanglement of international banking and foreign policy concerns, examines the nature of coordination between large commercial banks and the foreign policy apparatus of their home governments in Germany and Japan. The study also considers the implications of those bank-government relations for the United States.

The expanded international influence that major commercial banks have acquired over the last decade illustrates the extraordinary strength of the forces of economic interdependence that continue to transform relations among nations. One could argue that the largest commercial banks exerted an equally consequential impact on international relations before World War I or perhaps during the early interwar years;[2] but at least a half a century has passed since these institutions played the kind of role in allocating politically significant resources that they play today. The sheer volume of banks' financial intermediation across national borders in the early 1980s has never been approached in history.

One measure of the expanded international role of the world's largest

2. Herbert Feis wrote one of the few detailed comparative studies of the interaction between commercial banking and foreign policy, and perhaps the best, over fifty years ago: *Europe: The World's Banker, 1870–1914: An Account of European Foreign Investment and the Connection of World Finance with Diplomacy before the War* (Yale University Press for the Council on Foreign Relations, 1930). This now-classic study considers how the international financial entanglements of the European powers helped to precipitate World War I; in the cases of French and German foreign investment, in particular, Feis argues that political manipulation of the recipient (borrower) was often a first-order consideration.

commercial banks is the spectacular growth of the Eurocurrency market. The gross volume of deposits in that market rose from $110 billion in 1970 to $2.1 trillion as of December 1982; the net volume, after subtraction of interbank claims, grew from $65 billion to $960 billion.[3] Primarily through their intermediary function in this market, banks have served as the chief conduit in the petrodollar-recycling process in the wake of the oil shocks of 1973–74 and 1979–80, accepting massive deposits from members of the Organization of Petroleum Exporting Countries (OPEC) and other countries in surplus and on-lending those funds for a profit. Following the first oil shock, the largest banks became critically important in channeling funds into approximately one dozen non-oil-exporting developing countries, the smaller non-oil industrial countries, oil exporters outside the Middle East and North Africa, and Eastern Europe.[4] Throughout 1975–82, the growth of bank lending to all developing countries averaged over 20 percent per year.[5]

Despite a marked slowdown in new commercial international lending during the second half of 1982 and 1983, the banks have remained an important source of funds for many of the richer, more trade-oriented developing countries and the smaller industrial countries. In an international financial environment where the persistence of large payments imbalances seems inevitable and official financing available to countries in deficit is nearly certain to remain inadequate, the banks are likely to continue to play a major recycling role for many years to come.

Consider the magnitude of some of the most important international relationships that industrial countries' commercial banks have collectively undertaken since the mid-1970s. Loans by these banks to the non-OPEC developing countries grew from $63 billion at year-end 1975 to $247 billion in December 1982.[6] As of 1982 commercial banks accounted for over half of all external finance provided to the developing world as

3. Morgan Guaranty Trust Company of New York, *World Financial Markets* (May 1979), p. 13, and (June 1983), p. 17.

4. Between 1973 and mid-1980 bank claims on the twelve non-oil-exporting developing countries in question multiplied more than sixfold, to a total of just under $100 billion. The twelve countries are Argentina, Bolivia, Brazil, Chile, Colombia, India, Ivory Coast, South Korea, Philippines, Taiwan, Thailand, and Turkey. Morgan Guaranty, *World Financial Markets* (March 1980), pp. 1–13, and (December 1980), p. 12.

5. Morgan Guaranty, *World Financial Markets* (June 1983), pp. 2–3.

6. Bank for International Settlements (BIS), *Forty-Seventh Annual Report, 1st April 1976–31st March 1977* (Basle: BIS, 1977), p. 114; and BIS, *International Banking Developments—Fourth Quarter 1982* (BIS, 1983), table 3.

a whole[7] and for more than 60 percent of the external debt of twenty-one major developing country borrowers, compared with about 30 percent of their debt in 1974.[8] Through their roles as borrowers, advisers, and creditors vis-à-vis the OPEC states, large banks have managed to secure influential relationships with these nations as well. At year-end 1982 industrial countries' commercial banks held deposits of $135 billion from the OPEC states, down somewhat from peak deposit levels during early 1981 but still more than two and one-half times their level at year-end 1975 ($52 billion); loans from the same banks to OPEC members totaled $79 billion at the end of 1982, five times the $14 billion in outstanding loans at the end of 1975. Finally, commercial bank loans to Eastern Europe and the Soviet Union amounted to roughly $53 billion at the end of 1982, more than twice their 1975 volume.[9]

The new dimensions of individual commercial banks' international relationships have also been striking. In 1979, for example, a single Japanese commercial bank, the Bank of Tokyo, played a pivotal role in arranging $8 billion of credit for the People's Republic of China.[10] In 1982 Citicorp derived a phenomenal $150 million of income, or more than 20 percent of its global earnings, from a single foreign country, Brazil.[11] And although more than a thousand banks are involved in international lending today, a mere fifty banks account for about two-thirds of the total dollar amount.[12]

Although the new prominence of banks in international affairs has resulted largely from huge increases in the volume of their cross-border lending and deposit taking, other factors have also been significant. Principal among them have been major advances in many large banks' capabilities to gather and process information from disparate geographic points. The number of banks engaged in transnational branching rose by 90 percent between 1970 and 1978, while the number of foreign branches

7. Art Pine, "Lenders' Jitters: International Bankers Take Steps to Restore Faith in Their System," *Wall Street Journal*, September 15, 1982.

8. Morgan Guaranty, *World Financial Markets* (May 1982), p. 9.

9. BIS, *Forty-Seventh Annual Report*, p. 114; BIS, *International Banking Developments—Fourth Quarter 1982*, tables 3, 4. The figures for the Soviet Union and Eastern Europe exclude commercial bank loans to Yugoslavia, which summed to an additional $9 billion at year-end 1982.

10. "Private Banks Reach Agreement with China on Terms of Syndicate Loan," *Japan Economic Journal*, April 3, 1979.

11. *1982 Citicorp Annual Report and Form 10-K*, p. 51.

12. Leo C. deGrijs, "Transitions: Developing Nations Face a Test of Will," *American Banker*, July 27, 1983.

and agencies they maintained increased 72 percent, U.K. and French banks excluded.[13] The creation of global networks of operating units and representative offices, the development of new and highly sophisticated internal communications systems, and the strengthening of in-house analytic capabilities have permitted a number of these institutions to track and probe more deeply than ever before into events of political as well as economic consequence around the world.

Although American banks overwhelmingly dominated international financial markets through the 1960s and early 1970s, banks from a number of other countries began to play a more important role in international finance during the second half of the 1970s.[14] One measure of the relative shift in international standing of American banks has been a decline in their representation among the world's largest banking institutions, a fact of some significance because of the influence of relative size on a bank's competitive position in the international marketplace.[15] (Only part of this decline was the result of currency changes during the period, including the general decline in the value of the dollar.) As of year-end 1982, the fifty largest commercial banking companies in the world included fifteen Japanese banks, six German banks, and seven American banks; and Western European institutions on the list collectively outnumbered those from the United States by a factor of more than three. The ten largest banks in the world included only two American banks in 1982, compared with seven in 1970.[16]

Similarly, American banks' preeminent position in various international markets has suffered some erosion since the mid-1970s. Between year-end 1975 and year-end 1981, U.S. banks' share of industrial country

13. During the same period, banks from the United Kingdom and France lost large numbers of branches and agencies located in former colonies. U.K. banks alone experienced a decline of over 3,000 branches and agencies during this period. Diane Page and Neal M. Soss, *Some Evidence on Transnational Banking Structure* (Washington, D.C.: U.S. Office of the Comptroller of the Currency, 1980), pp. 14–16.

14. This change occurred even as American banks retained a competitive advantage in many areas of international finance, because of the advanced state of American banking technology and the existing scope of large American banks' foreign branch networks, among other factors.

15. For a further discussion of the causes and significance of the decline in U.S. banks' relative size, see C. Stewart Goddin and Steven J. Weiss, *U.S. Banks' Loss of Global Standing* (Washington, D.C.: U.S. Office of the Comptroller of the Currency, 1980).

16. "The Top 500 in World Banking," *Banker* (London), vol. 133 (June 1983), pp. 177–81; and "World Banking—The Top 300," *Banker* (London), vol. 121 (June 1971), p. 640. Size was measured by total bank assets less contra accounts.

commercial bank loans to OPEC states fell from approximately 58 percent to 32 percent.[17] Over the same interval American banks' share of similar claims on non-OPEC developing countries slipped from 65 percent to 36 percent. (This occurrence has not been altogether bad from a U.S. perspective, however, in light of those countries' increasingly serious debt service problems.) For four major non-OPEC developing country borrowers in East Asia (South Korea, Taiwan, the Philippines, and Thailand), the decline was from 81 percent to 50 percent.[18] It is also noteworthy that between the twelve months of 1976 and the first five months of 1979 American banks' share of publicized syndicated credit commitments throughout the rapidly growing Asia/Pacific region eroded from 70 percent of total market commitments (actual loan participations) to 20 percent. Over the same period there was a threefold increase in European banks' share of the same credits to 38 percent of the total and a tenfold jump in Japanese banks' share to 23 percent.[19]

Given the limited time frames they cover, none of the above figures offers definitive proof of long-term trends.[20] Nevertheless, the figures do provide evidence of the expanding financial role that European and Japanese banks have begun to play in important overseas markets. At this point, it is clear that American, Japanese, and European banks currently share the premier positions of influence throughout the financial world.

The Focus of the Study

One question prompted by the broad changes now occurring in the international banking environment is: to what extent, and in what ways, do the major commercial banks in several advanced industrial countries

17. These figures on U.S. banks' share of international lending should be considered rough estimates. Based on analysis of data in BIS, *Forty-Sixth Annual Report, 1st April 1975–31st March 1976* (Basle: BIS, 1976), pp. 86–87; U.S. Federal Reserve System, *Federal Reserve Bulletin*, vol. 66 (January 1980), p. A63; and Morgan Guaranty, *World Financial Markets* (October 1982), pp. 1–9.

18. Morgan Guaranty, *World Financial Markets* (September 1976), p. 11, and (October 1982), p. 3.

19. R. A. Nigel Henley, "The U.S. Banks Bow Out of the Pacific Market," *Euromoney* (July 1979), pp. 90–93.

20. Furthermore, data for the early 1980s indicate some strengthening in American banks' share of commercial loans to selected Asian countries relative to 1979. Morgan Guaranty, *World Financial Markets* (October 1982), p. 3.

either influence or assist in implementing the foreign policies of their governments? At issue is the tendency of some of the world's leading commercial banks and their home governments to work together to pursue one or the other's international objectives. Of particular concern here will be the capacity and willingness of those governments to achieve national objectives by attempting to influence commercial banks' international allocation of credit.

As a general rule large banks headquartered in North America, Europe, and Japan variously assess their own international performance according to an assortment of commercial criteria: short or long-term profitability, prestige and reputation, minimization of loan losses, maximization of asset growth, and improvement of market share or perhaps establishment of a niche in a specialized corner of the market. Despite their predominantly entrepreneurial orientation, however, large commercial banks occasionally find themselves engaged in international activities that are of more than passing interest to their home governments. Often a government's interest reflects regulatory concerns, such as ensuring that banks properly manage their international assets and liabilities to protect depositors and preclude disruption of financial markets, or maintaining control over monetary policy. At other times, however, some governments have perceived in commercial banks' international activities a means of advancing specific policy objectives of the state—for example, diversifying raw materials sources, expanding exports to reduce a trade deficit or create jobs, providing financial support (in some cases disguised aid) to a country whose economic and political stability is of fundamental importance to the state, or conversely denying such support to an objectionable foreign regime.

In other instances, banks have sought and obtained the assistance of their home government in furthering commercial objectives abroad. In many cases, the resulting government support for commercial banking activities has been tied to the government's own objectives. Official support in these instances has sometimes taken the form of concessionary funding provided out of foreign currency reserves, loan guarantees and cofinancing packages offered through government export-support programs, or bailout assistance in the form of partial assumption of risk or help in negotiating refinancing for a problem credit, perhaps to a sovereign borrower. Whether the prevailing direction of influence runs from government to banks or banks to government, commercial outcomes in these cases are likely to be determined by nonmarket factors.

To the extent that this happens, government policy affects the international allocation of financial resources by commercial banks. Some governments, moreover, may perceive commercial international banking as a deliberate tool of foreign policy.

In seeking to explore differences in the specific terms of accommodation between the state and indigenous commercial banks in several industrial countries, a fundamental concern will be the actual *extent* of that accommodation (that is, the degree of bank-government coordination) as well as the prevailing direction of influence. A larger focus will be the cohesiveness of foreign economic policy emanating from these countries: do banks and government tend to work toward shared or complementary objectives in the international sphere, or do their actions regularly appear disjointed, the result of a lack of communication, mutual distrust, or possibly even conflict of purpose?

Although this study concentrates on the Federal Republic of Germany and Japan, two of the non-Communist world's preeminent sources of political-economic power and international banking strength, the underlying concern is with the United States itself. In the realms of both international finance and foreign economic policy, West Germany and Japan offer two of the world's most striking examples of success in the extended postwar period, as measured by the rapid rise in their leading banks' international stature, particularly during the 1970s; the steady increases in German and Japanese exports since the late 1950s, surpassed today only by those of the United States among non-Communist countries; and the relative strength over time of the deutsche mark and yen. By studying the relationships between commercial banking and foreign policy in these two countries, one should be able to develop criteria for assessing the efficacy of the same interaction in the United States.

Institutional relationships between leading international commercial banks and the official foreign policy machinery of government are significantly different in West Germany, Japan, and the United States; the contrasts among these relationships reflect differing historical experiences, domestic institutional arrangements, and attitudes among relevant elites, as well as the nature of the specific problems that each country's political economy confronts. Furthermore, although the prevailing patterns of German and Japanese government-bank relations are quite distinct from one another, they are both noticeably less adversarial in tone than their American counterpart. This fact appears to reflect a greater convergence of international interests between banks and government and stronger bank-government working relationships in Germany and Japan, combined with those governments' relatively more skillful use of incentives to influence bank behavior when deemed necessary.

Recent scholarly research has demonstrated that structural differences in national financial systems contribute to the differing capacities of governments to intervene in their countries' industrial economies.[21] Case studies support the conclusions that the state tends to lead the process of industrial adjustment in Japan, working through a financial system in which banks play a primary role. By way of contrast, banks, companies, and the government tend to reach negotiated solutions to problems of industrial adjustment in Germany, where the financial system can be categorized as credit-based and bank-dominated. In the United States, in juxtaposition to both Germany and Japan, "A decentralized financial system with a strong securities market has contributed to the concentration of power and decision making in the corporation itself."[22] The same differences in national financial structure also wield enormous influence on bank-government relations in the international sphere.

As this study will document, banks and government in Germany and Japan are able to communicate and occasionally work together in the international sphere in ways found far less frequently in the United States. As a consequence, German and Japanese banks often serve more as partners to their governments, albeit junior in status but still positioned both to exert marked influence over official policy and to help execute it. The German and Japanese governments appear to display considerably more sensitivity to the long-term operating interests of their countries' leading international banks; at the same time, these governments are better able to draw upon the international capabilities of their countries' commercial banking systems to achieve important official policy objectives.

Such bank-government coordination in Germany and Japan raises

---

21. See John Zysman, *Governments, Markets, and Growth: Financial Systems and the Politics of Industrial Change* (Cornell University Press, 1983). Zysman has constructed models of three distinct types of financial systems, each with specific political implications. The three systems are: (1) a credit-based system with administered prices (such as France or Japan); (2) a credit-based, bank-dominated system (such as Germany); and (3) a capital market–centered system with resources allocated by competitively established prices (such as the United States).

22. Ibid., p. 269.

significant questions about the current ability of the U.S. government to formulate and execute foreign economic policy and about the ability of American banks to compete abroad. Such questions will demand growing attention in the United States over the coming years as non-American banks play an expanding role in international finance, and as the U.S. government confronts an increasingly complex array of international economic problems in which American and other industrial countries' interests are not the same.

Several qualifications to the analysis should be stated at the outset. First, the focus of this study is the tendency of banks and governments to work together internationally, particularly to achieve foreign policy objectives; as such, regulation of international banking activities by each government will be of only peripheral concern.

Second, the study will not attempt to deal with all facets of international banking but rather will concentrate on international lending by commercial banks and to a lesser degree on their deposit-taking activities. This emphasis will result in cursory treatment of other aspects of international banking, such as bond underwriting and foreign exchange dealing. But it includes the core of most large banks' international business and is of sufficient breadth to provide a window on banks' relations with their home governments in dealing with international policy issues.

Third, the analysis will not attempt to reformulate existing dominant explanations in the field of international political economy. Rather, through examining the degree and terms of accommodation between commercial banks and the foreign policy machinery of their home governments, the investigation will seek to draw on several of those explanations to provide insights into relatively unexplored data. Furthermore, in light of the nature of that data, the analysis will make primarily qualitative rather than quantitative assessments.

Finally, the study aims more to provoke discussion than to supply definitive answers. The ultimate purpose of this analysis is to raise questions about a set of complex political-financial relationships in the world's most important industrial countries, relationships largely hidden from public view.

PART ONE

The Federal Republic of Germany

CHAPTER TWO

The German Banking System

THE relationship between commercial banking and foreign policy in the Federal Republic of Germany is subtle and paradoxical, eluding easy definition. German banks often behave internationally in a manner highly complementary to their country's foreign policy interests, yet the German government can require such behavior only under the most extreme circumstances, such as a national emergency. While German banks and their government have occasionally reached understandings in areas where private financial and foreign policy interests overlap, their traditional preference has been not to formalize those understandings and certainly not to publicize them. Rather, as a means of securing each other's support in the international sphere, both the German government and German banks have relied on a natural convergence of interests and a well-developed system of highly discreet, ad hoc communication.

The modern relationship between international banking and foreign policy in the Federal Republic, while reflecting the impact of rapid changes in the international financial environment since 1965, has been molded fundamentally by several major determinants of German economic life that have remained surprisingly constant over the last one hundred years. Two determinants have influenced this relationship decisively and provide a useful analytic means for cutting into its complexity: (1) the liberal, loosely regulated character of the German financial sector, combined with the central role of banks in German economic decisionmaking;[1] and (2) the export drive that has served as a

---

1. *Liberal* in this context refers to economic liberalism, with its emphasis on laissez-faire business-government relations, a free market economy, and free trade. For a discussion of economic liberalism as it applies to post–World War II Germany, see

primary motivating force behind both German foreign policy and German international banking. Largely because of these factors, an elite core of powerful banks has emerged in German financial and economic life. These banks provide a natural partner for the German government in a number of different international areas where the commercial interests, financial skills, and knowledge of the former overlap with the policy objectives of the latter.

Successive German regimes have viewed enhancement of German industrial and commercial interests abroad as a fundamental foreign policy objective. Given that the largest German banking institutions have identified with and strongly supported the advancement of those same interests, banks and government have enjoyed a natural, extensive mingling of interests beyond German borders. At the same time, however, German banks and government have rarely defined their interests as absolutely identical. The government of the postwar Federal Republic, similar to peacetime German governments from the time of German unification until the advent of the Third Reich, has had few mechanisms at its disposal to prohibit German banks from participating in international loans or taking other foreign actions. But German governments have traditionally possessed a range of mechanisms for *positively* influencing the international behavior of German banks, for encouraging (although not requiring) their commitment of financial resources abroad in ways they probably would not have chosen alone. In this qualified sense, leading German banks have served the German state as "subsidiary agents of their foreign policy" since at least the days of Bismarck.[2] In doing so, however, these banks have also behaved as private entrepreneurs, simultaneously serving their own commercial interests.

German governments have hesitated to intervene directly to influence the behavior of German banks in specific transactions. Thus in recent times guarantees have been a favored governmental mechanism to enhance the appeal to German banks of certain broad categories of transactions, such as export financing, that stimulate demand for industrial goods or contribute to expanded German economic ties overseas.

Andrew Shonfield, *Modern Capitalism: The Changing Balance of Public and Private Power* (Oxford University Press for the Royal Institute of International Affairs, 1965), p. 239ff.

2. Fritz Stern, *Gold and Iron: Bismarck, Bleichröder and the Building of the German Empire* (Knopf, 1977), p. 429.

This type of broad inducement permits policy formulators within the government to influence German banks' international lending patterns without having to issue policy directives, or even suggestions, to a single bank. (The availability of official guarantees does serve as a policy signal to the banks, however, making governmental preferences clear.) The mechanism leaves banks ultimately free to make their own credit and portfolio decisions, in keeping with the liberal tradition that has long played a key role in German finance.

In a limited variety of instances, however, the government of the Federal Republic has shown a willingness to dig progressively deeper into its bag of incentives to encourage German banks to take positive financial actions abroad. During the late 1970s and early 1980s, the German government occasionally issued guarantees under nonroutine circumstances covering at least a portion of specific international loans. The likelihood of such governmental action tended to increase according to the importance of the foreign policy objectives at hand and the direct contribution of a given loan toward meeting those objectives; that tendency was always tempered, however, by the degree of financial risk that the government might have to absorb. In cases where both foreign policy stakes and financial risk have been moderate to high, the government has occasionally engaged in bargaining with German banks to persuade them to undertake financial transactions with as much risk for the banks' accounts as possible. Additional policy instruments at the government's disposal have included moral suasion and implied governmental cooperation in future times of need.

The Structure

The organization of the German banking system constitutes both essential background for this study and a point of entry for examining the bank-governmental relationships that are its focus. Reflecting the liberal tradition in German banking, dominant characteristics of the system include free competition in the provision of financial services and limited public regulation. The system's competitive, open nature is evident from the large number of operating institutions, a remarkable degree of diversity, and a low level of concentration. At the end of 1982, approximately 4,930 separate banking institutions existed in the Federal Republic, of which 1,560 (31.6 percent) were small credit cooperatives

Table 2-1. *Structure of the German Banking System, Year-End 1982*

Institution	Number of organiza- tions	Assets (billions of dollars)[a]	Percentage of system assets
Commercial banks	240	252.6	22.2
Big banks[b]	6	97.6	8.6
Regional banks and other commercial banks	97	114.8	10.1
Foreign banks operating branches	58	24.0	2.1
Private bankers	79	16.2	1.4
Central giro institutions	12	184.6	16.2
Banks with special functions	16	77.7	6.8
Kreditanstalt für Wiederaufbau (KfW)	1	28.0	2.5
Savings banks	595	250.0	22.0
Credit cooperatives and their central institutions[c]	2,272	176.8	15.5
Mortgage banks	38	165.1	14.5
Private	25	101.3	8.9
Public	13	63.8	5.6
Installment sales financing institutions	113	13.4	1.2
Postal giro and postal savings bank offices	15	18.1	1.6
Total	3,301	1,138.5	100.0

Sources: Deutsche Bundesbank, *Monthly Report*, vol. 35 (March 1983), p. 32–33, 44–45; and Kreditanstalt für Wiederaufbau, *Annual Report for the Year 1982*, balance sheet fold-out. Figures are rounded.

a. Deutsche marks converted to U.S. dollars at the rate of DM 2.38 = $1.00. Excludes assets of foreign branches and foreign subsidiaries.

b. Deutsche Bank AG, Dresdner Bank AG, Commerzbank AG, and their subsidiaries in Berlin.

c. The Bundesbank's monthly reporting statistics cover only those credit cooperatives whose balance sheet total on December 31, 1972, amounted to DM 10 million or over, and smaller institutions that on November 30, 1973, were required to render returns. At year-end 1982, this reporting procedure resulted in the exclusion of approximately 1,560 small credit cooperatives with balance sheet totals averaging less than DM 20 million.

with balance sheet totals averaging less than DM 20 million ($8.4 million).[3] At the other end of the institutional spectrum, four banks— three in the commercial sector and one in the noncommercial sector— held leading positions in the system with consolidated assets ranging from $45 billion to $83 billion. Deutsche Bundesbank (German central bank) statistics, which generally do not cover the smaller cooperative banks and certain other financial institutions, yield a breakdown of the rest of the financial system, as shown in table 2-1.

The variety of operating institutions is profuse, whether measured by size, organizational structure, or functional type. The commercial banking sector, which accounted for 22 percent of the system's total assets, includes the "Big Three" commercial banks with their national branch

3. Deutsche Bundesbank, *Monthly Report*, vol. 35 (March 1983), pp. 32–33, 44–45.

networks, other commercial banks that are essentially regional in character, branches of foreign banks, and private bankers (organized in the legal form of sole proprietorships, general partnerships, or limited partnerships). Indicative of the low level of concentration in the overall German financial system, the Big Three commercial banks recently held only 9 percent of the system's assets, a modest figure both in absolute terms and in comparison with the market shares of the largest commercial banks in most other industrialized countries. At the same time, however, it should be noted that within the commercial banking sector, which maintains a dominant market position in handling business transactions between Germany and other countries,[4] these three banks accounted for a considerable 39 percent of assets.

The noncommercial banking sector, which held the remaining 78 percent of assets in the system at year-end 1982, can be subdivided into the following major categories:

—Central giro institutions: These banks, which include Germany's eleven *Landesbanken,* serve as clearing houses to the savings banks, and some have also become major international lenders. Most giro institutions are owned by an association of savings banks in their region and/or by the local state.

—Banks with special functions: These banks include the government-owned Kreditanstalt für Wiederaufbau (KfW), which grants project loans, long-term export financing, and aid to developing countries.

—Savings banks, credit cooperatives and their central institutions, mortgage banks, and other banks (including installment sales financing institutions and postal giro and postal savings bank offices).

Regulation

The regulatory structure itself has played an important role in establishing the open quality of the financial system. First, a minimum of regulatory hurdles checks entry into the system. The German Banking Act stipulates that any person wishing to conduct banking business in the country must obtain a license from the Federal Banking Supervisory Office, but the act goes on to limit strictly the grounds on which the

---

4. Bank-Verlag Köln, *The Banking System of the Federal Republic of Germany,* revised by Juergen Stein (Cologne: Bundesverband deutscher Banken, 1977), p. 14.

office can refuse to grant a license.[5] Furthermore, the burden of proof as to an applicant's lack of qualifications rests with the Supervisory Office. Second, the act imposes extremely few restrictions on bank activities. In keeping with the German tradition of universal banking, the first paragraph establishes an especially broad definition of "banking business." Beyond this definition, the act restricts banks from engaging in very few types of business (the section entitled "Prohibited Business" contains only three brief provisions), and the sense of the law is that banks may engage in any activity not expressly forbidden.[6]

The limited scope of German bank regulation also extends to the international sphere. The Federal Banking Supervisory Office has been able to obtain only skeletal information to date about the operations of German banks' foreign subsidiaries, even though the parent banks conduct much of their international business and a growing volume of business with domestic customers through them. The pivotal 1978 "gentlemen's agreement," which stipulated what data German banks should voluntarily provide the Supervisory Office on their Luxembourg subsidiaries, ran a total of six sentences and did not call for even such basic information as a breakdown of loans according to country of borrower.[7] According to a second gentlemen's agreement reached during

5. According to par. 33 of the Banking Act, the Federal Banking Supervisory Office may refuse to grant a license for a new bank only if it is inadequately capitalized, if its managers or proprietors are untrustworthy or not professionally qualified, or if the bank has fewer than two managers. Deutsche Bundesbank, *Banking Act of the Federal Republic of Germany*, translated by the Deutsche Bundesbank from the text in the *Federal Law Gazette* of May 3, 1976 (Deutsche Bundesbank, undated).

6. In accord with pars. 10–12 of the Banking Act, the Federal Banking Supervisory Office has been relatively strict in applying its powers relating to the liquidity and capital adequacy of banks. Several further rules are intended to limit loan concentrations. Writing in 1982, however, Richard Dale observed, "Until now the capital adequacy criteria have not been applied on a consolidated basis, nor does the SO [Supervisory Office] have the statutory authority to do so. . . . There are currently no plans for assessing liquidity on a consolidated basis." Furthermore, although the Supervisory Office has legal authority to conduct its own audits of banks, "Bank supervision is based on annual auditors' reports to the supervisory authorities rather than on-site examinations by the regulators themselves." Richard Dale, *Bank Supervision Around the World* (New York: Group of Thirty, 1982), pp. 29–33.

7. The 1978 agreement calls only for a grouping of assets according to type of country, such as European Community countries, other industrialized countries, developing countries, OPEC countries, and Comecon countries. With regard to data on *individual* loans booked in foreign subsidiaries, the agreement requires only that such loans be "mentioned, respectively commented as far as the risks are remarkable. Name and address, however, shall be enciphered, to maintain the host country's banking secrecy, if necessary." In addition, according to one prominent Düsseldorf banker,

August 1981, banks should also provide the Supervisory Office and the Bundesbank with quarterly "consolidated figures" covering all wholly owned or nearly wholly owned foreign subsidiaries. While terming this second agreement "a step in the right direction," the Bundesbank still noted that the "German bank supervisory authorities neither have sufficient insight into the operations of these subsidiaries nor can require the German parent banks to make adequate provision for risks."[8] The second agreement does not call for the names of borrowers or data on subsidiaries less than about 95 percent owned, and as of late 1982, Germany's eleven landesbanks collectively refused to comply even with it.[9]

The Banking Supervisory Office, lacking a large staff or strong legal mandate and unable to obtain comprehensive data, has a restricted capability to regulate German banks.[10] Even the Supervisory Office's location in West Berlin, removed from the principal financial and political crossroads of the Federal Republic, would seem to hamper the office's effectiveness. The federal government has maintained the Supervisory Office there, along with the headquarters of a number of other government agencies, largely for symbolic reasons relating to the political importance it attaches to the city; the location also seems an appropriate

some major German banks for years have kept the Federal Republic's bank regulators further in the dark by basing the annual reports of pivotal subsidiaries, such as those in Luxembourg, on different reporting periods from that of the parent bank. "Gentlemen's Agreement on the Reporting of German Banks about their Foreign Subsidiaries," provided in June 1980 by Federal Banking Supervisory Office, Berlin; and interview with senior official of one of the Big Three German commercial banks, Düsseldorf, July 18, 1980.

8. Deutsche Bundesbank, "Bank Supervision on the Basis of Consolidated Figures," *Monthly Report*, vol. 33 (August 1981), pp. 25–26.

9. In the United States, in contrast, comprehensive bank supervision has been conducted on the basis of consolidated figures for a number of years; for any given U.S. bank, detailed supervision has covered all subsidiary and affiliate operations in which it maintains a share ownership of 25 percent or more. Deutsche Bundesbank, "Bank Supervision on the Basis of Consolidated Figures," p. 26; and David Shirreff, "The Challenges of Ingelore," *Euromoney* (January 1982), pp. 74–75.

10. The Supervisory Office's legal mandate might be strengthened substantially if the recommendations of an official Commission of Inquiry into Basic Banking Questions (the Gessler commission) are incorporated into a revised banking act. Formed in 1976, the Gessler commission reported its findings in May 1979, which included a call for the consolidation within group accounts of all subsidiaries more than 50 percent owned. However, formal revision of the Banking Act, a matter that has been under discussion since at least 1974, was still pending as of mid-1983. See *Bericht der Studienkommission "Grundsatzfragen der Kreditwirtschaft,"* Schriftenreihe des Bundesministeriums der Finanzen, Heft 28 (Bonn: Wilhelm Stollfuss Verlag, 1979).

symbol, however, of the distance of financial regulation from the mainstream of West German economic and political life.[11]

The Bundesbank, one of the most powerful and autonomous central banks in the world, also plays a significant regulatory role. Headquartered in Frankfurt, Germany's principal financial center, the Bundesbank possesses primary responsibility for German external and domestic monetary policy and thus exerts an important influence on the operations of the banks. As summed up in a recent study of German banking, the Bundesbank's principal functions are those of "banker to the federal government, issuer of bank notes, intermediary for inter-bank transactions, controller of the money supply, lender of last resort to banks and maintainer of the value of the Deutsche Mark."[12] Among its principal powers, the Bundesbank can influence bank liquidity and market interest rates by varying the minimum reserve ratios of banks and setting the discount rate at which they may borrow from the central bank. To a far greater degree than the Banking Supervisory Office, however, the Bundesbank has traditionally identified with the outlook and interests of the German banking community and has regularly helped to represent its viewpoints to the appropriate ministries in Bonn.[13] As a general rule, the commercial banks "can get their point of view aired at the right place at the right time [in Bonn] through the Bundesbank," observed a former senior official of the bank.[14]

11. In terms of the broader relations beyond the regulatory sphere that exist between German banks and their government, the Supervisory Office would appear similarly removed. Paraphrasing the words of one senior Supervisory Office official on the subject of the large banks' input into German foreign policy: "We don't know. [For that] you must go to Frankfurt and Bonn, and in Bonn particularly to the Economics and Finance Ministries. . . . The key to our system is that it is very free. Banks can do whatever they're not explicitly forbidden from doing. And as you can see from the Banking Law, there are very few regulations." Interview with senior officials of the Federal Banking Supervisory Office, Berlin, June 23, 1980.

12. Philip Thorn and Jean M. Lack, eds., *Banking and Sources of Finance in the European Community* (London: Banker Research Unit, 1977), pp. 150–51.

13. The backgrounds of two of the last three Bundesbank presidents suggest a pattern of ties to Germany's banking establishment. Karl Klasen, president from 1970 to 1977, came from the management of the Deutsche Bank and returned to its Supervisory Board after leaving the Bundesbank. Karl Otto Pöhl, who assumed the presidency in 1980, once worked as head of public relations for the Federation of German Banks.

14. Interview with former senior official of the Bundesbank, Frankfurt, July 9, 1980. It should be stressed, however, that exceptions to this rule exist. For instance, one major exception occurred during January–March 1979, when the Bundesbank wanted a more restrictive credit policy than the German banking community and actually opposed its viewpoints in Bonn.

At the same time, the Bundesbank's independent status has kept it detached from the policy-formulating processes of the German government (outside of the bank's own domain of monetary policy). Despite its relatively close links with the Banking Supervisory Office, the Bundesbank, in the words of a senior official of the Federation of German Banks, "is a bank for banks, not a regulatory board. They feel like a bank. They can understand banks."[15] The Bundesbank has arguably played a more important role as a conduit between German banks and the foreign economic policy apparatus of government (for example, in the crisis created by the U.S. freeze of Iranian assets in 1979) than as a regulator in a narrowly conceived sense. In any event, the principal responsibility for regulating the activities of German banks has resided with the Banking Supervisory Office in Berlin.

In summary, regulation of German banking, although slowly becoming more structured and formalized, remains relatively weak. As the author of a 1980 International Monetary Fund memorandum concluded:

Thus, it is fair to say that on the whole most regulations under the Banking Act are defined in a rather general way and have been applied liberally by the authorities. As a result, the banking sector enjoys an amount of freedom of action which probably is not matched by banks in many other countries.[16]

The Role of Large Banks

A natural result of Germany's laissez-faire financial environment has been the emergence of a uniquely German strain of universal banking, in which a vast number of the nation's banks are free to function as truly multipurpose financial institutions. Nearly all German private commercial banks and a number of additional banks, such as the central giro institutions of the savings banks, pursue a wide range of financial activities, including investment and merchant banking as well as the retail and wholesale functions of American banks.[17] The great deal of

15. Interview with official of the Federation of German Banks, Cologne, July 2, 1980.

16. Klaus-Walter Riechel, "Functional and Structural Aspects of the German Universal Banking System," Departmental Memorandum 80/26, Central Banking Service, International Monetary Fund, March 27, 1980, p. 15.

17. The following more detailed description of German universal banking functions has been offered by the Federation of German Banks: "Nearly all the private commercial banks are universal (or multipurpose) banks: they collect deposits of all amounts and different running periods, they lend money at short, medium and long-term and to every extent, they deal with securities of all kinds . . . , carry out payment transactions and deal with foreign exchange, currency, coins and precious metals. All kinds of business

specialization evident within the system has resulted primarily from conscious choice and not from legal impediments confining banks to particular functional areas. Many institutions, while remaining multi-purpose in at least a technical sense, have committed most available resources to carving out a limited market niche for themselves, usually one capitalizing on in-house strengths. For example, areas of speciali-zation for private bankers have included export finance, securities trading and underwriting, industrial finance, property management, and real estate finance. In parallel fashion, most regional commercial banks, as their name implies, have concentrated resources on the development of business within a specific geographic area, although some have acquired functional specializations as well.

In the competitive intensity of the German marketplace, almost all banks have had to specialize in order to survive or at least to ensure maximum profitability. A very few universal banks, however, have competed so effectively across the full range of banking services that they have climbed to predominant positions in almost every sector of German finance. These exceptional institutions are today the largest in the system in terms of assets and among the largest in the world. Their full importance cannot be assessed accurately through measures of their share of total German banking assets; as already observed, the degree of concentration in the overall system is relatively low, even if the largest private universal banks do control a sizable portion of assets in the system's commercial sector. Instead, to understand completely the premier position of these banks, one must look to their leadership role within the German financial community and beyond to their position of influence over German industry and within the German polity.

At the top of the list are the Big Three commercial banks: Deutsche Bank, Dresdner Bank, and Commerzbank. All three institutions are structured as publicly held share corporations and maintain principal headquarters in Frankfurt or Düsseldorf. Deutsche, with over $83 billion of assets at the end of 1982, ranked then as the eleventh largest bank in the world; remarkably, this single institution has financed or handled payment for as much as 25 percent of German trade in recent years.[18]

are effected nationally and internationally. . . . Furthermore, the private commercial banks are deeply engaged in the services of property management, investment advice and investment saving." Bank-Verlag Köln, *The Banking System of the Federal Republic of Germany*, p. 13.

18. Interviews with official of the Federation of German Banks, Cologne, July 2, 1980, and with senior officer of the Deutsche Bank, New York City, November 30, 1982.

All three banks ranked among the world's twenty-five largest throughout 1976–80; as a result of the recent German economic recession and an 18 percent weakening of the deutsche mark against the dollar during 1981–82, however, Commerzbank was not on that select list as of year-end 1982.[19] Deutsche, Dresdner, and Commerzbank are each unrivaled in the extent of their domestic branch networks, which span all parts of Germany; Commerzbank, the smallest of the three, maintained approximately 875 domestic branches during the early 1980s, and the combined total for the three exceeds 3,000.

In addition to the Big Three private commercial banks, a public institution of rapidly growing national and international influence is the Westdeutsche Landesbank Girozentrale (WestLB), formed in 1969 through a merger. Headquartered in Düsseldorf and owned jointly by the federal state of North Rhine–Westphalia, various local savings bank organizations, and regional authorities, WestLB functions both as the country's largest central giro institution and as a universal bank specializing in long-term finance. Although much of its business is concentrated in its home state, WestLB has been a major participant in the Eurocredit markets since the mid-1970s. It ranked as the world's twenty-sixth largest bank at year-end 1982.[20]

The influence of Germany's largest universal banks, and particularly the Big Three private institutions, is difficult to overestimate. Within the financial system, they dominate the development of new banking services, the self-policing of the industry, and the formulation of industry policy positions on subjects ranging from proposed federal legislation to Bundesbank monetary policy. Much of the influence of the largest banks over the banking community's policy positions has a semi-institutionalized character and derives in part from those banks' privileged status in the national peak banking associations.[21] These associations, in turn, play a major role in representing the banking industry en masse to the federal government and the public. According to German law, for instance, the federal government must consult the appropriate peak associations whenever new laws affecting banking are being considered. Similarly, the Banking Act requires that these associations be consulted

19. Commerzbank ranked as the world's thirty-ninth largest bank as of year-end 1982 (ranking according to assets less contra accounts). See "The Top 500 in World Banking," *Banker* (London), vol. 133 (June 1983), pp. 177–79.

20. Ibid., p. 179.

21. These peak associations are centrally organized federations that assist in defining and advancing the interests of German banks in a particular institutional category, such as all commercial banks.

before the Federal Banking Supervisory Office may draw up principles to determine the adequacy of bank capital and liquidity. The most influential peak banking association is the Cologne-headquartered Federation of German Banks, representing all indigenous commercial banks in the nation. The Big Three banks, in turn, are highly influential in determining the federation's policies and positions. These three banks, and in particular the Deutsche Bank, lead in funding the federation and preparing its staff positions, and as of 1981, managing directors of these banks sat on its presidium and chaired three of its four most important working committees, including those for credit policy and questions of law.[22]

In self-policing the financial system, the dominance of the big banks is typified by their role on the Eurobond Subcommittee of the Central Capital Market Committee, also known by its German abbreviation, ZKMA. The ZKMA, described by Michael Kreile as "a club of the chief issue banks,"[23] was formed by the country's leading banks in 1957, with the agreement of the Economics Ministry, to control and coordinate access to the German capital market. The subcommittee, established in 1968 to arrange queueing of foreign issues in the domestic DM market, now greatly exceeds the ZKMA in importance.[24] Characterized by several critics as a "self-perpetuating oligarchy" and a "self-service store,"[25] the six-member subcommittee included senior officials of the

22. The degree of individual member banks' influence over the federation's stands on questions of banking and public policy is directly proportional to the quality of the staff work the banks supply to the federation as input. The Big Three, led by the Deutsche Bank, provide the most extensive and highest-quality staff support, and these banks have deliberately (and successfully) worked to keep the association's in-house analytic capability limited in order to maximize their own impact.

23. Michael Kreile, "West Germany: The Dynamics of Expansion," in Peter J. Katzenstein, ed., *Between Power and Plenty: Foreign Economic Policies of Advanced Industrial States* (University of Wisconsin Press, 1978), p. 212.

24. The unpublicized and nebulously defined operations of the subcommittee may give it influence far exceeding the timing of foreign bond issues' entry onto the German market. When the subcommittee requested that the Deutsche Genossenschaftsbank (DG Bank), a nonmember, postpone a DM 100 million issue for the Republic of Austria in May 1978, many observers believed the subcommittee objected primarily to the DG Bank's generous terms, 5¼ percent over ten years, and not to the then-prevailing volume of foreign deutsche mark issues. Pamela Clarke, "The German Capital Markets: Why DG's Austrian Issue Was Postponed," *Euromoney* (July 1978), pp. 95–96.

25. Patrick Myall, "How Closed is the Banker's Closed Shop?" *Euromoney* (February 1979), p. 69; and comment made by Ernst-Otto Sandvoss, chairman of the Board of Management, Deutsche Girozentrale–Deutsche Kommunalbank, quoted in Darrell Delamaide, "West Germany III: Keeping Order in the Capital Markets," *Institutional Investor,* international edition (June 1980), p. 114.

five largest banks in the country in 1980. The banks represented by all six members controlled over 90 percent of the new-issue market for DM Eurobonds at that time. In addition to its membership, several aspects of the work and operating style of the subcommittee are noteworthy because they reflect key functional characteristics of the German financial system. The subcommittee's operations demonstrate collective supervision by the nation's leading banks of their own activities as an alternative to government regulation; the management of a crucially important German financial market through informal consensus of elite participants, worked out behind closed doors; and the performance by leading German banks of a significant semipublic function.[26]

The influence of the largest universal banks extends beyond the financial community to Germany's critically important industrial sector. Under the universal system, banks may own shares and (at least for the moment) controlling interests in nonbank companies, including companies they lend to; vote shares of customers they represent (proxy authority); and participate in the oversight of nonbank companies through memberships on their supervisory boards held by top bank officers. As Germany's official Monopolies Commission observed in understated fashion in a study covering the years 1973–75, "Interrelationships between banks and non-banking corporations, frequently industrial enterprises, represent a form of conglomerate concentration particularly characteristic of Germany."[27] Similarly, a more recent Monopolies Commission report concluded that "there exists a tendency of large banks to acquire large firms."[28] Experts have found the full extent of bank influence over the German corporate sector difficult to gauge, but sufficient statistical evidence exists to support assertions that the influence is quite strong, and that the largest banks wield the preponderant portion of it.[29]

26. A senior Bundesbank officer attends all subcommittee meetings with the status of guest or observer. This person can be quite influential because of the subcommittee membership's considerable reluctance to take actions conflicting with the expressed wishes of the Bundesbank. However, in many other countries the central bank performs the same queueing function directly.

27. "The First Bi-Annual Report by the Monopolies Commission (Summary)," *German Economic Review* (Stuttgart), separate print, vol. 15 (1977), p. 157.

28. "West Germany: Monopolies Commission," *Journal of World Trade Law,* vol. 13 (September–October 1979), p. 458.

29. A large part of the measurement problem derives from banks' reluctance to provide relevant data, on occasion even to the German federal government. The Monopolies Commission reported in 1976, for instance, that it had intended "to determine by means of a special empirical survey to what extent participations of banks in non-

Data gathered by the Monopolies Commission in 1975, for example, revealed that banks, through their direct shareholdings, exercised significant voting rights of more than 5 percent in fifty-six of Germany's one hundred largest share companies. In a total of thirty cases the voting rights held by banks exceeded 50 percent, while in forty-one cases they amounted to at least 25 percent, sufficient to exercise blocking interest (veto control) under German corporate law. The influence of the Big Three commercial banks was especially important, as their shareholdings alone represented more than 25 percent of voting rights in eleven of the firms.

Proxy rights and directorships have substantially enhanced the influence of the Big Three banks as well. The commission's research further disclosed that these banks held proxies at the 1975 annual meetings of fifty-four of Germany's one hundred largest share companies. In the case of four of the ten largest share companies, the Big Three banks held proxies totaling 25 percent or more of voting rights, and hence maintained control of management by veto. Moreover, some observers have claimed that the banks commonly exchange proxies among themselves under a German business custom known as "loaned votes," thereby permitting a bank to multiply its voting power in any enterprise in which it has a particular interest.[30] The Big Three banks' control of directorships has been similarly extensive. Of 179 such directorships held by all banks in the one hundred largest share companies in 1975, the Big Three accounted for 102. Of the thirty-one cases where bankers were chairmen, representatives of the Big Three held twenty-one of these positions.[31]

---

banking enterprises coincided with positions held by banks in supervisory boards and with voting rights of shares held in custody by the banks, and whether such cumulative positions of influence were concentrated in certain industries." However, "because of the unsatisfactory response of essential parts of the banking sector, no such analysis could be performed." "The First Bi-Annual Report," p. 166.

30. According to the "loaned vote" practice, it is possible that banks may exchange proxies without referring back to the shareholder on each occasion when his vote is passed on for casting by another trustee. See Shonfield, *Modern Capitalism,* p. 250; and *Bericht der Studienkommission "Grundsatzfragen der Kreditwirtschaft,"* p. 308.

31. See "West Germany: Monopolies Commission," pp. 457–61. Every management board member of a bank is allowed to sit on the supervisory boards of ten nonbank companies. No restriction at all applied until 1965, when official discovery that Hermann Abs of the Deutsche Bank sat on at least thirty boards prompted promulgation of a "Lex Abs." Indicative of the unrivaled status of Deutsche is the fact that during the late 1970s it could claim 54 representatives among a total of 182 bankers sitting on the supervisory boards of all companies listed on the Frankfurt Stock Exchange. See Frederick Kempe, "The Universal Banks Resist Reform," *Euromoney* (July 1979), pp. 175–76.

The relationship between Germany's largest banks and corporations contains important elements of reciprocity. Industry executives also sit on the supervisory boards of the Big Three, and many of the largest industrial companies own shares in these banks. German tradition encourages private corporations and their lead banks to operate as a team. The Big Three, in particular, derive a large measure of their influence not from the exercise of brute force over client company managements, but from the often-unparalleled expertise they can offer those companies. This expertise typically extends well beyond financial matters, as the largest German banks maintain an intimate knowledge of both the daily operations of important commercial customers and trends in their industries.

Possessing the competent staff and the vantage point to take a broad view of a company's operating environment, the big German banks have often functioned as a highly valued source of new business ideas, even a force working for intra-industry coordination and rationalization. As early as 1920, Alfred Marshall concluded, "The German banks have surpassed even those of America in the promptitude and energy with which they faced the risks of turning a large flow of capital into an enterprise . . . to which the future belongs."[32] Fifty years later, Andrew Shonfield could still remark on "the sheer technical competence of the banks, especially in matters concerned with industrial innovation."[33] And John Zysman, writing in the early 1980s, portrayed the banks as "the 'prefects' in the German system of organized capitalism and the leaders in the process of [negotiated industrial] adjustment which that system facilitates."[34]

In summary, the several huge, highly diversified banking institutions that have thrived in the laissez-faire German financial environment are an exclusive elite within the German economic system. These premier houses as a group have constituted a logical partner not only for German business but for the German federal government as well. As such, some banks have acquired, in Shonfield's phrase, "a recognized special status—an almost para-statal position, as the natural and trusted ally of public authority."[35] The partnership of German government and finance

32. Alfred Marshall, *Industry and Trade: A Study of Industrial Technique and Business Organization; and of Their Influences on the Conditions of Various Classes and Nations* (London: Macmillan, 1920), p. 558.

33. Shonfield, *Modern Capitalism*, p. 262.

34. John Zysman, *Governments, Markets, and Growth: Financial Systems and the Politics of Industrial Change* (Cornell University Press, 1983), p. 260.

35. Shonfield, *Modern Capitalism*, p. 262.

has focused on important policy areas where the banks possess relevant expertise or commercial interests that overlap with state objectives. To a significant degree this cooperation has hinged on the absence of far-reaching government regulatory intervention in German banking affairs; unencumbered by extensive adversary dealings with the banks, the federal government has enjoyed decided freedom to maneuver in establishing a consultative dialogue with them on matters of policy.

The appeal to government policymakers of an ongoing dialogue with the largest universal banks has been enhanced by the latter's elaborate links well beyond the financial system. These banks have emerged not only as excellent sources of information and analysis on the German economy, but as natural conduits between government and the corporate world.

The Export Drive and Foreign Policy

In the field of foreign policy, Germany's principal financial houses and the government seek a "quiet consensus" when matters of international banking and state become intertwined.[36] In recent years the greatest overlapping of interests between German banks and foreign policy formulators has occurred in the area of German trade, particularly exports, and it is here that the two groups' occasional direct partnership has become most apparent. Exports have played a critical role in both the definition of the Federal Republic's foreign policy and the expansion of leading German banks' international financial activities. Under the watchful eye of both government and banks, the drive to export emerged as one of the most powerful growth-stimulating forces operating on the post–World War II German economy. Drawing upon an abundant labor supply, German technical and industrial capabilities, and unified domestic opinion in its favor, the drive has turned the Federal Republic into the second largest exporting nation in the world.[37] In 1981 West German exports totaled $176.1 billion, behind only those of the United States.[38]

36. Interview with chief officer in the United States of a major German bank, New York City, March 27, 1980.

37. For an elaboration of this point, see Kreile, "West Germany," p. 193.

38. International Monetary Fund, *International Financial Statistics,* Supplement on Trade Statistics, Supplement Series, no. 4 (Washington, D.C.: IMF, 1982), pp. 118–21. U.S. exports totaled $233.7 billion in 1981.

Table 2-2. *Sales and Export Ratios of Selected German Industries, 1981*

Sales in billions of U.S. dollars[a]

Industry[b]	Sales	Export ratio
Motor cars and other road vehicles	52.2	44.3
Chemicals	51.7	40.8
Mechanical engineering	50.5	45.8
Electrical engineering	46.2	31.7
Mineral oil processing	27.7	4.9
Iron and steel	19.5	40.0
Metalware	15.2	23.2
Textiles	13.5	23.4
Cement and bricks	12.3	9.8
Plastic processing	12.1	19.7
Wood processing	11.7	10.3
Coal mining	10.5	17.6
Steel drawing and cold rolling mills, steel shaping	10.3	19.7
Steel and light metal structures	9.8	20.8
Nonferrous metals	9.3	28.5
Clothing	9.2	14.2
Total, all German industry	488.3	27.3

Source: Dresdner Bank, *Report for the Year 1981*, p. 31.
a. Converted at rate of DM 2.26 = $1.00.
b. Most important industrial sectors as measured by sales.

At the same time, the small size and limited absorptive capacity of the German domestic market have rendered a number of key German industrial sectors highly export-dependent. In 1975, for example, the aggregate (direct plus indirect) export dependence of the investment goods industries amounted to 47.4 percent. Figures for other industries include: machine-building, 56 percent; automotive, 52 percent; iron-producing, 67 percent; and chemical, 48.5 percent.[39] Direct exports alone are also strikingly high as a percentage of total sales of many industrial sectors, as illustrated in table 2-2.

The factors prompting the government's commitment to export growth and the development of export markets reach to the core of the Federal Republic's economic livelihood. As of 1981, exports supplied an impressive 25.6 percent of the gross domestic product (up from about 15 percent in the mid-1960s, and compared with 8.1 percent in the United

39. Kreile, "West Germany," p. 201.

States) and 20 percent of the nation's jobs.[40] For a nation that must import 97 percent of its oil and most other raw materials, exports have further represented to the government a critically important source of foreign revenue; during the 1970s export growth became essential simply to cover oil price increases if the nation's current account were to be kept near long-term balance. Exports have also been the only feasible means of maintaining sufficient demand in certain key industrial sectors (such as nuclear power plant manufacturing) to ensure their continued existence. For German banks, the stakes in export growth have included lucrative international financing opportunities and the continued health of not only firms but entire industries to which the leading houses are deeply committed.

The highly complementary interests of government, industry, and banks in the export sphere have provided a cornerstone for their cooperation on a wider range of foreign economic policy issues. At one time or another these associated issues have included development and diversification of foreign raw materials sources for the German economy and expansion of ties with foreign countries that offer potentially attractive markets for German products (more recently, for German direct investment as well). A discernible recent trend also pointed toward increased bank-government cooperation in areas where there is an overlap between commercial financial relationships and high-level foreign policy interests (for example, in Portugal in 1978 and Poland in 1980).

Although the direction of influence between German banks and government, like that between banks and industry, has often been two-way, the German government has usually been the more equal partner in the relationship. The banking community may be well positioned to advocate its views to the government on a wide array of international policy matters, such as foreign trade and export credit policies, but Bonn is even better positioned to offer inducements to the banks to behave in a manner consistent with its own objectives. By adjusting the terms of loan guarantees available through Hermes, the German export credit program, the government interministerial committee responsible for

40. Exports as percentage of gross domestic product from IMF, *International Financial Statistics*, Supplement on Trade Statistics, no. 4, p. 52. Employment statistic from Export-Import Bank of the United States, *Report to the U.S. Congress on Export Credit Competition and the Export-Import Bank of the United States for the Period July 1, 1980, through December 31, 1980* (Export-Import Bank, 1981), p. 45.

Hermes has frequently sought to stimulate (or discourage) German bank commercial interest in entire categories of international transactions, including transactions with particular countries. Still another tool of influence at Bonn's disposal has been the cofinancing capability of the government-owned Kreditanstalt für Wiederaufbau, which joins with German commercial banks to extend international loans on occasion. Although used sparingly in deference to the banking system's laissez-faire principles of organization, an ultimate tool at Bonn's disposal has been moral suasion backed by the implicit threat of less governmental cooperation, perhaps even tacit resistance, in the future.

In the past, on matters of "high politics" involving German strategic interests, the German banking and business communities generally were not consulted and rarely, if ever, enjoyed the upper hand. For example, during the days of the Adenauer administration's cool treatment of the Soviet bloc, banking and business interests did not vigorously or effectively oppose the government's restrictive policies toward granting guarantees for long-term export credits to Comecon countries. Similarly, business and financial interests played a subservient role in formulation of the *Ostpolitik* (Eastern policy) conducted by the Social Democratic party–Free Democratic party coalition from 1969 onward. In Kreile's words, "*Ostpolitik* stands out as an area of 'high politics' par excellence. It was essentially formulated both by the relevant government departments (Chancellor's Office and Foreign Office) and by the foreign policy establishment of the Bundestag parties. Business hardly ever dared to intervene in this sensitive core area of foreign policy."[41]

As the 1970s progressed, however, the interests and even the continued health of German banks and industry became increasingly intertwined with high German foreign policy, particularly vis-à-vis the Soviet bloc countries. *Ostpolitik,* although not the product of private-sector pressure on the German government, created the circumstances in which German banks and industry undertook dramatically increased commitments to Eastern Europe. The policy's indirect commercial consequences have included the creation of as much as $6 billion in outstanding German bank loans to Poland at year-end 1981 (probably only 40 to 50 percent covered by German government guarantees),[42] and the German

41. Kreile, "West Germany," pp. 204–05, 208.
42. John Tagliabue, "Payments Reported by Poland," *New York Times,* January 13, 1982; and Edward Cowan, "U.S. to Pay Part of Polish Debt; Default Avoided," *New York Times,* February 1, 1982.

private sector's enthusiastic support for the construction of a 2,800-mile large-diameter (56-inch) natural gas pipeline from Urengoi in northwest Siberia to the Soviet Union's western border. As of mid-1982, the estimated hard currency cost of that pipeline was $5 billion, and it appeared likely to provide billions of deutsche marks of export contracts to a sagging German economy, not to mention major financial opportunities for German banks. Even more significant for German industry and banks have been the potential benefits of the overall pipeline expansion program currently under way in the Soviet Union. This program, scheduled to produce 9,600 miles of new 56-inch pipeline capacity in addition to the 2,800-mile Urengoi line, could generate up to $15 billion in European pipe and machinery exports (and credit requirements) by 1985.[43]

Inevitably, once *Ostpolitik* facilitated increased German commercial interdependence with the Soviet bloc countries, German high foreign policy could not ignore the results. Thus a clear concern for German industrial and banking interests was apparent in the German government's ambivalent response throughout 1980 to the Carter administration's call for allied economic sanctions against the Soviet Union following its military intervention in Afghanistan. The same concern essentially explains the German government's reluctance during 1982 to join U.S. economic sanctions against both the Soviet Union and Poland following the Warsaw regime's imposition of martial law.

The domestic consensus in favor of export growth has been so strong that the leading banks have made uncharacteristically blunt statements urging still further governmental and public support for it. A recent official pronouncement of the Dresdner Bank typifies the general export positions publicly advocated by the Big Three:

> The clouds on the horizon of world trade are dark enough. We can and must not afford to jeopardise our export possibilities, which have anyway grown fewer, and to foster the growing pressure from imports. . . . For German industry, dependent as it is on the export of finished goods and the import of raw materials and energy, it now seems more important than ever to set foreign trade on as wide a basis as possible and to strengthen its position on promising markets.[44]

The forums available to Germany's largest banks for expressing views

43. Ed. A. Hewett, "The Pipeline Connection: Issues for the Alliance," *Brookings Review,* vol. 1 (Fall 1982), pp. 18–19.

44. Dresdner Bank, *Report for the Year 1978,* pp. 32, 36.

on exports and related foreign policy issues are hardly limited to public statements, however. A variety of contacts, both institutionalized and informal, exists between the banking and foreign policy communities. The institutionalized role of the banking associations in representing member banks' views to government has already been cited. For the Federation of German Banks, in particular, this role has regularly included matters with foreign policy content.[45] The banking community has found additional institutionalized forums for expressing its views in several interministerial committees of the federal government charged with coordinating foreign economic policy, such as the one responsible for allocating export credit guarantees (the Hermes interministerial committee). Although voting rights on this committee extend only to senior civil servants representing the Ministries of Economics, Finance, Foreign Affairs, and Economic Cooperation, bankers and export industry representatives participate in committee sessions as advisory members.[46] Bankers also sit in an advisory capacity on the interministerial committee handling insurance for direct foreign investments.[47] The boards of public institutions, such as the Kreditanstalt für Wiederaufbau, have provided bankers further organized access to foreign policy formulators.[48] Prominent bankers as well as industrialists also frequently sit on formal advisory councils to the federal ministries. The most important such body with respect to foreign economic policy has been the Foreign Trade Advisory Council of the Ministry of Economics, whose forty-one members recently included five bankers and seventeen directors of export-oriented industrial corporations.[49]

In comparison with institutionalized contacts, informal links have played an even more important role in promoting communication between Germany's largest banks and foreign policy machinery. In the post–World War II years, a succession of leading German bankers has

45. See, for example, John Tagliabue, "German Banks Seek Bonn Pledge on Poland," *New York Times*, December 21, 1981.

46. Hermes Kreditversicherungs-Aktiengesellschaft (Hermes AG), "The German System of Export Credit Insurance," document no. 9 Tr/1M (May 1980), p. 2.

47. Hans-Eckart Scharrer, "Die Rolle der Banken," in Hans-Peter Schwarz, ed., *Handbuch der Deutschen Aussenpolitik* (Munich: Piper, 1975), p. 221.

48. The KfW board, whose chairman is the minister of finance, has included in recent years the minister of economics, the minister of foreign affairs, the president of the Bundesbank, the minister for economic cooperation, and representatives of the principal German banking associations, among others. The banking association representatives have invariably included some of the country's most influential bankers.

49. See Kreile, "West Germany," p. 202.

had access to the chancellor on far-reaching policy matters involving German banking, industry and international relations.[50] These men have included Robert Pferdmenges (Bankhaus Sal. Oppenheim), Hermann Abs (Deutsche Bank), Jürgen Ponto (Dresdner Bank), and Wilfried Guth (Deutsche Bank). Senior executives from the leading banks frequently accompany the chancellor or cabinet ministers on official international trips. Phone exchanges, office visits (including visits by cabinet ministers to the commercial banks), and working lunches and dinners also regularly bring top bankers and foreign policy officials of the Federal Republic together. The role of informal, ad hoc communication in helping banking and governmental elites to work toward agreement on many major issues of foreign policy cannot easily be overemphasized.

A Historical Note

The large banks' crucial role in the German economy and polity reflects patterns that, despite interruptions, have characterized German finance for over one hundred years. The period from 1870 to 1914, in particular, was a watershed era for German banking, producing many of the institutions, institutional relationships, and public- and private-sector attitudes toward international lending that reemerged to shape German finance during the postwar years.

Although several major German commercial banks existed as early as the 1850s, the establishment of the Deutsche Bank by the industrialist Georg von Siemens in 1871 marked the beginning of the consolidation of German banking and German banks' systematic development of deposit business. (It is noteworthy that the German Empire was created in the same year.) Between the early 1870s and 1885, German financial power became heavily concentrated in Berlin, not only the center of wholesale demand and purchasing power in the empire but also its seat of government.[51]

By the early 1900s, four great banks, known as the "four Ds," dominated Berlin and German finance in terms of accumulated capital and business volume: the Deutsche Bank, Disconto-Gesellschaft, Dresdner

50. Scharrer, "Die Rolle der Banken," p. 221.
51. J. Riesser, *The German Great Banks and Their Concentration in Connection with the Economic Development of Germany* (Government Printing Office, 1911), pp. 44–47, 85, 87, 653–55.

Bank, and Darmstädter Bank. (The Commerz Bank headed the second tier of banks. Later, during 1929–31, the Disconto-Gesellschaft and Darmstädter Bank merged into the Deutsche and Dresdner Banks, respectively.)[52] The mandate of the most powerful of the four Ds, the Deutsche, was to promote German commercial relations with other countries and simultaneously fuse German industrial and banking interests.[53] All of the great banks practiced the "mixed" or universal form of banking still characteristic of German finance.

By the turn of the century, the great banks possessed extremely close ties to German industry. Through their "over-generous" granting of long-term loans and representation on clients' supervisory boards, the banks wielded decisive influence over most of Germany's largest companies.[54] Another distinctive characteristic of German finance at that time was its close working relationship with the imperial government, a relationship in which formal official supervision of banking activities played a minimal role.[55] In the international sphere, the partnership of German banks and government worked largely to advance vital German trade interests, dictated by the German economic system's increasing dependence on the development of export markets. Indicative of Germany's enormous industrial growth during the period, German exports rose from fourth to second largest in the world shortly after 1880 and maintained that position until the start of World War I.[56]

Feis captures much of the flavor of relations between the German government and the great banks during the period 1870 to 1914, particularly on matters of international policy:

For the advancement of [German international interests] the government trusted to a large degree to the instinct of the private investor and the judgment and initiative of the Great Banks. It did not wish to introduce itself formally and regularly into the affairs of the money market or of the banks. . . .

It was by private, direct, unofficial but steady communication with the directing heads of the important banks that the Kaiser and the Foreign Office assured themselves of the adjustment of capital movements to their judgments

52. Gustav Stolper, *German Economy, 1870–1940: Issues and Trends* (New York: Reynal and Hitchcock, 1940), p. 50.

53. Marshall, *Industry and Trade*, p. 567.

54. Shonfield, *Modern Capitalism*, p. 247.

55. Herbert Feis, *Europe: The World's Banker, 1870–1914: An Account of European Foreign Investment and the Connection of World Finance with Diplomacy before the War* (Yale University Press for the Council on Foreign Relations, 1930), pp. 78, 163, 187.

56. Stolper, *German Economy, 1870–1940*, p. 52.

and policies. Such communication permitted secrecy, flexibility of judgment, and formulation of terms of common advantage. . . .[57]

Two disastrous world wars and a financially chaotic interwar period irrevocably altered numerous aspects of German bank-government relations. At the very least, the German economic system is far more liberal today, and successive governments of the postwar Federal Republic have probably been more circumspect than any of their predecessor regimes in using German banks as tools of state economic or mercantilist policies. Yet the extent to which the big German banks succeeded in reconstituting themselves along traditional lines following World War II, despite the opposition of the occupying powers, remains truly remarkable. Although those powers attempted to impose the American principle of "state banking" on the German financial system, limiting any one bank's operations to a single *Land,* the Deutsche and Dresdner Banks both managed to reestablish central control over virtually their entire national branch networks by 1950, and Commerzbank achieved the same result by 1958.[58] Similarly, the largest German banks, unimpeded by extensive regulatory supervision, succeeded in reasserting themselves as influential partners to both German industry and government in the postwar years.

One cannot simply extrapolate from the German bank-government dynamics of the late nineteenth and early twentieth centuries to understand the subtleties of the modern "quiet consensus" between Bonn's foreign policy apparatus and the German big banks on many issues of international policy. Nevertheless, scrutiny of the period from 1870 to 1914 does provide clues as to the foundations on which modern German bank-government relations are built. In this context, Shonfield's observation on the postwar reconstruction of the German economy holds particular relevance to the postwar development of institutional relations among German banks, government, and industry:

The defeat, division, and chaos which Germany suffered in the 1940s did not wipe out the legacy of the past; it only lifted temporarily the pressure of history. When the Germans began to reconstruct their economy, they built upon the familiar structural foundation and plan, much of it invisible to the naked eye, as if guided by an archeologist who could pick his way blindfold about some favorite ruin.[59]

57. Feis, *Europe: The World's Banker,* pp. 163, 166.
58. "The law was changed to suit the facts in 1954," notes Shonfield. *Modern Capitalism,* p. 242.
59. Ibid., p. 240.

CHAPTER THREE

Bank-Government Relations: Cases of Limited Interaction

As Germany's international banking and official foreign policy communities pursue their own concerns and objectives, complementary patterns of behavior regularly result. Free market forces, mutually reinforcing interests, and excellent communication frequently work together to define the positive tone of relations between these two communities.

The extent of direct involvement between German banks and their government varies according to the circumstances of the financial transaction at hand. The foreign transactions of the largest German banks can be roughly categorized, in fact, according to the interest they arouse in the German foreign policy community. As a rule, the latter's interest in a particular deal and willingness to influence it will reflect both the political content and the financial risk entailed. The vast majority of German banks' international lending and deposit-taking activities fall in the category of little or no interaction at all. The exceptional cases of direct coordination will be discussed in the next chapter; cases in which coordination has been nonexistent or limited to government provision of incentives or signals in the financial marketplace will be considered here.

First, there is a large category of transactions that have negligible political ramifications for the German government and thus arouse little or no interest on the part of its foreign policy machinery. Consequently, German banks are left to make independent entrepreneurial decisions in this area, one of very considerable commercial value to them. Examples of transactions in this category include most general working capital or balance-of-payments loans by German banks to foreign governments; most loans by these banks' foreign branches to commercial entities in host countries, including the local subsidiaries of German companies; interbank loans; and the vast majority of deposits.

Standard Trade Credits

A second major category of transactions involving somewhat greater bank-government interaction is that of German export credits and loans to finance foreign raw material projects that will provide some portion of their output to the German economy. German banking and foreign economic policy interests converge in this credit category, and the total volume of financing is perhaps the largest of any subgroup of German commercial international loans.[1] The interaction between the German government and banks is generally limited here to the government's routine offering of loan guarantees (for a fee, which banks try to pass on to the borrower) and the banks' weighing of the availability of such guarantees in decisions on whether or not to extend financing.

The German government typically offers export and raw materials guarantees on the basis of its assessment of the political and commercial risk inherent in the underlying loans, not on the basis of specific foreign policy objectives. The primary intent of the government in issuing such guarantees is to stimulate exports and secure raw materials at a macro level. As a consequence, the government's interest in specific transactions is negligible. From the lending perspective, the availability of a Hermes export or raw materials credit guarantee becomes of interest to a German bank when it is sufficiently uncomfortable with the level of financial risk to be willing to pay a fee to eliminate most of it.[2]

The mechanism for bank-government interaction in this credit cate-

1. Herbert Wolf, "Worldwide German Banking—II," *Bankers Magazine* (Boston), vol. 163 (November–December 1980), pp. 96–97.
2. In the case of individual credits disbursed to German exporters, Hermes guarantees covered up to 85 percent of the commercial risk and 90 percent of the political risk as of 1980. In the case of buyer credits that German banks extended directly to foreign importers, Hermes guarantees covered up to 95 percent of the banks' risk. Export-Import Bank of the United States, *Report to the U.S. Congress on Export Credit Competition and the Export-Import Bank of the United States for the Period July 1, 1980, through December 31, 1980* (Export-Import Bank, 1981), pp. 49–50; and interview with officials of Hermes AG, Hamburg, June 25, 1980.

gory is usually the Hermes interministerial committee.[3] This committee, whose voting members include senior civil service representatives from the Ministries of Economics, Finance, Foreign Affairs, and Economic Cooperation, is charged with awarding individual guarantees in response to applications from German banks and export suppliers. German bankers and export industry representatives also sit on the committee in an advisory capacity, although they cannot attend all meetings. In unusual instances involving particularly large or problematic guarantees, the final decision rests with the full German cabinet, consisting of the chancellor and the heads of the various ministries. In the standard instance, however, the procedures for allocating guarantees for exports or supplies of raw materials are formal and systematic. The political content of the underlying loans is relatively low, consisting of their contribution to the achievement of broad objectives of German foreign economic policy. The risk in these transactions is low to moderate: low enough to cause the government to assume it on a quasi-commercial basis in return for a premium, high enough for the resultant guarantee to induce banks to take a course of action they very likely would not have adopted without the guarantee.

Under normal circumstances, the Hermes guarantee mechanism serves to influence the allocation of German bank credit toward export financing in general and specifically toward those foreign borrowers most likely to be of direct benefit to the German economy. The mechanism involves no stated understandings between German bankers and foreign policy formulators; nor does it provide a means for the government to order banks to extend particular international credits. The mechanism simply lowers the level of risk inherent in certain classifications of transactions in return for a fee. Banks are left free to behave entrepreneurially, although the market conditions they face have been altered distinctly by governmental action.

Exceptional Trade Credits

A third category of bank-government interaction covers trade transactions of still more interest to the German federal government; in

3. The interministerial committee possessed responsibility for reviewing and deciding on all applications for Hermes guarantees exceeding DM 5 million (roughly $2.7 million) as of year-end 1980. In practice, responsibility for many of the smaller and more routine transactions is delegated to a subcommittee. Export-Import Bank of the United States, *Report to the U.S. Congress on Export Credit Competition*, p. 46.

addition to their impact on the Federal Republic's macro trade flows, these transactions hold some particular relevance to German foreign policy. In these cases, the German government appears to grant or deny Hermes cover on grounds other than pure assessment of commercial risk. When the government has restricted availability of Hermes cover to a country for political reasons (for example, Chile and South Africa), the level of guarantees has been lower than would have been dictated by assessment of commercial risk alone. In a few instances where the government has expanded Hermes cover for political reasons, the government has shown a keen sensitivity to the financial risks it must incur; ultimately the financial risk factor serves to limit the extent that the government will consider using the guarantee instrument for political purposes. An important qualification characterizing all transactions within this category is that they are trade-related. Another is that the government's efforts to influence financial flows are linked primarily to the offering or withholding of guarantees in the marketplace. Individual banks are still left to make their own credit decisions, as the Hermes instrument relies on the market mechanism to achieve its influence; open exchanges between bankers and public policy formulators are not necessary, nor are indirect understandings.

A variety of different features can cause a financial transaction to fall within the exceptional trade credit category, relating to either the importance of the specific underlying export or import to German foreign economic policy or the political significance of the foreign trading partner. Among the most salient examples in recent years of such exceptional trade credits, together with the distortions in normal conditions they reflect, are the following:

—The government's guarantee, and joint financing with German banks, of DM 3.7 billion in nuclear reactor sales to Brazil in 1976 (reflecting higher assumption of Brazilian risk by the German government than economic and political risk considerations alone would have dictated, and governmental involvement producing a far larger volume of DM-denominated credit, and at more favorable terms, than Brazil would have been able to obtain on its own in the market);

—The government's restriction of Chilean export credit guarantees to DM 2.5 million per transaction during the late 1970s and early 1980s (constituting a restraint on Hermes cover for Chile below what standard risk considerations alone would have dictated during much of the period);

—The government's restriction of South African export credit guarantees to DM 50 million per transaction, also during the late 1970s and

early 1980s (a political signal to other countries of the German government's disapproval of South African apartheid policies; yet because of
exceptions to the restriction, an intentionally insignificant limit on
German–South African trade and financial dealings);

—The government's expansion by DM 500 million of total Hermes
guarantees available for exports to Poland, combined with a relaxation
of Hermes repayment terms, in March 1980 (reflecting higher assumption
of Polish risk by the German government than standard Hermes commercial risk considerations alone would have dictated).

Nuclear Exports to Brazil

The West German government reached an agreement with the government of Brazil in 1975 establishing the framework for Brazil's
purchase of between two and eight nuclear reactors and accompanying
advanced nuclear technology from the West German private firm of
Kraftwerk Union (KWU). Negotiations on the official bilateral agreement began in approximately June 1974. As one observer noted, "It was
difficult to distinguish between the various levels of routine meetings
concerning technological cooperation, actual sales negotiations, and
high-level political talks."[4] The agreement included joint declarations
by the German minister of science and technology and the Brazilian
minister for mines and energy specifying areas of cooperation.

The internationally controversial deal, which represented the first
sale of a full nuclear fuel cycle outside the established nuclear weapons
states, supplied KWU with desperately needed orders to assemble new
reactors at a time when the small domestic German market was saturated
and the country's nuclear power plant manufacturing industry was
suffering from an overcapacity of almost 30 percent.[5] The West German
government, in assisting in the negotiation of the underlying sales
agreement and guaranteeing the financial package (as well as participating in it), helped to obtain a crucial export contract for an industry in
which the government had already sunk $5 billion in research and

4. Helga Haftendorn, *The Nuclear Triangle: Washington, Bonn and Brasilia;
National Nuclear Policies and International Proliferation*, Occasional Paper no. 2,
Studies in German Public and International Affairs (Washington, D.C.: Georgetown
University, School of Foreign Service, 1978), pp. 14, 22, 24.

5. William W. Lowrance, "Nuclear Futures for Sale: To Brazil from West Germany,
1975," *International Security*, vol. 1 (Fall 1976), p. 157.

development costs.[6] In addition, the contract added stability to 13,000 jobs at KWU, helped to diversify the German reactor industry's export markets, and enabled the government to secure access to major new uranium supplies that were expected to be found in Brazil. The German banks, for their part, benefited from a sizable expansion of their credit relationship with a significant sovereign borrower under relatively riskless terms.

The financial transaction itself, concluded in July 1976, covered the first two nuclear power plants and consisted of two parallel term loans, each for approximately DM 1.85 billion (equivalent to about $740 million apiece at the time).[7] One of the loans was an all-German bank syndicated credit organized by Dresdner Bank and covered by a 95 percent German government guarantee, administered through Hermes. The government-owned Kreditanstalt für Wiederaufbau (KfW) extended the second loan, also under a 95 percent Hermes guarantee. Each credit had a scheduled term (including drawdown period) of twenty years, exceedingly long for a commercial loan although not unusual for state-supported financings of nuclear power plant exports. The term will almost certainly run considerably longer, however, because of construction delays in Brazil.

Although German government officials have remarked that the entire package carries "all market rates," it is highly likely that the KfW provided approximately 35 percent of its share of the financing at a preferential interest rate of 7.25 percent fixed.[8] In addition, it is noteworthy that the German government provided the participating German banks with special assistance on funding. Given the magnitude of the overall credit and its denomination in deutsche marks, funding could

6. Norman Gall, "Atoms for Brazil, Dangers for All," *Foreign Policy*, no. 23 (Summer 1976), p. 158.

7. Interview with officials of the Kreditanstalt für Wiederaufbau, Frankfurt, July 7, 1980; and with officials of one of the Big Three commercial banks involved in the financing, Frankfurt, July 11, 1980. At least two published reports have stated that the amount of the financings was higher: "more than DM 4 billion," according to Lowrance, and DM 4.3 billion, according to a Hamburg newspaper. Lowrance, "Nuclear Futures for Sale," p. 151; and "Banken Geben Brasilien Viel Geld," *Hamburger Abendblatt*, July 24, 1976.

8. Interview with officials of the KfW, Frankfurt, July 7, 1980; and interview with officials of one of the Big Three German commercial banks involved in the credit, Frankfurt, March 10, 1981. Several published reports have indicated, apparently erroneously, that the Brazilians received much more than this amount at a preferential rate. According to Gall, "Half of the debt will be financed at 7.25 percent by the Kreditanstalt für Wiederaufbau," while Lowrance wrote that "the basic loan rate to Brazil is a low 7.25 percent," apparently for the entire package. Gall, "Atoms for Brazil," p. 158; and Lowrance, "Nuclear Futures for Sale," p. 151.

indeed have been a problem for these banks. However, through a complex scheme worked out between the banks and the Hermes inter-ministerial committee and apparently approved at the cabinet level, the German government permitted the banks periodically to transfer a major portion of their accumulated claims arising from the credit, along with the associated Hermes cover, to intermediaries for refinancing in the German capital market.[9]

The German government and banks alike have consistently main-tained that there was nothing unusual about the Brazilian financing. As Edward Wonder wrote shortly after the financing was consummated, "Those closest to the nuclear industry [within the Federal Republic] perceived nuclear energy as a conventional commercial undertaking, a matter of marks and pfennigs from which questions of a political nature should be excluded."[10] By its very nature, however, the Brazilian deal involved special political considerations. The Germans proceeded in the face of strong objections from the U.S. government that the deal could lead to the proliferation of nuclear weapons.[11] The magnitude of the sale alone made it unusual: it represented the largest single foreign trade contract that the Germans had yet negotiated,[12] and the associated Hermes guarantee was also probably the largest issued up to that date. Moreover, the Dresdner-syndicated financing ranked among the largest single commercial credits yet extended to a developing country. In directly assuming at least DM 3.5 billion of the credit risk for the parallel loans, the German government took on enormous Brazilian exposure at a time when strictly commercial assessments of Brazilian economic risk already were wavering. A *Euromoney* assessment of Brazil, for example, noted in June 1976, a month before the conclusion of the German-Brazilian financial package:

[Brazil's] appetite for foreign capital wrought an alarming increase in its overseas debts which now total more than $22 billion; international bankers' eagerness to

9. Interview with officials of one of the Big Three commercial banks involved in the credit, Frankfurt, July 11, 1980.

10. Edward Wonder, "Nuclear Commerce and Nuclear Proliferation: Germany and Brazil, 1975," *Orbis*, vol. 21 (Summer 1977), p. 292.

11. Wonder has noted in this regard, "West German nuclear-export policy, as revealed in the Brazilian deal, . . . [is] determined much less by economic and security factors operating at the international level than by political and economic pressures originating within Germany. . . . Bonn's clash with Washington, then, becomes more understandable if one realizes that the predominantly domestic and economic sources of West German policy do not readily complement the international security concerns of the United States." Ibid., p. 281.

12. "Banken Geben Brasilien Viel Geld."

participate in the Brazilian economic miracle diminished. It became more difficult to syndicate loans to Brazil, spreads widened in response to banks' reluctance to participate and, even today, *it can be difficult to put a medium-term syndicated credit for Brazil through the markets.*[13]

Although the German government encouraged provision of the overall financing package through the involvement of the KfW and through special funding arrangements, the primary mechanism for interaction between the German government and the major German banks was the Hermes guarantee. The German government assured the participation of German banks by offering a nearly total guarantee of their exposure. While the government was clearly assuming a commercial risk greatly exceeding what German banks would have been willing to undertake alone, it was nevertheless sufficiently confident of Brazil's ability eventually to repay that it extended the maximum percentage export guarantee available under standard Hermes operating procedures.

Restricted Trade Cover for Chile

During the late 1970s and early 1980s, the West German government maintained a limit of DM 2.5 million per guarantee on export transactions with Chile.[14] Under the Hermes program, transaction limits have occasionally applied to countries "in cases of limited creditworthiness."[15]

13. "Brazil—the Lenders and the Borrowers," *Euromoney* (June 1976), p. 48 (emphasis added).

14. The following discussion is based primarily on interviews with senior officials of the Ministry of Finance (June 30, 1980) and the Ministry of Economics (July 1, 1980), both in Bonn; and with a senior official of one of the Big Three commercial banks, Düsseldorf, July 18, 1980.

15. Hermes Kreditversicherungs-Aktiengesellschaft, "Germany: Major Features of the Export Credit Financing System," provided by Hermes AG in April 1981, p. 4. Hermes officials claim that no formal classifications of countries exist within the guarantee program beyond a distinction between countries eligible for cover on economic grounds and those that are not. However, guarantee limits on individual transactions did apply to a number of countries during 1980, including Chile, South Africa, Romania, Yugoslavia, and Egypt. West German foreign policy considerations influenced establishment of limits for the first two countries (according to a senior Finance Ministry official), while predominantly economic considerations were responsible in the last three cases. In the words of one voting member of the Hermes interministerial committee, "There is still enough leeway in the [Hermes] instrument to introduce under extraordinary circumstances a political element." Overall Hermes exposure ceilings and term limits also appear to apply to a further short list of countries, intended principally as a means of diversifying and limiting the government's risk. Interviews cited in preceding footnote, as well as interviews with officials of Hermes AG, Hamburg, June 25, 1980.

The motives of the German government with regard to Chile, however, were primarily political in nature.

At least during 1979–81, the Chilean guarantee ceiling reflected official objection to the repressive domestic policies of the Pinochet military regime far more than misgivings about the levels of risk associated with lending to the country. (Indicative of the perception that this risk was low is the fact that major German banks, usually more conservative than their government in assuming financial exposure in nonindustrialized countries, joined large international banks from the United States and other countries in displaying a decided readiness to lend in Chile during these years.)[16] The Chilean case is revealing as an instance in which the political and foreign economic objectives of the West German government came in conflict. The result was a relatively ineffective attempt by one faction within the government to use the German banking system to make a political statement, with the attempt hampered by both disunity of purpose within the government and the limited usefulness of the Hermes instrument as a negative political tool.

Hans Matthöfer, finance minister from 1978 until 1982, led efforts within the German government to restrain official and commercial ties with Chile; although influential elements within the Social Democratic party supported him,[17] he is widely given credit for almost single-handedly imposing the special guarantee ceiling on export credits to the country. At the same time, however, free trade advocates within the Economics Ministry and elsewhere in the German government remained interested in the economic and commercial benefits that the Federal Republic could derive from expanded Chilean relations. The compromise policy result was a low Hermes guarantee ceiling that was still high enough to permit official cover for a steady flow of small German export transactions. Also, when larger exports of particular value to the German economy were involved (for example, Siemens power plant components manufactured in Berlin), either the cabinet or the Hermes interministerial committee apparently authorized exceptions to the DM 2.5 million guarantee limit. Not surprisingly, German banks displayed much more

16. Chile was able to obtain a large volume of new Eurocurrency bank credits during the approximate period of the case: $867 million in 1979, $1,322 million in 1980, and $2,204 million in 1981. Morgan Guaranty Trust Company of New York, *World Financial Markets* (October 1982), p. 12.

17. Interview with senior official of one of the Big Three commercial banks, Frankfurt, March 9, 1981.

single-mindedness of purpose in their Chilean interests than did their government. The country represented to them an attractive and rapidly expanding market during 1979–81 in which they were eager to acquire new business.

The principal mechanism for interaction between German foreign policy machinery and German-based international banks in the Chilean case was again the Hermes guarantee. Beyond the direct impact of the guarantee's restricted availability on risk calculations that German banks made when assessing potential financial transactions, the restriction sent a somewhat confused official signal to the banks, suggesting to them lukewarm interest on the part of the government (or at least the finance minister) in their continued lending. Absence of extensive Hermes cover for export transactions did force the banks to allocate and monitor their Chilean exposure more carefully. But in a country where banks were disposed to lend actively anyway, official reluctance to issue guarantees imposed a minimal constraint.

As has been stated, the federal government is not well equipped to restrict German banks from engaging in commercial activities that they would otherwise pursue. Complete prohibition of dealings with a foreign country remains feasible if multilateral sanctions have been imposed, perhaps through the United Nations, or if the security or strategic interests of the German state are in jeopardy.[18] But when the government's foreign policy objectives are either only moderately important or unclearly defined, effective restriction of German bank activity is unlikely to occur. The government's restrictions on Hermes cover probably reduced German bank lending in Chile during 1979–81, but they by no means eliminated it. This fact reflects both the German government's uncertain commitment at the time to the policy objective of restraining commercial ties with Chile and the limited effectiveness of Hermes cover as a political instrument in influencing German commercial relations with a prosperous country. The Chilean case also illustrates the difficulty that Bonn probably faces whenever it attempts to pursue policy objectives, particularly those of only moderate priority, that conflict with the commercial and export goals of German banking and industry.

Restricted Trade Cover for South Africa

The German cabinet set a DM 50 million official guarantee limit for individual trade credits to South African importers in November 1977,

18. See *Aussenwirtschaftsgesetz* (German Foreign Trade Law), pars. 22 and 27.

and a "guidance" limit of the same amount continued in effect as of mid-1983. This restriction, which resembles the one imposed in the Chilean case, also appeared to be based primarily on noneconomic factors. As evidenced by many German banks' positive attitudes toward lending in South Africa during the late 1970s and early 1980s, financial risks alone would have dictated more relaxed restrictions and possibly no limit on individual transactions at all.[19]

The German government's foreign policy interests in South Africa, similar to those in Chile, have reflected a conflict between economic or commercial concerns and those of a more purely political nature. In South Africa, however, higher economic stakes influenced the policy outcome. South Africa has represented a crucial source of raw materials for the German economy, including manganese, chrome, uranium, and tin, as well as a major market for German exports and investments.[20] In 1979 German imports from South Africa totaled a record DM 3.6 billion, while exports to South Africa totaled DM 3.1 billion; outside of Western Europe, South Africa ranked as Germany's eighth largest import source and sixth largest market.[21] Throughout this period, however, the German government appeared sensitive to both international and domestic pressure to restrict German commercial ties with South Africa in light of its apartheid practices.

The German government's Hermes restrictions represented a subtly

19. For one reference to German banks' enthusiastic interest in South Africa, see "Capital-Report Südafrika: Wirtschaftswunder," *Capital* (Hamburg) (June 1980), pp. 153–55. As noted earlier, Hermes' stated policy has been to impose ceilings on the amount of guarantees for single transactions only on the grounds of a borrower's "limited creditworthiness." In the case of South Africa, however, considerations of creditworthiness probably called for a *term* limit on guarantees, but not a transaction limit. As reported in one journal shortly after the German cabinet set its South African policy, "Bankers in Johannesburg say that international finance remains generally available to South African borrowers. Private industry has been able to raise long-term capital without any appreciable difficulty. The only squeeze applies to central government and the public corporations. . . . [and is] expressed not so much by withholding funds as by limiting the term of any loans to no more than three years and insisting on a clear premium." Quentin Peel, "International Finance Remains Available for South Africa," *Banker* (London), supplement, vol. 128 (May 1978), p. xii.

20. As of the late 1970s, according to a South African source, as many as 60,000 jobs in West Germany's automobile, engineering, electrical, and chemical industries depended directly on German–South African trade. Furthermore, "a severance in the supply of manganese and chrome . . . would result in one-quarter of German industry closing its doors and the number of unemployed rising to seven million. . . ." "Foreign Reports: Bonn," *South Africa International* (Johannesburg), vol. 10 (July 1979), p. 43.

21. Bundesministerium für Wirtschaft, *Leistung in Zahlen, 1979* (Bonn: Referat Presse und Information, 1980), pp. 66–69.

conceived policy response, probably intended to please all parties while minimally affecting German–South African trade. The unusual guarantee limit constituted concrete action taken by the West German government in opposition to apartheid; by focusing on the size of individual transactions, the limit also probably served to reduce German banks' visibility in the South African market. The limit was sufficiently high, however, to suggest that it was the product of economic and commercial factors rather than political ones. Such an interpretation, described as "clever" by a voting member of the Hermes interministerial committee in 1980, proceeded along the lines that, despite South Africa's prevailing economic strength, economic prospects for the country were hurt by the possibility of a black takeover. (To paraphrase the same German government official, one need only look at Ghana or Zaire.)[22] Thus opponents of apartheid were left relatively satisfied by a visible political action taken against South Africa; simultaneously, Germany's free trade lobby was left satisfied by an explanation of the governmental action in terms of economic and commercial rationales.

In fact, the Hermes restriction has had only a modest impact on German–South African economic ties. The DM 50 million limit, twenty times larger than the one for Chile, has been loose enough to permit German banks to finance export shipments of moderate size to South Africa under Bonn's official guarantee. In addition, it is probable that the German government has occasionally permitted exporters to link individual DM 50 million guarantees to cover larger transactions. (One such authorized circumvention of the limit, according to a source within one of the Big Three commercial banks, permitted a considerably larger guarantee for a loan or loans to finance German export of a coal liquefaction plant during 1979.)[23]

Expanded Trade Cover for Poland

Poland approached the Bonn government in early 1980 for assistance in the midst of a financial crisis that threatened the Poles' ability to cover essential imports and meet current debt repayments to Western creditors, primarily banks. Although the Poles pursued a number of strategies

22. Interview with voting member of Hermes interministerial committee, Bonn, July 1, 1980.
23. Interview with senior official of one of the Big Three commercial banks, Düsseldorf, July 18, 1980.

during 1979–81 to obtain new financing from Western sources, the one of particular interest here is their request for new Hermes guarantees that would enable them to obtain additional trade credits from German banks. In March 1980 Poland was widely perceived as "plagued by slow growth, the effects of a poor harvest and a crippling debt service ratio."[24] At that same time, according to reliable German sources, the German government had already guaranteed export and other credits to Poland totaling at least DM 4.18 billion. Although economic considerations may have provided much of the rationale for the German government's accumulated exposure to Poland before March 1980, commercial risk considerations would not have justified Bonn's extension of large additional guarantees as of that date.[25]

The decision of the German government to offer Poland DM 500 million in new trade guarantees was almost certainly reached at the cabinet level. It reflected the considerable importance that consecutive postwar German governments have attached to strengthened German-Polish ties and to a politically and economically viable Poland. Successive Bonn administrations have accepted the burden of a special German obligation to the Polish people in light of the painful historical association of the two countries. In addition, since 1970 the German federal government had relied on improved West German–Polish relations to obtain permission for thousands of Germans living east of the Oder-Neisse line to emigrate to the Federal Republic.[26]

Current and past West German governments have also maintained substantial interest in Poland as a long-term export market and raw materials supplier, and such economic links became particularly attrac-

24. Roger Boyes, "Lambsdorff to Discuss Polish Debt," *Financial Times* (London), March 17, 1980.

25. According to sources at one of the Big Three commercial banks, the German government's offer of new guarantees may have represented a revival of a German proposal originally made to Poland at least a year earlier. These sources state that the Poles had previously declined the additional guarantees because they were not needed at the time (1978 to early 1979) to obtain market financing. (Interview with officials of one of the Big Three commercial banks, Frankfurt, March 10, 1981.) Significantly, however, perceptions of Polish creditworthiness were far more positive in 1978–79. Thus previous offers of Hermes cover may have reflected a different weighing of commercial and political considerations by the German government, with somewhat greater emphasis on the former.

26. Sixty thousand ethnic Germans were able to emigrate between 1970 and 1975, and a resettlement protocol signed in October 1975 called for Poland to permit a further 120,000 to 125,000 to emigrate over the following four years. German Information Center (New York), *Relay from Bonn*, vol. 7 (March 15, 1976).

tive to Bonn during the late 1970s as a means of lessening the Poles' economic dependence on the Soviet Union. Further motivation for the German cabinet to offer support for bank export credits involved the Soviet invasion of Afghanistan: the Schmidt administration was committed to keeping open vital trade links with Eastern Europe despite the intervention, but German banks were uninterested in financing exports to Poland if it required them to assume considerable additional Polish risk.

By responding positively to the Polish government's request for additional trade guarantees, the German government decisively altered the credit factors weighed by German banks when considering the extension of new trade financing to the Polish state. The additional guarantees, announced by West German Economics Minister Otto Graf Lambsdorff during a visit to Warsaw on March 16–17, provided DM 500 million of new cover for Polish imports of steel spare parts, textiles, and chemicals from the Federal Republic. The guarantees were structured to permit loan repayment terms substantially more lenient than both accepted market practice and Hermes operating procedures usually required: although financing terms for the imports in question typically ranged from 90 to 180 days, this Hermes cover extended from three to five years.[27] In effect, Poland received the capability to raise an additional DM 500 million in three- to five-year commercial loans from German banks, all under the guarantee of the German government.

What makes this case exceptional is not that the German government extended Poland new cover to obtain bank financing for German exports, but rather that the government based the new cover on an assessment of political factors. Economic and commercial criteria, reflecting either Poland's creditworthiness or the types of goods being covered, were of secondary importance. Considerations of creditworthiness did play a pivotal role, however, in limiting the amount of new Hermes cover that the German government was willing to extend. The Poles had originally sought DM 2 billion in fresh Hermes guarantees.[28] Although the German government placed moderate to great political importance on obtaining a new flow of Western funds into Poland during early 1980, it showed a

27. Christopher Bobinski, "Lambsdorff Disappoints Poles on Credit," *Financial Times* (London), March 18, 1980; and interview with chief financial officer of a German corporation active in East European trade, Cologne, July 2, 1980.
28. Bobinski, "Lambsdorff Disappoints Poles on Credit."

clear reluctance at that particular time to absorb so large an amount of additional Polish risk for its own books. Thus the DM 500 million figure represented a compromise solution that took into account both the political need to offer some amount of new cover and the financial desirability of offering an amount far short of the sum sought by the Poles.

In summary, Poland ultimately obtained the new financial resources covered by the German cabinet's decision not from an allocation of public funds but through the German banking system. The German government used the Hermes guarantee in this case as a political instrument to effect a flow of funds from that system into a particular country, yet, as far as can be ascertained, without making a direct approach to German banks.

Loans Supported by the Kreditanstalt für Wiederaufbau

No discussion of German bank-government interaction in the international sphere would be complete without consideration of the role of the government-owned KfW.[29] An official brochure describes it as "a bank with functions of a politico-economic character" and an institution that "complements the activities of the commercial banks." Founded in 1948, the KfW functioned originally as an agency to distribute Marshall Plan–related aid intended to finance reconstruction of the German economy. But over the years the KfW has grown into an important agency for the execution of German foreign economic policy, charged with financial responsibilities relating primarily to developing countries, including a handful of state-trading economies (such as Yugoslavia and Romania). Thus, while the KfW today continues to commit almost half of its DM 60 billion in assets to domestic development, the agency also grants long-term financing for German export sales to the developing world, often in tandem with German commercial banks and on terms

29. The agency's original name was the Reconstruction Loan Corporation, which Hermann Abs, its first general manager and later chairman of the Deutsche Bank, translated into the present German name. The German federal government owns 80 percent of the KfW's share capital, and the governments of the German states own the remaining 20 percent.

that the latter would be reluctant or unable to provide.[30] The KfW additionally administers a substantial portion (40 percent in 1981) of the German government's official assistance to developing countries, frequently in conjunction with the agency's financing of German exports to them.

It is in the financing of German exports, generally to developing countries, that the agency's cooperation with German commercial banks in the international sphere has been closest. Many of the KfW transactions have been trade credits of country-specific foreign policy significance to the German government. (One of the most important KfW joint financings with commercial banks in recent years, supporting the export of nuclear reactors to Brazil in 1976, was discussed above.)

The KfW's primary objectives in extending international credit apart from straight development aid are dual: to promote German exports and to provide some degree of financial assistance to developing countries, particularly ones of political or economic consequence to the German state.[31] During 1981, for example, the KfW committed DM 3.4 billion ($1.5 billion) in loans and grants to finance the export of German capital goods, including ships and aircraft, and the expansion of German enterprises abroad.[32] Such KfW financing has tended to be at noncommercial rates and terms, subject to the guidelines of the international consensus on state-supported credit financing of exports. On occasion, KfW involvement in a cofinancing package with German commercial banks appears to have the effect of drawing the banks into a sector of the international market in which the government desires their active participation. Alternatively, such involvement can improve the compet-

30. The tenor of KfW loans has generally been longer than those that German commercial banks are able to grant. In addition, KfW loans usually carry attractively low fixed interest rates, in contrast to the less predictable floating rates of most commercial bank loans. The KfW is forbidden to conduct banking business that German commercial banks would otherwise do.

31. The KfW law, amended in 1969, specifically identifies the international functions of the KfW as granting loans and issuing guarantees "in connection with export transactions of domestic enterprises" and granting loans "which serve to finance projects deserving of assistance in foreign countries, especially in connection with development aid, or which are necessary for funding foreign debtors' liabilities to creditors in the Federal Republic, or are of special governmental or economic interest to the Federal Republic of Germany." Kreditanstalt für Wiederaufbau, *Law*, amended version as of June 23, 1969 (Frankfurt: KfW, undated), p. 5.

32. Kreditanstalt für Wiederaufbau, *Annual Report for the Year 1981*, p. 41. The DM 3.4 billion figure includes DM 393 million of grants (as opposed to loans) to foreign buyers to finance German ship exports.

itiveness of a commercial financing bid that German banks might already be attempting to offer a foreign buyer.

The international lending function of the KfW (as opposed to its development aid role) can influence the German financial system's allocation of resources in two distinct ways. First, the KfW funds the major portion of its international lending by borrowing from institutional investors (such as insurance companies and pension funds) and banks and by issuing securities. In essence, the agency thereby serves as a financial intermediary between German commercial funding sources and foreign borrowers that might not represent familiar or attractive risks to investors. In a typical case, institutional investors will lend to the KfW at the low rates they would grant the German government, receiving in return a KfW obligation that has the same market rating as a federal government obligation. The KfW will then relend these funds abroad under Hermes cover; thus the German government provides a direct guarantee of the agency's intermediary role.

Second, as typified by the Brazilian nuclear deal, the KfW occasionally engages in cofinancing with German commercial banks. KfW participation in a foreign credit, combined with the nearly certain availability of Hermes cover for all lending parties involved in the same credit, can serve as a double policy signal to German commercial banks of the government's interest in the underlying transaction. Additionally, KfW involvement will likely produce a blended rate to the borrower that is more competitive than what commercial banks alone would be willing to offer.

The inexpensiveness of KfW international financing primarily reflects the agency's below-market composite cost of funds. Although the KfW obtains the bulk of its funding for foreign loans from the commercial sources just identified, a portion of its funding also comes from extremely cheap European Recovery Program (ERP) monies accumulated by the German government during the immediate postwar years.[33] A second factor tending to reduce the interest rates charged by the KfW is that it is not compelled to show a profit. The institution is almost totally tax-exempt and is forbidden by law from distributing any profits that do

33. In 1953 all postwar economic aid funds were combined in the Federal Republic under the European Recovery Program (ERP) Special Fund. During 1981 the KfW disbursed DM 379 million ($170 million) of ERP funds in the form of export credits, untied financial loans abroad, and loans for investments abroad, out of total such loan disbursements of DM 2,232 million ($990 million). See ibid., p. 19.

accrue. (Still, profits can be useful to the KfW insofar as they provide an additional means of subsidizing credits, particularly to domestic borrowers.)[34]

On occasion the KfW has been able to increase further the competitiveness of German banks' syndicated financings of larger exports to developing countries by mixing in development aid. (During 1981 the agency received all of its development aid funds directly from the federal budget.)[35] When an aid element is at least 25 percent of the total value of a loan, the German government has been able to list all of the funds provided by the KfW for the transaction in Official Development Assistance (ODA) statistics compiled for Germany.[36] The KfW's inclusion of development aid has also provided a means for effectively reducing the overall cost of export financing below the minimum rates set by the international consensus on state-supported credit financing of exports. (Such mixed credits, an increasingly important component of German development assistance to the more advanced developing countries,[37] did not violate Organization for Economic Cooperation and Development [OECD] guidelines as of late 1982 so long as the aid element amounted to at least 25 percent of the value of the transaction.)

As of June 1980 countries classified as "developing" by the KfW and receiving "substantial" buyer credits from it to purchase German exports included Algeria, Argentina, Brazil, Colombia, Greece, Indonesia, Malaysia, Mexico, Morocco, Peru, the Philippines, Portugal, Romania, Spain, Syria, Taiwan, Thailand, Venezuela, and Yugoslavia.[38] Reflecting the motives of German foreign policy on which KfW assistance is often predicated, this list includes several oil-exporting countries; a number of states that provide important export markets for Germany;[39] and a number of countries providing the Federal Republic

34. Interview with official of the KfW, Frankfurt, March 10, 1981.
35. KfW, *Annual Report for the Year 1981*, p. 19.
36. This accounting practice is in keeping with OECD guidelines. See ibid., p. 15, footnote; supplementary information provided in interviews with officials of the KfW, Frankfurt, July 7, 1980, and March 10, 1981.
37. KfW, *Annual Report for the Year 1981*, pp. 55–56.
38. As described by an official of the KfW, Frankfurt, July 7, 1980.
39. Yugoslavia, Spain, Greece, Brazil, and Algeria ranked respectively as Germany's sixth, seventh, tenth, sixteenth, and nineteenth most important non–European Community customers in 1979. Bundesministerium für Wirtschaft, *Leistung in Zahlen, 1979*, pp. 68–69.

major supplies of raw materials other than petroleum.[40] In the case of almost every loan transaction with all of these countries, the KfW has alternatively borrowed funds from private German sources and reloaned them, joined with German commercial banks to structure a syndicated or dual financing package at better than commercial terms when viewed compositely, or done both.

The U.S. institution most similar to the KfW is the Export-Import Bank. Although these two public banks do not perform strictly analogous functions and currency fluctuations may cause an understatement of the KfW's relative size when expressed in dollars as of year-end 1981, some comparisons between the two banks may still prove useful. In overall size, the KfW was more than 65 percent larger at year-end 1981 with DM 61.3 billion ($27.1 billion) in assets. (The Export-Import Bank held $16.2 billion in assets at the close of its 1981 fiscal year, September 30.)[41] In terms of the percentage of national exports financed, the Export-Import Bank was the much more significant institution. During 1981 the KfW's new export-financing commitments directly covered a mere 0.9 percent of German exports. Even if the KfW's 1981 financial cooperation (development aid) commitments are included, the institution probably financed less than 1.5 percent of German exports for the year.[42] In contrast, the Export-Import Bank's loan authorizations during fiscal 1981 equaled approximately 2.3 percent of U.S. exports.[43] The two

40. These include Brazil, Indonesia, Malaysia, Morocco, Peru, and Thailand. Klaus Esser and Jürgen Wiemann, *Key Countries in the Third World: Implications for Relations between the Federal Republic of Germany and the South* (Berlin: German Development Institute, 1981), p. 39.

41. KfW, *Annual Report for the Year 1981*, p. 83; and Export-Import Bank of the United States, *Fiscal 1981 Annual Report*, p. 18.

42. New export-financing commitments (both loans and grants) totaled approximately DM 3.4 billion ($1.5 billion) during 1981. Financial cooperation loan and grant commitments to developing countries totaled an additional DM 3.4 billion. In 1981 the KfW disbursed more than 45 percent of such financial cooperation funds to German enterprises furnishing "supplies and services" (exports) to developing countries. KfW, *Annual Report for the Year 1981*, pp. 15, 51, 57.

43. These loan authorizations amounted to $5.4 billion during fiscal 1981. The bank's total authorizations (including guarantee and insurance authorizations) aggregated to $12.9 billion, equal to roughly 6 percent of annual U.S. exports. It should be noted, however, that the German government also guaranteed 9 percent of German export sales through the Hermes insurance program during 1981. Export-Import Bank of the United States, *Fiscal 1981 Annual Report*, p. 1; and Hermes Kreditversicherungs-AG, *Annual Report for the 64th Business Year Ended 31st December, 1981*, p. 24.

banks' total trade-related and other international loans, however, were roughly comparable in size at the end of their respective 1981 fiscal years. The Export-Import Bank's balance sheet showed $15.8 billion in loans receivable (nearly all in support of U.S. exports), while the KfW reported DM 30.1 billion ($13.3 billion) in export credits, financial cooperation loans to developing countries, untied financial loans abroad, and loans for German investments abroad.[44]

In the end, what makes the KfW remarkable is not its absolute size, but rather its special role as a catalyst in German commercial bank financing of exports to developing countries, combined with its versatility as a quasi-commercial instrument of German foreign economic policy. A noteworthy 18 percent of German exports went to developing countries in 1981, and the KfW, together with the Hermes insurance program, has helped to promote the availability of commercial bank credit to finance these export sales.[45] As an instrument of foreign economic policy, the KfW has also played a highly successful role in coordinating joint public-private financings of selected export sales that the German government has wished to encourage (such as the Brazilian nuclear power deal of 1976).

Untied Credits of Political Significance: A Loan to Portugal

On selected occasions the German government has also issued general guarantees for bank credits not tied to German trade. Although these credits have not been associated specifically with German exports, the securing of raw materials for the German economy, or German commercial projects or other direct investments abroad, they have nevertheless provided sufficient political benefits to the government to prompt

44. Export-Import Bank of the United States, *Fiscal 1981 Annual Report,* p. 18; and KfW, *Annual Report for the Year 1981,* p. 84.

45. Deutsche Bundesbank, *Monthly Report,* vol. 34 (March 1982), p. 75. In this context, the programs of the AKA Ausfuhrkredit-Gesellschaft mbH (often known simply as AKA), a syndicate of fifty-eight commercial banks, have also significantly enhanced the availability of commercial export credit in Germany. The AKA's B fund, the only one of its three funds that is governmentally supported, provides financing for supplier credits to developing countries with repayment terms between one and four years. Export-Import Bank of the United States, *Report to the U.S. Congress on Export Credit Competition,* pp. 45, 48–49.

its intervention in the market. General untied guarantees of this type, very possibly issued without consultation between the government and the banks, have materialized when government officials have strongly desired consummation of a particular foreign loan but have doubted that the market would effect the necessary financial intermediation on its own. At the same time, government officials, weighing objectives other than commercial profit, have felt sufficiently comfortable with the level of associated financial risk to accept it for the government's own account.

Bonn has granted extremely few such guarantees. One reason is that the Finance Ministry must account for them in its annual public report detailing the federal budget. Heavy use of public resources to guarantee large banks' international credits not tied to German trade would inevitably unleash damaging criticism on any governing administration— from its parliamentary opposition as well as other quarters.

Portugal was the outstanding recipient of untied commercial bank credits guaranteed by the German government during the late 1970s.[46] By year-end 1977 the socialist government of Mario Soares urgently required international financial assistance to stabilize a fragile domestic economy and to cover mounting import bills; the country's current-account deficit for 1977 had risen to $1.5 billion, equal to nearly 25 percent of the gross national product.[47] Portugal's credit standing was poor, but most Western governments shared the view that, unless the country could obtain substantial financing relatively quickly, growing pressure from both extreme left- and right-wing domestic political elements threatened the collapse of its new democratic institutions.[48]

A group of OECD countries and Venezuela had tentatively agreed midway through 1977 to provide a $750 million medium-term loan to the Portuguese, but the two group members committed to providing the bulk of these funds, the United States ($300 million) and West Germany ($200 million), did not actually make their shares available until 1978. The United States formalized arrangements for its contribution first, signing an agreement with the Bank of Portugal in early March 1978 to lend it

46. Both Yugoslavia and Argentina received such financing during the 1960s and early 1970s. In 1983 the Bonn government issued another untied guarantee covering a DM 1 billion bank loan to the German Democratic Republic (see chap. 4).

47. "Aiding a Vision in Portugal," *New York Times*, March 25, 1978.

48. See Reginald Dale, "Portugal Rejoins Europe," *European Community*, no. 201 (May–June 1977), p. 32; also David Herbert, "Lisbon: World Help Is Needed," *Euromoney* (February 1978), pp. 126–28.

$300 million for ten years at 8.15 percent annual interest.[49] Technically a U.S. congressional appropriation to the Agency for International Development program, the loan was to be administered by the Treasury Department.

Neither the United States nor Germany was willing to disburse funds until the Portuguese reached an agreement with the International Monetary Fund on new economic austerity measures, which was concluded in early May.[50] When the German Ministry of Finance finally made arrangements to fulfill its own loan commitment, its approach to the dilemma of providing the agreed-upon assistance and conserving scarce budgetary resources was arguably ingenious. The U.S. government had relied on public funds to provide its share of the OECD jumbo credit, but the German Finance Ministry instead offered a guarantee to the German commercial banking community that served as a catalyst to private provision of the resources. In a scheme that went far to harness the competitive efficiency of the marketplace to the advantage of the Portuguese, the Finance Ministry invited German banks to bid for the mandate to lead-manage a fixed-rate term loan of DM 420 million ($200 million) for the Portuguese government under Bonn's guarantee. One of the prerequisites for bidding (endorsed by the German government and conceivably designed by it) was that interested banks had to offer additional unguaranteed credit to the Portuguese government. The larger the amount of supplementary unsupported credit a bank was willing to include, the greater were its chances of winning the overall mandate. The German government, indifferent as to which banks actually provided the credit, left selection of the winning bid to the Portuguese. Not opposed to deriving some income for itself from the arrangement, the German government further announced its intention to charge the selected bank(s) a fee for the guarantee.[51]

49. See Robert N. McCauley, "A Compendium of IMF Troubles: Turkey, Portugal, Peru, Egypt," in Lawrence G. Franko and Marilyn J. Seiber, eds., *Developing Country Debt*, Pergamon Policy Studies 36 (Pergamon Press, 1979), pp. 152–54; and Paul Lewis, "11 Countries Agree on $750 Million Loan to Portugal," *New York Times*, June 23, 1977. Also see "U.S. Agrees To Lend Portugal $300 Million," *Wall Street Journal*, March 2, 1978. According to the *Journal* article, the loan was interest-free for the first two years.

50. See "Portugal, IMF Agree on Austerity Steps that Unlock Loans," *Wall Street Journal*, May 5, 1978.

51. The German Finance Ministry has declined to disclose the exact fee that it charged, but a prudent guess would be 0.75 percent of outstanding guaranteed principal. Banks would normally try to pass on such a fee to the borrower.

The resultant credit package was labeled by *Institutional Investor* one of the "most outstanding" and "noteworthy" international financings of 1978; to another observer, Robert N. McCauley, it merely confirmed "the fellow-traveling of mark and flag in Portugal."[52] After a period of moderately intense competition for the mandate among Germany's largest banks during early summer of 1978, the Portuguese government selected Westdeutsche Landesbank and Commerzbank on a joint basis to manage a pair of term credits, which the two banks had proposed, totaling $350 million. The first of the two financings, denominated in deutsche marks and representing Germany's $200 million official contribution to the $750 million OECD assistance loan, was handled administratively by Westdeutsche and signed in early July. The parallel financing for $150 million, denominated in dollars, represented the additional amount of unguaranteed credit that the two banks were willing to underwrite in the Euromarket for the Portuguese; this second loan was handled administratively by Commerzbank and signed later the same month.[53]

The overall arrangement enabled Portugal to make a successful approach to international credit markets at a time when considerable uncertainty existed within worldwide commercial banking circles as to whether Portuguese risk was a marketable quantity. The dual structure of the package, in particular, provided the Portuguese a benefit worth potentially much more than Germany's $200 million commitment to participate in an OECD loan. By linking German banks' provision of a nearly riskless credit with their syndication of a much less attractive one, the package played a critical role in reestablishing Portugal as a creditworthy name in the Euromarket. As summarized in the financial press,

Portugal met its first true test [of acceptance by the marketplace] with the $150 million loan and passed with flying colors. . . . "Portugal approached the

52. See "The Best Deals of the Year: Three to Get Portugal Ready," *Institutional Investor*, international edition (December 1978), pp. 5, 66, 86–87; and McCauley, "A Compendium of IMF Troubles," p. 155.

53. The borrower of record for the DM 420 million transaction was Banco de Portugal; the rate was fixed, but other details were not made public. The borrower of record for the $150 million transaction was the Republic of Portugal; technically a floating-rate multicurrency loan, it carried an interest rate margin of 1.0 percent and had a term of seven years. See "The Best Deals of the Year," pp. 86–87; advertisement and "Market Commentary: Publicized Eurocredits," *Euromoney* (September 1978), pp. 87, 165; and advertisement and "Market Commentary: Publicized Eurocredits," *Euromoney* (October 1978), pp. 198, 221.

market with restraint and dignity," said one banker. "It recognized that it should not press too far and too fast."[54]

The successful structuring of the $150 million loan helped facilitate the relatively smooth completion of a $300 million international commercial term loan to the Portuguese the following month, priced identically; the six-bank lead-management group for this final loan, which included three American banks and Dresdner Bank, succeeded in placing about one-third of it each in the United States, Europe, and Japan.[55] From the point of view of the German Ministry of Finance, the overall Westdeutsche-Commerzbank package helped to stabilize a European neighbor foundering both politically and economically. Working through the German commercial banking system, Bonn succeeded in both meeting an official multilateral financial commitment and advancing its political interest in a democratic Portugal without disbursing public funds. The Finance Ministry did have to incur a contingent liability through the issuance of a sizable guarantee, but the associated risk was one that ministry officials obviously assessed as reasonable and acceptable. Finally, through inclusion of a guarantee fee, it is possible the Finance Ministry will generate a moderate amount of income for itself before the DM 420 million loan is repaid.

Conclusion

German banks have pursued the overwhelming majority of their foreign transactions in response to free market forces, without consulting the Finance Ministry, the Economics Ministry, the Bundesbank, or any other government agency. Conversely, the federal government has not sought to look after the international interests of Germany's banks as an overriding and independent objective of German foreign policy. Yet even as staunch a defender of free trade as Peter Hermes, a former state secretary of the Foreign Office, has argued, "Admittedly, [German] foreign policy does as a rule promote foreign trade interests and the role adopted by the State is one of active support." He has also acknowledged

54. See "The Best Deals of the Year," *Institutional Investor*, p. 86.
55. Ibid.; see also "Market Commentary: Publicized Eurocredits," *Euromoney* (November 1978), p. 166.

the existence of "significant exceptions" to Bonn's principle of separating politics from trade.[56]

Many of the international transactions of German banks have no foreign policy content to begin with, while in other cases market forces have combined with the natural interests of the banks to produce financial decisions acceptable to the official foreign policy community. On occasion, however, the German government has sought to influence in a deliberate fashion the nature and focus of German banks' international attention. In a majority of these cases, the government's provision of general incentives in the marketplace has accomplished the desired redirection of the banks' international lending patterns. For instance, in the case of standard trade credits, the German government has routinely offered guarantees for export financing based on its assessment of the political and commercial risk inherent in the underlying loans. The banks, for their part, have weighed the availability of such guarantees in decisions on whether or not to extend financing.

Under exceptional circumstances, the German government has granted or denied trade credit guarantees on grounds other than pure assessment of commercial risk. The government has also encouraged German commercial bank financing of German exports to selected developing countries and a handful of state-trading economies through the cofinancing programs of the Kreditanstalt für Wiederaufbau. In addition, the government has infrequently guaranteed "untied" commercial credits of particular political significance to it.

In a few highly unusual but revealing instances, the German government has resorted to direct negotiation with German banks, sometimes combined with the provision of special incentives, in an effort to effect particular commercial financial outcomes. These instances will be considered next.

56. Peter Hermes, "Foreign Policy and Foreign Trade Interests," *Aussenpolitik (German Foreign Affairs Review)*, vol. 27, no. 3 (1976), pp. 247–48.

CHAPTER FOUR

Bank-Government Relations: Cases of Direct Negotiation

FORMAL, explicit coordination rarely occurs between the government and banks in Germany, and one would not expect it in light of the laissez-faire traditions that underlie both German commercial banking and relations between the German public and private sectors. Yet when such explicit coordination does occur, the financial transactions involved tend to be of profound foreign policy significance as well as of major commercial consequence for the banks. In those instances where the government has resorted to direct negotiation to influence the banks' international behavior, German bankers almost certainly would not have accommodated the government's foreign policy interests to the same extent of their own volition.

These rare cases illustrate the kind of ad hoc collaboration that is possible between the German banking and foreign policy communities at critical moments. Even under the most exceptional circumstances, the extent of collaboration in the international sphere has still proved limited; neither the government nor the banks have been able to prescribe each other's behavior in detail. But when direct cooperation has occurred, it has usually had a marked impact on both the competitive position of German banks and the responsiveness of the Federal Republic's foreign policy machinery to changing international circumstances.

The following cases represent major instances of direct negotiation between Germany's banks and foreign policy machinery during the period from 1975 to 1980. In most of the cases, the government sought to persuade banks to extend credits perceived to be in the German national interest by senior public officials, often including the chancellor and various cabinet ministers. German banks typically responded by asking for guarantees, thereby forcing the government to weigh foreign policy considerations against financial risk. Not surprisingly, in those cases where negotiations occurred, both the financial risk and the foreign policy stakes tended to be high. Determined to expose as few budgetary resources as possible to such risk, the government resorted to moral suasion and almost certainly on occasion to implied assurances of future support in an effort to induce German banks to accept a major portion of the risk. The government usually behaved as the more powerful partner in these exchanges; nevertheless, the banks enjoyed considerable leverage because they possessed the final say on whether or not they would extend credit.

The cases that will be considered in this context are the following:

—The German government's negotiation with both German banks and the Indonesian government to arrange financing to complete the Krakatau steel project in 1975–76;

—The government's consultation with the Federation of German Banks and member institutions to devise financial measures to support the U.S. government's freezing of Iranian assets in late 1979 and early 1980;

—The government's unsuccessful efforts to enlist the support of German banks in obtaining a solution to the Turkish financial crisis in 1980;

—The government's successful application of pressure on German banks to extend a DM 1.2 billion term credit to the Polish government in 1980.

The Krakatau Steel Project

During the early 1960s the USSR intended the Krakatau steel plant near the northwestern tip of Java to be a centerpiece of its aid program to Indonesia. After a sharp reduction in Soviet influence within the country in 1965, however, the partially completed project lay abandoned until the beginning of the next decade, when President Suharto and Ibnu Sutowo, then president of the state oil company, Pertamina, pushed jointly for resuming construction. At that time, Sutowo reorganized Krakatau as a limited-liability company, with Pertamina the majority shareholder. Siemens, Salzgitter, and a number of other large German companies became major subcontractors for the project, and by the end of 1973 these companies had received Krakatau-related orders substantially in excess of DM 1.2 billion. In May 1975 the German financial magazine *Capital* labeled these accumulated orders of German firms "the largest export deal in German economic history."[1]

Given Indonesia's vast oil wealth as well as the direct involvement of the prestigious Pertamina organization in the project, German firms originally had few worries about payment for their services. In February 1975, however, Pertamina experienced a severe liquidity crisis, and Indonesia's central bank was forced to assume responsibility for its financial obligations. In subsequent months, as Indonesia's economy and international credit standing suffered from the ramifications of the Pertamina crisis, the future of the Krakatau complex came into doubt.

As construction progress on Krakatau approached a standstill for a second time, the cash-poor Indonesian government became desperate to arrange external financing in an effort to induce the project's German contractors to continue work. In September 1975, at a time when German banks were refusing to provide such financing because of Indonesia's faltering credit standing, Indonesian Finance Minister Ali Wardhana and central bank governor Rachmat Saleh traveled to Bonn for "an exchange of views on mutually interesting questions in the economic sphere" with Economics Minister Hans Friderichs and other German government officials.[2] At approximately the time of these meetings (and perhaps during them), the Indonesian government urged the German government to issue guarantees covering the necessary commercial financing. The German government's response was that Bonn lacked the legal authority to guarantee general credits for Krakatau. However, if the underlying loans could be connected directly to German-Indonesian trade, then a guarantee arrangement might be possible.[3]

The West German government had significant interests in trying to accommodate the Indonesian request. To begin with, too many German export contracts were at stake to risk their termination. Many Economics Ministry officials were annoyed at the prospect of having to come to the rescue of large and sophisticated German corporations caught overex-

1. "Grösster Auftrag Aller Zeiten," *Capital* (Hamburg) (May 1975), p. 122.
2. "Indonesischer Finanzminister bei Friderichs—Zufriedenstellende Bilanz," *Nachrichten für Aussenhandel* (Frankfurt), September 15, 1975.
3. Interview with senior officials of the Ministry of Economics, Bonn, July 4, 1980.

tended in a remote land.[4] Nevertheless, refusal by the German government to offer any support could have adversely affected not only the performance of some of Germany's premier industrial names but also much of the country's export-dependent industrial sector. The German government was further motivated by the growing importance of Indonesia to German foreign economic policy. Despite Indonesia's current financial problems, its long-term potential as a market for German exports was considerable, a consequence of both the archipelago's huge population and its underdeveloped natural wealth. This potential had become all the more apparent during the early 1970s as the Suharto government had sought to diversify Indonesian trade away from Japan and the United States and to cultivate West Germany as a third major partner.[5] Strong bilateral ties held additional appeal to German foreign policymakers because of Indonesia's promise as a major world supplier of raw materials needed by the German economy, including oil, natural gas, tin, bauxite, nickel, and copper.

Krakatau differs crucially from the trade-related cases in which the German government simply issued Hermes guarantees to prompt the bank financing it desired. Here, as in the Portuguese case, major general-purpose funding was required, not just funding to cover German exports or to develop raw materials supplies for the German economy. Legally the German cabinet could not have authorized a Hermes guarantee for such a broad purpose. An untied guarantee, issued directly by the Finance Ministry (similar to the Portuguese pattern) and not through Hermes, would still have been a possibility, provided that the guarantee was demonstrably "in the particular state interests of the Federal Republic" or in the service of "promotion-worthy intentions."[6] However, provision of such a guarantee in this instance very likely would have created two problems: a serious domestic political controversy, in which the government might have been accused of risking public funds to subsidize the country's leading corporations, and a barrage of developing country requests for similar guarantees.

The financing package for Krakatau announced by the Deutsche Bank

4. "Indonesien-Kredit: Die verschwundenen Millionen," *Wirtschaftswoche* (Düsseldorf), July 30, 1976.

5. See O. G. Roeder, "Indonesia: Move to Off-Set Japan, U.S.," *Far Eastern Economic Review* (October 23, 1971), p. 45.

6. See *Haushaltsgesetz 1981* (German Budget Law), par. 9.2.b.

in July 1976 was the product of over ten months of negotiation among the German Ministry of Economics, leading German banks, the Indonesian government, and a number of German industrial firms. Hailed by Deutsche Bank director Hans-Otto Thierbach as "a milestone in the further development of German-Indonesian economic relations," the financial arrangement called for an all-German bank syndicate to provide the Indonesians DM 1.175 billion (roughly $470 million at the time) to continue construction of the steel complex. Of this amount, DM 450 million (ten-year term) was earmarked to pay for German exports and carried the Federal Republic's guarantee issued through Hermes. A German industrial consortium guaranteed the remaining DM 725 million (five-year term). According to conditions that Bonn officials (probably within the Economics Ministry) helped to devise and possibly negotiate for this second portion, Pertamina would be required to ship two million tons of crude oil annually over a five-year period to a wholly owned subsidiary of Veba AG, a German oil company controlled by the German government through a 43.7 percent equity position. Pertamina would accrue receivables from Veba worth approximately DM 300 million per year for the shipped oil, but Veba's payments would never leave Germany; rather, they would be funneled to a specially created Pertamina subsidiary in Düsseldorf, and from there directly back to the German bank syndicate to repay principal and interest.[7]

The entire arrangement neatly served the interests of the German government and represented a considerable accomplishment for the Ministry of Economics. The ministry had played an important role in obtaining the flow of financial resources sought by the Indonesian government after German banks had originally refused to extend credit. The deal improved official bilateral relations between Bonn and Jakarta, and at the same time the German government was able to protect German export orders probably worth far more than the financing. The German government issued direct guarantees worth less than half the total value of the financial package; moreover, it helped to lay the groundwork through the arrangement for a significant term supply of oil from a source that rarely supplied the German market. German banks, for their part, ended up with a DM 1.2 billion loan based almost exclusively on Hermes and German corporate guarantees.[8] The German industrial consortium

7. "Indonesien-Kredit."
8. Interest spreads and fees on the transaction were not publicized, so one can only speculate as to the profits the banks earned from the transaction.

that guaranteed part of the loan, presumably consisting of most of the German contractors benefiting from the financing, faced only modest risk itself because of the securing of Indonesian oil reserves as informal collateral for the loan through the Veba contract.

Direct negotiations between leading German banks and the German Ministry of Economics occurred in this case in part because of the complexity of the overall transaction and in part because of the German government's desire to effect a bank financing that, because of domestic political considerations as well as financial ones, it felt unable to guarantee in its entirety. Strong working communications between senior German bankers and Economics Ministry officials helped to produce a final transaction that served both the commercial interests of the banks and the foreign policy objectives of the German government.

Freezing Iranian Assets: The German Response

In a move with far-reaching financial and political ramifications, the U.S. government froze all official Iranian assets within its jurisdiction on November 14, 1979, ten days after the seizure of hostages at the U.S. embassy in Tehran. During the next four to six weeks, Washington sought to pressure its principal European allies and Japan into taking supportive action. Through successive visits of senior American foreign policy officials to Bonn during December 1979, Washington showed particular interest in persuading the German government to impose strong parallel financial sanctions.

The Iranian crisis posed foreign policy questions of major consequence to the German government. In broad terms the crisis posed a dilemma between official German-American bilateral relations on the one hand and long-standing German financial and commercial ties on the other. This case stands out as an instance of negotiation leading to implementation of foreign policy measures highly sensitive to the financial sector's interests; it also illustrates German bank behavior consciously supportive of the foreign policy objectives of the German state. Unlike other cases of negotiation, foreign policy formulators were not requesting the financial sector to commit a particular flow of resources; rather, at issue was the disposition of Iranian deposits already held with German banks and the establishment of guidelines governing future German-Iranian business relations. As a consequence, the question of issuing official guarantees played no significant role here. Financial risk considerations did remain central, as German banks and the government alike sought to avoid actions that might trigger substantive Iranian defaults on German credits. The possibility of inflicting permanent damage on German-Iranian commercial relationships posed an incalculable risk beyond the immediate financial one as well.

Close economic and financial relations have linked Germany and Iran for decades. As recently as 1978 Iran was the Federal Republic's largest customer in the Middle East by a wide margin, importing DM 6.8 billion worth of German goods. During the Iranian political turmoil of 1979, German exports to the country still amounted to DM 2.35 billion, falling behind only those to Saudi Arabia within the region that year.[9] Conversely, Iran was Germany's largest supplier of oil as of 1978, providing 18 percent of total oil imports, and in 1979 it continued to supply over 10 percent of Germany's oil imports.[10] Even beyond the extent these reciprocal trade figures suggest, the German commercial and banking sectors have long prided themselves on extremely close Iranian business connections. Many German firms, including banks, had pursued business in Iran since at least the 1920s. Furthermore, a strong anticolonial bias in Iran has traditionally worked in favor of German companies because Germany never claimed colonies in the area. By the end of 1977 approximately 8,000 Germans lived in Iran, and even in early 1980 as many as 250 German firms still employed roughly 500 German expatriates in the country.[11]

Although the U.S. freeze occurred on November 14, Washington did not begin to put serious pressure on Bonn to take supportive action until late November at the earliest. When such pressure did materialize, a primary initial effect on financial and economic officials within the German government was to cause confusion, because various offices in Washington (such as the White House, Treasury, and State Departments) tended to emit conflicting signals on the severity of the sanctions against Iran that they sought from the Germans. U.S. pressure reached a climax

9. Bundesministerium für Wirtschaft, *Leistung in Zahlen, 1979* (Bonn: Referat Presse und Information, 1980), pp. 68–69.

10. German Information Center (New York), *The Week in Germany*, vol. 11 (February 29, 1980); "Geordneter Rückzug aus Iran," *Frankfurter Allgemeine Zeitung*, December 1, 1979.

11. Memorandum from one of the Big Three commercial banks, Frankfurt, dated February 19, 1981. Higher figures were reported in "Folgen eines Iran-Boykotts Begrenzt," *Frankfurter Allgemeine Zeitung*, May 19, 1980.

during the first half of December when a delegation of senior State and Treasury Department officials traveled to Bonn to discuss the German role in sanctions, followed by Secretary of State Cyrus Vance a week later.[12] At minimum the State-Treasury team wanted the German government to show tacit support for the freeze by prohibiting German banks from building up large nondollar deposits from the Iranian government. However, many senior German government officials anticipated or felt by early December U.S. pressure to impose more severe restrictions on financial flows between the Federal Republic and Iran and to move against Iranian assets within German jurisdiction.[13]

Within a day after the State-Treasury delegation's visit to Bonn, the German government made its first public announcement of sanctions by disclosing the suspension of Hermes guarantees for export credits to Iran. The announcement was apparently timed, as reported in one press account, "to defuse growing United States criticism of alleged allied inaction in supporting American measures against Iran."[14] In fact, the action had minimal practical effect, as no German firm had actually requested a Hermes guarantee for an Iranian trade credit since the U.S. freeze had begun almost a month earlier. The announcement did buy time for the German government, however, which was essential for it to devise more substantive sanctions that at the same time were sensitive to German banking and commercial interests.

Negotiations between the German banking community and the German government played a pivotal role in the government's formulation of policy measures to support the U.S. asset freeze. The government began detailed discussions with the banking community by late November, and a close dialogue continued through at least early January 1980. Throughout this period, in the words of one senior Economics Ministry

12. See Roger Boyes, "Bonn Halts Iran Trade Credits," *Financial Times* (London), December 10, 1979; and John M. Geddes, "Bonn Lists Sanctions on Iran," *New York Times*, December 8, 1979.

13. During late November and early December 1979, several senior German officials, including the economics minister, publicly sought to allay fears about the "danger to the free flow of capital" in Germany in connection with the Iranian crisis. On December 10, the *Financial Times*, reporting the German government to be under "considerable pressure" from Washington to offer support, added that "Bonn would only be able to move against Iranian assets if the security of West Germany or world peace was directly threatened." Jonathan Carr, "Bonn Shocked by Iran Assets Move," *Financial Times* (London), November 30, 1979; Boyes, "Bonn Halts Iran Trade Credits."

14. Geddes, "Bonn Lists Sanctions on Iran."

official near the process, "there was constant consultation, a constant exchange of views, information and opinions."[15]

Although the German foreign trade law grants the federal executive branch, with the consent of the Bundesbank, authority to impose restrictions on international capital and payments movements, both the Economics and Finance Ministries were reluctant to take this kind of formal unilateral action against Iran; any such move would have conspicuously violated the Federal Republic's long-standing public commitment to unrestricted world trade and payments flows.[16] Possibly as early as late November 1979, the Finance Ministry consequently asked the Federation of German Banks if its members would be willing to take *voluntary* action to curb their Iranian business. Following a period of initial soundings of both bank association representatives and prominent bankers, the Finance Ministry suggested in late December that German banks adopt a "gentlemen's agreement" committing themselves to refrain from extending new credits to Iran and opening new accounts for Iranian customers, among other restrictive measures.[17]

Even before the Finance Ministry advanced its idea of a gentlemen's agreement, however, a consensus seems to have evolved within the banking community that voluntary sanctions would be commercially unacceptable over the long run. Such a consensus may have formed as early as December 7, the date of a critical meeting on Iranian sanctions attended by Banking Federation officials and senior German bankers.[18] In the end, even senior Bundesbank officials supported the Banking Federation's view that voluntary sanctions would not work: they might permanently damage German commercial relationships with Iran as well as leave German banks vulnerable to shareholder suits.

15. Interview with senior official of the Ministry of Economics, Bonn, July 4, 1980.

16. See Jess Lukomski, "W. Germany Backs Sanctions on Iran," *Journal of Commerce*, April 10, 1980; also Deutsche Bundesbank, "Mitteilung Nr. 7010/80: Bekanntmachung zu Sanktionsmassnahmen gegen Iran auf dem Gebiet des Kapitalverkehrs," *Bundesanzeiger* (Cologne), May 29, 1980; and "Die Sanktionen gegen Iran," *Frankfurter Allgemeine Zeitung*, June 7, 1980. For a discussion of the official German commitment to liberal world trade, see Peter Hermes, "Foreign Policy and Foreign Trade Interests," *Aussenpolitik (German Foreign Affairs Review)*, vol. 27, no. 3 (1976), pp. 247–56.

17. "Wolff für Sanktionen gegen Iran," *Frankfurter Allgemeine Zeitung*, April 12, 1980.

18. This meeting has been referred to as a "routine" one, and senior Banking Federation and Bundesbank officials may also have discussed other topics at it. Interview with senior officials of the Federation of German Banks, Cologne, July 4, 1980.

As a decidedly second-best policy option (particularly for the Economics Ministry), both the Economics and Finance Ministries consequently resolved to impose official sanctions, but only on one condition: the sanctions must take place within the context of unified action by all members of the European Community (EC). Given the Soviet Union's veto of United Nations sanctions against Iran on January 13, however, as well as French hesitancy in joining common Western action against Iran, unified EC measures at an early date appeared a dim possibility by the middle of January 1980.

An impasse between German banks and the German government over the sanctions issue could have resulted at this point, but did not, in part, because of a growing perception by the bankers of their own vulnerability in the crisis and their increasing dependence on the government's good will. With loans to Iran exceeding deposits by perhaps DM 1.5 to 2 billion, German banks faced an uncomfortable net exposure in the crisis.[19] Furthermore, just as the banks had shied away from a publicized, voluntary gentlemen's agreement to restrict Iranian business, they were also fearful of severe official sanctions that might place them at a competitive disadvantage with other European banks in Iran. The Banking Federation and its most influential members thus saw a need on this occasion to "show understanding to the government, . . . [to] make sacrifices in the German national interest," albeit for reasons that also made sound business sense.[20] A further prevailing perception among senior German bankers seems to have been that cooperation with the government now could be translated into help from it later. Within this context, the Banking Federation communicated to the government its willingness to help draft appropriate restrictions and to comply with any official pronouncements.[21] But on competitive grounds, the federation supported the government's desire to delay formal sanctions until the possibility of a common EC approach could be thoroughly explored.

The German government waited until May 23, one day after the EC's implementation of partial trade sanctions against Iran, to put into effect formal restrictions on capital and payments movements between the

19. "Bonn Besorgt: U.S.-Pfändung bei Krupp drängt uns in die Front der Feinde Irans," *Die Welt* (Hamburg), November 30, 1979.

20. Interview with senior official of the Federation of German Banks, Cologne, July 2, 1980.

21. As the managing director of one of the Big Three banks stated, his own bank agreed not to challenge the legality of any government orders in German courts. Interview, Frankfurt, July 11, 1980.

Federal Republic and Iran. At that time, the Bundesbank publicly activated sanctions limiting German banks' extension of new credit to Iran, opening of new accounts on behalf of Iranian customers, and acceptance of payments transactions for Iranian customers in currencies other than the dollar.[22] Yet German banks had apparently adhered to these sanctions informally ever since early January, when all European governments had *conditionally* agreed to them, contingent upon United Nations action that in fact never materialized.[23]

During this interim period (January–May 1980), German banks apparently policed their own financial dealings with Iran, thereby avoiding both the controversy that would have surrounded a formal gentlemen's agreement with their government and the commercial and political damage to Germany that would have accompanied official German unilateral sanctions. The financial restrictions that were imposed resulted from tacit coordination between the German banking community and the German government; as described by one German banking official, there was "a common understanding between banking and government. . . . Everybody knew and understood what the other part was thinking and planning."[24] A key intent of the measures was to produce minimal damage to long-term German-Iranian economic relations. The entire program actually cost German banks an inconsequential amount of business, as the U.S. freeze and offset actions had already stifled the bulk of Iranian international commercial and financial dealings. Throughout at least the first half of 1980, representatives of the largest German banks also continued to travel periodically to Tehran, reassuring the Iranians of German readiness to reestablish normal business relations at the earliest opportunity.

When faced with the necessity of formulating a policy restricting German-Iranian financial relations, the German Finance Ministry, Economics Ministry, and Bundesbank all showed a high degree of sensitivity to the commercial interests of German banks. Senior governmental officials vigorously solicited the views of German bankers on appropriate

22. The German government actually announced its restrictions on April 24, 1980. See Deutsche Bundesbank, "Mitteilung Nr. 7010/80"; and "Die Sanktionen gegen Iran."

23. An outline of the European governments' conditional points of agreement is contained in David Buchan, "Iran May Face More Financial Restrictions," *Financial Times* (London), January 10, 1980.

24. Interview with official of the Federation of German Banks, Cologne, March 12, 1981.

policy toward Iran, and the government clearly saw the international commercial interests of German banks in this case as a national concern of some priority. The communication between German banks and their government during late November 1979 through January 1980 decisively influenced the *means* chosen to implement financial measures against Iran; with their initial emphasis on tacit compliance and self-restraint, those means went far to accommodate the interests of the banks (as well as the government). The same process of communication also appears to have influenced the *severity* of the financial restrictions invoked.

The banks, while seeking to behave in accord with their own commercial and competitive interests, demonstrated their ability to adjust their behavior to support official German political objectives. For defensive as well as prudential reasons, German banks quietly limited their own Iranian business during early 1980; one consequence was that the German government was able to convey support to Washington for the asset freeze and simultaneously avoid implementation of official sanctions until a suitable multilateral framework could be established. As one senior Bundesbank official described the leading banks' position, "Iran brought home the fact of the inevitability of getting a much closer association with the government on international issues. . . . If Germany had fully joined the freeze, it would have been a very bad blow to the banks. They realized then that they must cooperate with the government because they might have to fall back on the government at some point in the future."[25]

The Turkish Financial Crisis

By early 1978 the Turkish government faced an external debt problem of critical proportions, brought on by deteriorating domestic economic conditions, unfavorable developments in the country's balance of trade (largely related to sharp increases in oil prices), and poor public-sector financial management. Turkey's current account had plummeted to a deficit in excess of $3.5 billion during 1977, following a four-year decline from a surplus position before the 1973 Arab oil embargo. The country's outstanding external debt, which had more than doubled in two years to reach $11.4 billion at the close of 1977, increased to more than $14.1

25. Interview with former senior official of the Bundesbank, Frankfurt, July 9, 1980.

billion by the end of 1978.[26] One direct consequence was an untenable debt service burden, with large amounts of short-term debt in arrears by year-end 1977 and substantial additional amounts soon to fall due. As 1978 progressed it became increasingly apparent that Turkey faced an acute need to locate new sources of medium- and long-term funds simply to cover essential imports and meet payments of interest and principal on existing loans.

Following the Guadeloupe summit in January 1979, the German government began efforts to coordinate multilateral financial assistance for the Turks on behalf of Organization for Economic Cooperation and Development (OECD) countries.[27] On various occasions after that the German Finance Ministry attempted to prod German banks to assist in structuring a framework for funneling fresh financial resources into Turkey and to participate directly in their delivery. This process of prodding provides further evidence of the remarkable ability of the German government to communicate with its country's leading banks, this time in an effort to promote international commercial lending patterns toward Turkey that would serve the foreign policy interests of the German state and its NATO allies. The Turkish experience, however, also illustrates the absolute limits to that ability that arise when the financial risk involved is sufficiently high to deter both the German banking community and the German government from accepting it.

Reflecting primarily strategic and military concerns, the German government placed paramount importance on attempting to sponsor a solution to Turkey's financial crisis. From Bonn's perspective, Turkey has represented a vital link in the NATO alliance, located in close proximity to the oil fields of the Middle East and flanking the Bosphorus, poised to pinch "the giant's nostrils," as Churchill once wrote.[28] For some time before the Guadeloupe summit, the German government had supplied Turkey with defense aid as well as free deliveries of surplus matériel from the German army. Turkey could hardly be counted upon

26. World Bank, *Turkey: Policies and Prospects for Growth* (Washington, D.C.: World Bank, 1980), pp. 31, 256.

27. Before the Guadeloupe summit, an initial debt relief operation had been arranged through an OECD consortium for Turkey in May 1978. It called for consolidation of $1.14 billion in arrears on guaranteed short-term and bilateral medium- and long-term debt, as well as amounts due over the period from May 1978 through June 1979. Ibid., pp. iv–v.

28. David Tonge, "Turkey: A Vital Ally for the West," *Financial Times* (London), January 21, 1980.

to buttress NATO's crucial southeastern flank, however, if the country could not overcome its own serious economic and political difficulties. In the context of Turkey's NATO role and buffer location between the Soviet Union and the Middle East, Chancellor Helmut Schmidt's initial coordinator for Turkish financial support, Walther Leisler Kiep, labeled "effective assistance for our Turkish friends . . . almost a national duty."[29] Substantial German-Turkish trade and other economic links possibly provided additional impetus to the German government's efforts to coordinate Turkish financial aid,[30] but in their absence high political considerations alone almost certainly would have prompted action by Bonn.

In seeking to coordinate with the German banking community to resolve Turkey's financial problems, the government contemplated a partnership with a group of institutions possessing historic and sizable links with the Turkish economy. The Deutsche Bank, an active lender to the Turkish government as early as 1888, ranked among the top banks in the world in volume of Turkish business during the 1970s. Similarly, the Dresdner Bank had been active in Turkey since cooperating with Deutsche in 1889 to found the Anatolian Railway Company.[31] These collective ties had facilitated outstanding German bank credit to Turkish entities estimated at more than DM 1 billion by the late 1970s.[32] However, prudential considerations greatly tempered the banks' enthusiasm for extending new credit to Turkey as the decade closed.

At the beginning of February 1980 Chancellor Schmidt had just

29. Walther Leisler Kiep, "Western Aid to Turkey," *Survival* (London), vol. 22 (January–February 1980), p. 24.

30. The German government had extended some DM 1.75 billion of Hermes export credit guarantees to Turkish public- and private-sector entities that were still outstanding as of year-end 1978. German exports to Turkey totaled DM 2.7 billion during 1976 and DM 2.3 billion in 1977, before Turkish financial problems began to cut sharply into the country's ability to obtain trade financing. In addition, the German economy has benefited from hundreds of thousands of Turkish immigrant workers who have obtained employment in the Federal Republic since the 1960s. For export figures, see Klaus Esser and Jürgen Wiemann, *Key Countries in the Third World: Implications for Relations between the Federal Republic of Germany and the South* (Berlin: German Development Institute, 1981), p. 181.

31. Herbert Feis, *Europe: The World's Banker, 1870–1914: An Account of European Foreign Investment and the Connection of World Finance with Diplomacy before the War* (Yale University Press for the Council on Foreign Relations, 1930), p. 319; and J. Riesser, *The German Great Banks and their Concentration in Connection with the Economic Development of Germany* (Government Printing Office, 1911), pp. 434, 445.

32. Interview with senior official of the Deutsche Bank, Frankfurt, March 9, 1981.

transferred immediate responsibility for coordinating multilateral assistance for Turkey to his finance minister, Hans Matthöfer. During the intervening months since Guadeloupe, the German government had enjoyed at least partial success in its efforts to organize a solution to Turkey's financial problems. In May 1979 the OECD governments, under German leadership, pledged $1.46 billion to Turkey in medium- and long-term bilateral credits, trade financing credits, and program loans; and in July 1979 the OECD governments completed negotiations on the rescheduling of approximately $1.0 billion of existing official bilateral and state-guaranteed debt falling due between then and June 1980. Encouraged by both the increased level of commitment of OECD governments and the concurrent offering of financial support by the International Monetary Fund (IMF), seven major private banks, including the Deutsche and Dresdner Banks, organized a new commercial loan of $407 million to the Turkish government in July 1979 (to be placed with a number of international banks). And in August the third major rescheduling of Turkish debt in sixteen months occurred, as approximately 250 foreign commercial banks agreed to convert more than $3 billion in existing short-term loans into primarily term obligations.[33] Yet as of February 1980 chronic and severe debt service problems still remained. Turkey continued to require massive amounts of new medium- and long-term funding, a problem certain to be exacerbated by a debt repayment hump and sharp acceleration in the country's debt service burden over the coming several years.[34]

Officials of the German Finance Ministry and the Deutsche Bank came together on at least three occasions during February 1980 to discuss Turkey. Each of the encounters was at the request of the Finance Ministry, and when viewed together, they provide a useful illustration of German bank-governmental negotiations in an area of limited converging interests, major foreign policy stakes, and high financial risk. All of the meetings occurred during a period when Finance Ministry officials were seeking to devise a long-term, if not permanent, solution to Turkey's financial predicament; efforts up to that time, in contrast, had focused primarily on getting Turkey through whatever crisis was immediately at hand.

The first encounter occurred in Frankfurt on approximately February 4, when Matthöfer and his deputy, Manfred Lahnstein, visited informally

33. See World Bank, *Turkey: Policies and Prospects for Growth*, pp. v, 33–35.
34. Ibid., p. 34.

with senior officials of the Deutsche Bank to discuss the international banking community's current reading of Turkish risk. In retrospect, it would appear that Matthöfer and Lahnstein were primarily seeking information in order to define their own options (such as how much money official sources would need to provide after private bankers had reached their own ceilings for new Turkish debt). They also used this occasion to remind Deutsche management of its moral obligation to support the Turkish economy, particularly in light of the substantial interest income that they believed the bank had earned since 1975 on short-term loans to the Turkish central bank. However, almost certainly to Matthöfer's and Lahnstein's disappointment, Deutsche officials responded that major banks worldwide would probably be willing to provide no more than $200 million in fresh balance-of-payments term financing to Turkey at this point without guarantees.

Roughly a week passed before the second encounter, when a senior Finance official called on top Deutsche management in Frankfurt for further discussions.[35] This time the official inquired whether Deutsche itself could structure a long-term financial solution for Turkey, taking both official and private funding sources into account, and then organize the package's private component in international credit markets. The Finance Ministry was looking to Deutsche for a "global concept" at this point, one that would establish definitively both the total resource amounts and terms Turkey would have to receive in order to achieve an acceptably low debt service level by the mid- to-late 1980s. Former Deutsche chief executive Hermann Abs had assisted the Indonesian government in drawing up a similar debt settlement in 1968, the Finance official recalled; could not Deutsche do the same now for a country whose stability the German government was heavily committed to supporting?[36]

The response of Deutsche management appears to have been one of bewilderment. Deutsche officials did not balk at the difficulty of the

35. Finance Ministry officials also talked with the management of the Dresdner Bank at roughly the same time. Interview with officials of two of the Big Three commercial banks, Frankfurt, March 9–10, 1981.

36. In 1968 the government of Indonesia requested Abs personally to work out a formula for a feasible debt settlement, taking into account Indonesia's existing import requirements and related factors. Abs devised such a formula and presented it to the Inter-Governmental Group for Indonesia (IGGI). However, Abs did not then *arrange* the debt settlement in international financial markets. Interview with senior official of the Deutsche Bank, Frankfurt, March 9, 1981.

analytic calculations, but rather disagreed with the Finance Ministry's implicit assumption that a single bank, even the venerable Deutsche, could implement such a global financial package for a country in as much trouble as Turkey. First, Turkey in 1980 was not Indonesia in 1968: a high dependence on imported oil, an unstable domestic political situation, and dramatically changed prospects for developing countries' economic growth all made Turkey a decidedly less attractive credit risk. (Furthermore, the Indonesian debt settlement had involved only government debt, rather than both government and commercial debt.) Second, as Deutsche officials had already communicated to the Finance Ministry, an extremely large new Turkish credit would probably be nearly impossible to syndicate and sell down in international financial markets. Most world-class banks either had all the Turkish exposure they wanted or lacked any incentive to acquire large amounts now.[37] Third, no extensive new lending operation to Turkey could be mounted on the basis of a "slanted front," in which Deutsche or even German banks collectively took the lead while large banks in other countries abstained from committing new funds. In light of the large number of international creditors clamoring at Turkey's door, any limited group of banks lending new resources faced the risk that their funds would be used to pay out their competitors.

A core issue closely associated with each of these three problems was the issuance of official guarantees.[38] Ultimately, Deutsche and other German banks were willing to lend substantial new sums to Turkey if the German government were prepared to accept most of the financial risk ("the friendly handshake" from the government, as one banker put it).[39] However, the government was reluctant to issue any guarantees whatever in this case.

37. In this regard, it is interesting to note the belief of a well-placed banker at the time that Turkey would need at least $6 billion to $8 billion in new money at reasonable terms, for at least four to five years, simply to permit the country to continue to engage in current business—"to go on living." Interviews with commercial banker, Frankfurt, July 8, 1980, and March 9, 1981.

38. Officials at one of Germany's Big Three commercial banks indicated that they sought to use the Portuguese guarantee of 1978 (discussed in chap. 3) as a precedent for an official guarantee of German private lending to Turkey. However, an official at another of the Big Three banks stated that his bank never considered the issuance of guarantees by Bonn to be a realistic possibility in the Turkish case. This official had still raised the Portuguese example "conversationally" during a discussion of Turkey with Finance Minister Matthöfer at the time (early 1980). Interviews with officials of two of the Big Three commercial banks, Frankfurt, March 9–10, 1981.

39. Interview with official of one of the Big Three commercial banks, Frankfurt, July 8, 1980.

From the Finance Ministry's perspective, guarantees of new bank loans to Turkey posed an impossible dilemma. German law forbade the finance minister from guaranteeing loans if he expected the guarantees to be called, and Matthöfer, a prominent public figure, clearly felt the risks, political as well as financial, to be too great.[40] Finance Ministry officials were also sensitive to the danger of issuing loan guarantees that would result in financial gains to third-country banks eager to collect on past-due loans to Turkey. A danger almost as great, particularly in an election year, came from the possibility of creating the appearance that the government was taking on financial commitments to help German banks get repaid in Turkey.[41]

While the question of the Deutsche Bank's role in designing a long-term solution to Turkey's financial problems was still unresolved, Matthöfer flew to Ankara on February 18 to lead talks on OECD aid. Here the third significant interaction of the month occurred, for included in Matthöfer's private entourage was the Deutsche Bank's central office manager in charge of Turkish lending. The latter's involvement resulted from the personal request of a high-ranking Bonn official to Deutsche cochairman Wilfried Guth that he designate someone to provide a commercial banking perspective on the trip. The presence of a Deutsche executive during Matthöfer's discussions with Turkish government leaders accomplished several objectives for the German finance minister. First, it provided him a means of communication with a group of Germany's most influential international bankers and a better feel during the discussions for both German bank interests and capabilities in Turkey. This conduit extended additionally to those sectors of German industry doing business in Turkey, for the Deutsche representative's superior at the bank's Frankfurt headquarters was also the chairman of the principal association for German business interests in Turkey. Second, Deutsche participation in the trip had the effect of making the bank both more aware of and involved in official German efforts to help Turkey.

The Matthöfer trip, although producing no major breakthroughs in the German government's efforts to achieve a long-term solution to Turkey's financial problems, was instrumental in helping German suppliers achieve a settlement of their substantial unguaranteed financial

40. Hermes guarantees of new export credits to Turkey were absolutely forbidden under German law as of February 1980 because Turkey was in default on several export credits already guaranteed under the Hermes program.

41. Interview with senior official of the Ministry of Finance, Bonn, June 30, 1980.

claims against Turkish importers.[42] From a Deutsche Bank perspective, the trip also helped to deflate senior Finance Ministry officials' hope that any single German bank could solve Turkey's complex financial predicament. Deutsche apparently never refused outright to put together a major new long-term financial package for the Turks. However, around the time of the trip and on subsequent occasions, the bank did work to convince Finance Ministry officials of its inability to implement such a package, despite its willingness to complete any necessary underlying analysis. In the words of one senior bank official, Deutsche was able and prepared to perform "the civil engineering" in the Turkish case, "but not the construction."[43] Over the ensuing months, although overall German bank-government relations remained good, a lingering, low-key stalemate resulted over the specific issue of Turkish support.

In many respects Deutsche acted as an analytic extension of the German Finance Ministry in investigating the prospects for arranging long-term financial assistance to Turkey. The full role that some senior ministry officials *hoped* Deutsche would play would have also required the bank to orchestrate the behavior of the international financial markets toward Turkey. Deutsche's reluctance to play that role in the Turkish case was primarily a function of the enormous financial risk involved, and neither the German government nor the bank could devise a scheme that made the risk tolerable to either party. Deutsche and other major German banks appeared to be waiting for the German government to offer concrete incentives for extending new Turkish credit. Concurrently, the banks provided the government very tangible assistance short of money (such as professional advice and information about the international banking system's views on Turkey), and they matched Bonn's moral arguments that they should support the Turkish economy with highly principled stands of their own, emphasizing prudential concerns. In the end, however, as one senior Deutsche official remarked, "We shall not let our government stand alone."[44]

Following the $407 million commercial bank loan of July 1979, German banks apparently did not provide Turkey with any significant new

42. Matthöfer apparently told senior Turkish financial officials while in Ankara that failure of the Turkish government to change its original unsatisfactory settlement terms would have a negative impact on the German government's continued readiness to lead OECD assistance efforts. The Deutsche Bank representative's participation in the meeting almost certainly proved helpful in making this point.

43. Interview with senior official of the Deutsche Bank, Frankfurt, March 9, 1981.

44. Interview with senior official of the Deutsche Bank, Frankfurt, July 11, 1980.

medium-term funds for four years.[45] Finally, in September 1983, after an extended period of somewhat improved economic conditions in the country, the Kreditanstalt für Wiederaufbau and Deutsche Bank quietly completed arrangements for a DM 1 billion ($372 million) joint export financing of four new frigates for the Turkish navy. Two of the vessels would be built in economically depressed shipyards in Hamburg and Kiel, while the other two ships were to be constructed in Turkey with equipment provided by German suppliers. Significantly, a Hermes guarantee covered all or nearly all of the financing package, in which commercial banks from several European countries in addition to Germany participated. According to one published account, "The banking consortium, made up of 13 banks . . . is led by the Deutsche Bank. . . . The [Turkish Finance] ministry said the U.S. and Switzerland would also be contributing to the project that is aimed at modernization of the Turkish navy."[46]

A Term Credit to the Polish Government

From late 1979 through 1981, the Polish government pursued a number of strategies to obtain financial resources from Western governments and banks to help stabilize the faltering Polish economy. An earlier case focused on Bonn's raising of Hermes export credit guarantee exposure for Poland, a tactic permitting the German government to work essentially through market forces to stimulate increased German commercial lending to Poland. In this closely related case, the German government used a combination of direct pressure and a specific guarantee to persuade German banks to extend a major syndicated credit to help Poland meet immediate foreign currency needs.

45. In 1981 German and other foreign banks did agree to a further rescheduling of old credits to Turkey. In 1982 a Dresdner Bank subsidiary, Dresdner (South East Asia) Ltd., assumed a second-tier manager position in a $200 million three-year syndicated Eurodollar loan to a Turkish agricultural bank. In May 1983 Commerzbank helped lead-manage a $100 million one-year oil import facility for Turkey. And in July 1983 Hypobank International SA secured a fourth-tier participation in a $200 million five-year credit to the Turkish government. German banks did not take on major leadership positions, however, in any publicized medium-term Eurocredits to Turkey throughout the period. Euromoney Syndication Guide (data service) (London: Euromoney Publications, Ltd.), data as of August 1983.

46. "W. European Banks Back Turkish Frigate Purchase," *Financial Times* (London), September 9, 1983.

During the fourth quarter of 1979, according to well-informed German banking sources, Polish financial officials realized they could not cover approximately DM 3 billion in principal and interest owed West German banks during 1980.[47] The shortfall was part of a much larger debt service problem, as Polish principal and interest payments due Western creditors during 1980 totaled $7.2 billion, the equivalent of nearly 70 percent of Poland's anticipated hard currency earnings for the year. Because Poland owed 40 percent of its existing hard currency debt of $19.4 billion to West German creditors, Polish officials logically turned to their financial contacts in Frankfurt for assistance.[48]

In December 1979 Poland's Deputy Finance Minister Marian Krzak called on the managements of Deutsche, Dresdner, and possibly other banks in Frankfurt, Düsseldorf, and Munich to seek fresh loans. Although informed German bankers were clearly aware of the seriousness of Poland's need for new credit, a consensus seems to have prevailed among them that German banks would not have to incur more Polish exposure simply to recover past loans because the Russians could not afford a substantive default by a Warsaw Pact country in Western financial markets. Sustained with this confidence, leading German banks informed Krzak that they would be unable to commit major additional financial resources to Poland in 1980—unless support for new loans could be obtained from the German government. The banks thus had no problem with providing new funds to Warsaw, only with new Polish exposure. With this unsubtle distinction in mind, the banks at the very least did not discourage Krzak from seeking the support they desired directly from the German government.

During the winter of 1979–80 the Polish government did approach the German government on the matter of issuing guarantees for a new commercial credit to Poland; according to a source at one Frankfurt bank, some discussions on the matter occurred directly between Chancellor Schmidt and Polish Party Chief Edward Gierek.[49] Schmidt,

47. Interview with officials of one of the Big Three commercial banks, Frankfurt, July 10, 1980.

48. Francis Ghiles, "Poland Reassures Its Creditors," *Financial Times* (London), August 13, 1980; and Nicholas Cumming-Bruce, "Jan Woloszyn's Struggle for Poland," *Euromoney* (October 1980), p. 100. Estimated share of Polish debt owed West German creditors provided during interview with officials of one of the Big Three German banks, Frankfurt, July 10, 1980.

49. Interview with senior officials of one of the Big Three commercial banks, Frankfurt, July 11, 1980.

especially concerned about maintaining positive relations with East European governments following the Soviet Union's intervention in Afghanistan, personally became convinced of the necessity of new German commercial lending to Poland by the early spring of 1980 at the latest.[50]

A complex negotiating process then ensued between the German government and banks that finally resulted in an agreement in early August on terms and conditions for a major new German commercial credit to Poland. At an early stage in this process, the German government, through a variety of means, made clear to the leading banks that it expected them to commit additional resources to Poland. Around the beginning of April, for example, Finance Minister Matthöfer and his deputy used the occasion of a private Frankfurt luncheon with senior representatives of the Big Three banks and the Bank für Gemeinwirtschaft to press the German government's case.[51] Minister Günter Huonker of the federal chancellory telephoned the leading banks as well to emphasize the urgency of a new loan,[52] and Chancellor Schmidt took up the issue directly with the top management of the Deutsche Bank and possibly other major German banks.

The negotiating process established relatively quickly that German banks would extend a major new syndicated credit to Poland, and that the German government would formally guarantee a substantial part of it. From the outset of negotiations, both the banks and the government seem to have viewed large additional Polish exposure as undesirable but tolerable. Thus both parties drew sharp pragmatic distinctions between additional Polish exposure versus Turkish exposure, assessing the risk inherent in the latter as distinctly less palatable. One consideration was that the Polish government, unlike its Turkish counterpart, had paid punctually all principal and interest installments due to date.[53] A second factor was Poland's favorable prospects at the time for increased Russian support if necessary. Having reached informal agreement on the fact of a new loan, German banks and government moved on to set its terms.

The interests of borrower, lenders, and guarantor substantially dif-

50. Interview with senior official of the Ministry of Economics, Bonn, July 1, 1980.
51. Interview with senior official of the Ministry of Finance, Bonn, June 30, 1980; confirmed during interview with senior officials of one of the Big Three banks, Frankfurt, July 11, 1980.
52. Rudolf Herlt, "Banken beugen sich Bonn," *Die Zeit* (Hamburg), August 29, 1980.
53. Ibid.

fered. The Polish government wanted a long-term loan as large as possible. During early discussions with the German government, for example, Polish officials expressed their desire for a DM 2.0 billion financing.[54] The German Finance and Economics Ministries did not object to a loan of that size per se and were eager to see German banks meet the full wishes of the Polish government; however, the ministries also wanted to minimize the absolute size of the German government's guarantee. First, neither ministry relished the prospect of issuing a large guarantee for commercial balance-of-payments financing at a time when other debt-burdened East European countries were likely to cite the arrangement as a precedent and demand similar assistance.[55] Second, the ministries hoped to see any given guarantee generate the largest amount of German bank lending possible. And finally, the German government wanted to incur no more Polish exposure (and financial risk) for its own account than absolutely necessary. The bargaining stance of the lenders centered squarely on the risk element: German banks wanted as large a government guarantee of the total loan as possible, resulting in minimal additional Polish exposure for themselves.

During negotiations on the size of the overall loan and guarantee, Economics Minister Otto Graf Lambsdorff also played a pivotal role in representing the German government to the banks. If, as obliquely suggested by one senior Finance Ministry official, the banks did at one time seek a 100 percent guarantee, they did not pursue that tack publicly; nor did they pursue it for very long or with any success.[56] At some point during the spring the banks indicated to Lambsdorff their willingness to provide the full DM 2.0 billion sought by the Poles if the German government would guarantee DM 1.0 billion of that sum. Lambsdorff adamantly refused to consider a guarantee of so large an absolute

54. Ibid. This published figure was disputed, however, in interviews. According to an American banker closely involved in East-West trade, the Poles requested a DM 3 billion loan from German banks during February or March of 1980. In contrast, officials at one of the Big Three German banks indicated that the Poles had never asked for more than DM 1.5 billion. Interview with official of a major American bank, Vienna, March 15, 1981; and interview with officials of one of the Big Three commercial banks, Frankfurt, March 10, 1981.

55. By the beginning of July 1980 other East European countries, including Yugoslavia and Romania, were already soliciting financing terms from the German government similar to those for the German bank loan to Poland, even though its final details had not yet been agreed upon. Interview with senior official of the Ministry of Economics, Bonn, July 4, 1980.

56. Interview with senior official of the Ministry of Finance, Bonn, June 30, 1980.

amount, however, citing legal restrictions on the government's use of
the Hermes program. As a counteroffer, the minister proposed raising
the ratio of unguaranteed to guaranteed credit to 2:1; thus the government would issue a DM 500 million guarantee through Hermes if the
banks would come up with an additional DM 1 billion of unsupported
credit.[57] The banks agreed to the offer.

The specific reasons for the banks' willingness to compromise on the
guarantee issue are not absolutely clear, but they probably included a
strong wish to preserve good working relations with the Bonn administration over the longer term. Also influencing the banks' behavior may
have been the high spread being proposed for the loan (1.5 percent over
the banks' cost of funds in the London interbank market), as well as a
desire to demonstrate good faith to the Poles, whom the banks considered
important commercial clients despite their current hard times. Finally,
on July 4, Dresdner Bank announced it would lead-manage a DM 1.5
billion credit package for Bank Handlowy, the Polish state bank responsible for raising loans for the country in international financial markets;
one-third of the credit would be guaranteed by the German government.
In addition to Dresdner, the management group for the all-German
syndicate would include Deutsche Bank, Commerzbank, and the Bank
für Gemeinwirtschaft. The press release from Dresdner alluded further
to the facts that it still sought to enlarge the management group by
"another one or two banks," and that the package had not yet been fully
syndicated.[58]

As labor problems within Poland intensified during July, Dresdner
encountered serious difficulty trying to sell down the DM 1.0 billion
unguaranteed portion of the loan beyond the announced management
group. Dresdner reportedly attempted to bargain with the Finance and
Economics Ministries at this point for increased government cover, but
to no avail.[59] Rather, as described in one press account, "In an apparent
effort to influence the bankers' decision, Bonn privately made clear that
if the full DM 1 billion for debt servicing . . . were not raised, then state
backing for as much as another DM 500m would not be provided

57. Herlt, "Banken beugen sich Bonn."

58. Dresdner Bank, "Polen-Finanzierungspaket über 1.5 Mrd. DM," Mitteilung an
die Presse, Herausgegeben von der Informations- und Presseabteilung, Dresdner Bank
AG, Frankfurt, July 4, 1980.

59. Interview with senior official of one of the Big Three commercial banks,
Düsseldorf, July 19, 1980.

either."[60] In the end, in a further compromise between the German government and lending banks, the entire financing package was scaled down to DM 1.2 billion, and the governmental guarantee was reduced proportionately to DM 400 million. The Finance and Economics Ministries, perhaps in an effort to thwart attempts by other East European governments to seek similar general-purpose financial assistance, linked the guaranteed portion to long-term development of Polish coal resources that would eventually produce increased coal exports to the Federal Republic. However, German bankers and government officials alike actually expected the Warsaw government to apply the full DM 1.2 billion package toward easing Poland's immediate balance-of-payments problems.

If German banks, acting independently, had been willing to provide new unguaranteed credit to the Poles during 1980, at minimum they would have assembled a package bearing very limited resemblance to the one they offered under pressure from the German government (and with its partial support). For example, at the same time that the DM 1.2 billion package was constructed, a non-German syndicate was attempting to raise a separate credit for Poland. Its lead-management group, which included the Bank of America and four other major American banks, succeeded in raising only $325 million for seven years in international financial markets, far short of the goal of $500 million. Furthermore, after subtracting apparently politically motivated contributions to the syndicate by Moscow Narodny Bank and three other socialist-country banks, it becomes evident that non-German Western banks were willing to provide Poland only $250 million.[61] In contrast, the loan that German banks extended after German government intervention came to more than twice the actual amount of the non-German commercial loan and to more than two and a half times the amount that non-German Western banks were willing to contribute. The spreads on the German and non-German syndicated credits were the same, but, significantly, one-third of the amount provided by the German banks (the share guaranteed by the German government) carried a term of ten years, compared with the more conservative normal market term of seven years on the entire $325 million syndication led predominantly by

60. Jonathan Carr and Nicholas Colchester, "W. German Banks Offer DM 1.2 bn Credits to Poland," *Financial Times* (London), August 13, 1980.

61. Cumming-Bruce, "Jan Woloszyn's Struggle for Poland," p. 102.

American banks. (The term on the remainder of the German loan was also seven years.)

Press reports unanimously cited the German government's positive attitude toward the final structure of the Dresdner-led package; according to London's *Financial Times,* for example, "Bonn is pleased by the outcome. The result is a particular satisfaction—and relief—for the West German Chancellor, Herr Helmut Schmidt."[62] The fact that the German loan existed in a preliminary form by late June was probably instrumental in prompting sufficient confidence in Poland's financial prospects to make American and British banks willing to proceed with their own, smaller syndicated package, and the combination of the two loans produced a critically needed $1 billion in new Polish hard currency reserves. As the German Finance and Economics Ministries were fully aware, the two loans were a decisive factor in enabling Poland to obtain most of the full measure of credit it sought from international financial markets in 1980.

In summary, rigorous negotiations between the German government and leading German banks during 1980 determined both the amount and structure of a major new DM-denominated commercial term loan to the Polish government. The German government, sensing high political stakes and only moderate financial risk, used a combination of guarantees and suasion to encourage German banks to extend the credit. The banks, by consenting to acquire a moderately risky new financial asset, were able to obtain a partial guarantee covering their risk and substantial compensation resulting from a large interest spread.

The DM 1.2 billion credit is likely to have a far-reaching effect on future international coordination between Germany's banks and government. In part because of the uncharacteristic publicity accorded the government's pressure on the banks, the loan added at least a temporary, visible element of strain to German bank-government relations in the international sphere. To some degree, the refusal of the banks to lend to the Poles until the German government offered guarantees may have constituted a shrewd maneuver, reflecting the banks' calculation that high political stakes would inevitably force the issuance of official guarantees. Much of the publicity given to the Bonn government's prodding of the banks may have resulted from leaks to the press by the banks themselves, eager to maximize the government's responsibility

62. Carr and Colchester, "W. German Banks Offer DM 1.2 bn Credits to Poland."

for the final credit. In light of the growing severity of Poland's financial problems during 1981–82, especially following the imposition of martial law in December 1981, German foreign policy formulators are likely to be more cautious for some time to come when assessing the financial risks inherent in politically desirable commercial loans. Concurrently, the behavior of German banks in the Polish credit negotiations has probably reminded Bonn officials "how strong and tough" the banks can be, in the words of one involved American banker. As a result, in his opinion, "The [German] government will come to the bargaining table better prepared the next time."[63]

Conclusion

In recent years German foreign policy and German international banking have frequently appeared aligned because of a natural convergence of interests. The interests of Germany's banks and government in the international sphere have not always been either identical or complementary, however. When substantive differences have occurred, the government has often successfully relied on a range of incentives to modify the banks' commercial behavior. In other cases, personal contacts, strong institutional working relationships, and an element of mutual dependence have combined to facilitate ad hoc dialogue and negotiation between large banks and the government. Four recent examples of such direct negotiation were discussed in this chapter.

What does the future hold? During 1982–83, a time of economic recession in Germany and heightened uncertainty in international financial markets, German banks adopted a lower international profile in virtually all business areas other than export finance. Many large German banks were adversely affected throughout the early 1980s by the weak performance of key domestic industrial sectors and a growing volume of problem international loans. As German banking performance became strained during this period, the managements of the largest banks and officials of the federal government alike devoted increasing attention to the supervision of international risk and related prudential issues. The Federal Banking Supervisory Office gained a louder voice in its calls for more formal regulation of German banking; at the same time, political

63. Interview with official of a major American bank, Vienna, March 15, 1981.

influences on German commercial international banking probably re-
ceded somewhat as the banks struggled to improve profitability and
Bonn officials rethought the demands that could sensibly be placed on
the banks' stretched international capabilities.

(Interestingly, however, Germany's banks still worked closely with
German industry and the Bonn government during 1982 to arrange at
least $1.13 billion in Hermes-guaranteed, below-market financing in-
tended to cover German pipe and related machinery sales to the Soviet
Union.[64] And during the first half of 1983, both Bavarian premier Franz
Josef Strauss and Chancellor Helmut Kohl were involved in secret
deliberations that led to a DM 1 billion federally guaranteed bank loan
to East Germany.)[65]

Over the longer run, both the underlying strength of the German
banking system and a major role for German banks in international
finance appear assured. While the leading German banks may not
increase significantly the share of international business in their portfolios over the next five years, that share already stands between 20 and
40 percent for most of these banks, and it will almost certainly not
decline. Given the continuing dependence of the German economy on
exports, their promotion must remain a critical underlying concern of
German international finance. In a broader sense, German banks are
likely to retain their already strong interest in pursuing any business
related to the export and other overseas activities of German corporations. Thus the banks can be expected increasingly to "link international
business to strengths at home."[66] As the larger German banks achieve
renewed profitability, a strengthening of existing (but currently muted)
patterns of bank-government coordination seems likely on international
policy issues. Particularly in cases where the advancement of German
exports or the stability of important export markets is at stake, Germany's banks and government are likely to remain able to work together
effectively to advance both commercial and official objectives abroad.

64. Steve Mufson, "Anatomy of Continuing Soviet Pipeline Controversy," *Wall
Street Journal,* August 31, 1982.

65. The Bonn government and Strauss may have tried to use the loan, which came
as East Germany was experiencing severe debt service problems, to extract general
promises from the East German regime pertaining to intra-German relations. James M.
Markham, "Visit to East by Strauss Startles Bonn," *New York Times,* July 27, 1983;
"West Germany: Strauss Stumbles," *Economist,* vol. 288 (July 23, 1983), p. 40.

66. Interview with chief officer in the United States of one of the Big Three German
commercial banks, New York City, November 30, 1982.

PART TWO

Japan

CHAPTER FIVE

The Japanese Banking System

ANY ANALYSIS of the interaction between commercial banking and foreign policy interests in Japan must take into account both the specific domestic context of Japanese bank-government relations and the complex forces, internal as well as external, that have shaped modern Japanese foreign policy. Domestic institutional relationships go far to define the role of the country's banks as aggressive entrepreneurs in the financial marketplace and the accepted role of government in that marketplace as both a coordinator and a policeman. Japan's extreme dependence on imported natural resources, in turn, has combined with the preferences of influential domestic elites and the weight of recent Japanese history to give Japanese foreign policy a decidedly economic bent. Perceiving a hostile external environment and placing highest priority on the development of Japan's economic interests, the government has come to view the international capabilities of Japanese banks as a strategic resource.

Efforts to produce an overview of the dynamics between Japanese foreign policy and commercial banking are hampered by the amorphous nature of the connections between Japanese banks and government, the characteristic secrecy of their dialogue, and the fact that the banks' international capabilities and the government's attitudes toward their development are currently in flux. Nevertheless, much can still be said about these dynamics. In the Federal Republic of Germany, certain mechanisms have facilitated occasional close coordination between commercial banks and the official foreign policy apparatus. In Japan, analogous mechanisms have accommodated a nearly continuous dialogue between internationally active banks and the bureaucracy. Similarly, whereas Germany's top commercial banks have sometimes served as powerful, albeit junior, partners to government, the partnership between banks and government in Japan has called for greater, or at least more overt, deference by the banks toward the Ministry of Finance. Power in this most influential of ministries is personalized, and its officials can offer private Japanese banks guidance on any and all aspects of their business.

Both the Japanese government and the banking community encompass a multitude of viewpoints and interests, and conflict within each sector over policy issues is not uncommon. Mild conflict between the two sectors is frequently visible as well, as the banks appear to maneuver nearly continuously in their dealings with the authorities to achieve an improved entrepreneurial position. Yet the degree of coordination that Japanese banks and government are able to achieve in the international sphere remains remarkable in comparison to bank-government relations in either Germany or the United States. Even without the combination of respect and gratitude that many senior commercial bankers seem to feel toward their counterparts at the Ministry of Finance, an underlying homogeneity of attitudes would still contribute to a convergence of thinking on many international financial issues. This homogeneity serves as a major reconciling factor in Japanese bank-government relations, tempering the inevitable disagreements that arise.

Within the Japanese economy, the banks have provided critical support to Japanese industry. The banks' interaction with industry has taken place under the watchful eye of the state, which is indisputably the most powerful guiding force in Japan today. During most of the period since the end of World War II the Japanese government has maintained as its paramount policy objective domestic economic growth. In its efforts to direct the reconstruction and expansion of the Japanese economy, the government has actively influenced the banking system's domestic allocation of capital through both careful supervision of the system and direct financial intermediation.

Japan's international banking capabilities have been given a special national importance by the country's enormous vulnerability to external economic forces. Although domestic demand has been sufficient to stimulate, or at least to absorb, much of the phenomenal growth in output in the postwar period and subsequent years, the economy has nevertheless remained highly dependent on the rest of the world for mineral fuels, raw materials, and foodstuffs. Japan literally must import in order to survive. Conversely, Japan must export in order to acquire foreign exchange needed to cover mounting import bills. As Edwin Reischauer has observed, "No other major country [has] relied as heavily as Japan on resources and markets located so far away in distant areas of the globe. In this sense, Japan [has] moved in twelve decades [the 1850s to the 1970s] from being the world's most isolated country to being the most global."[1]

A natural convergence of private financial and official interests has often led large Japanese banks to subscribe voluntarily to the objectives of Japanese foreign policy. The banking community, as an influential member of the elite that has supported Japanese foreign policy throughout the postwar period, has contributed substantially to the formulation of that policy. Simultaneously, the governmental bureaucracy has generally recognized the international commercial interests of Japan's banks as worthy of official support. Furthermore, the Japanese government, primarily through the Ministry of Finance and the Bank of Japan (the central bank), has maintained a detailed knowledge of Japanese banks' offshore business and has used a variety of means to influence it.

The most informal and indirect methods available to the authorities for influencing Japanese international banking have been signals and incentives sent through the financial marketplace. Examples include providing official export insurance, designating certain overseas industrial ventures as "national projects," assuming creditor positions in large syndicated financings, and occasionally providing subsidized funding to private Japanese financial institutions. In some of these cases there has been no further governmental intervention and private banks have remained free to make their own business decisions; still, the official bureaucracy has made its preferences clear and has usually made accommodation more commercially attractive to the banks. In many instances, however, Japan's financial authorities have also relied on a combination of legally mandated supervisory powers and "administrative guidance" to influence the banks' international business pursuits. On these latter occasions, the financial bureaucracy has often been concerned primarily with matters of prudential oversight or monetary

1. Edwin O. Reischauer, "Foreword," in Robert A. Scalapino, ed., *The Foreign Policy of Modern Japan* (University of California Press, 1977), p. xvi.

policy. But Japan's strategic economic and hence political security has also regularly motivated official action.

The Structure

Japan's highly centralized government is able to use the Japanese commercial banking sector to serve a range of national objectives. The government has obtained this capability in part through its implementation of a structural policy for the entire banking system and in part through careful ongoing supervision of Japanese commercial banking. The government has obtained a further measure of influence by functioning as a key intermediary itself in Japanese financial markets.

Japan's financial system has been categorized as a credit-based, price-administered one, in which the state plays the leading role; this contrasts noticeably with Germany's credit-based, bank-dominated financial system.[2] For the Japanese authorities, the commercial banking sector has proven an important conduit for following and influencing activities in key industries. While the leading banks have tended to exert considerable influence over business, the relationship has had a degree of mutual dependence. One cannot accurately represent Japanese banks as omnipotent over the country's private sector. Still, the banks, responsive to strong central government signals, incentives, and supervision, have served as the most important financiers of Japan's corporate and industrial growth.

The Japanese banking system reflects higher concentration and greater specialization than its American counterpart. The Japanese government has kept concentration from advancing too far, though, and no "Big Three" institutions dominate banking in Japan as they do in the Federal Republic of Germany. As a consequence, Japan falls somewhere between Germany and the United States in terms of concentration.

Consisting entirely of indigenous privately owned institutions and the branches of foreign banks, the Japanese commercial banking sector will be defined broadly here to include all "ordinary banks" as they are sometimes known in Japan, or "all-banks" in the terminology of the

2. The categorizations are John Zysman's. He elaborates on the "price-administered" character of the Japanese financial system in *Governments, Markets, and Growth: Financial Systems and the Politics of Industrial Change* (Cornell University Press, 1983), pp. 245–51.

Bank of Japan.[3] Defined in this way, the commercial sector of the Japanese banking system contained 86 indigenous institutions at year-end 1982; this compared roughly in magnitude to the 182 such banks operating in West Germany on the same date, but differed fundamentally from the 14,960 domestically chartered banks in the U.S. commercial banking sector.[4] Japan's commercial banking sector consists of the following categories:

—Thirteen city banks, which are generally based in large cities and function as major wholesale lenders to Japanese industry. Most also maintain strong retail positions in urban areas of Japan and operate branch networks throughout the country. The largest city bank, Dai-Ichi Kangyo, ranked as the eighth largest bank in the world in terms of assets in 1982, and seven city banks ranked in the top twenty-five.[5] Although their international operations tended to remain modest through the mid-1970s, most of these banks subsequently came to regard the international field as their area of most rapid growth.[6] In accord with common practice, the Bank of Tokyo, the country's single specially chartered foreign exchange bank under the Foreign Exchange Bank Law of 1954, is classified here as a city bank.

—Ten long-term lending banks, comprising three long-term credit banks and seven trust banks. The long-term credit banks specialize in long-term loans to major industries to fund capital investments. Unlike the city banks, these banks are allowed to issue term debentures, a privilege that gives them a decided advantage in funding their long-term portfolios.[7] The operations of these banks are centered in Japan's major urban areas. The Industrial Bank of Japan (IBJ), the largest long-term

3. See Eric W. Hayden, "Internationalizing Japan's Financial System," An Occasional Paper of the Northeast Asia–United States Forum on International Policy (Stanford University, 1980), p. 2; Bank of Japan, Economic Research Department, *The Japanese Financial System* (Bank of Japan, 1978), p. 2.

4. See tables 2-1, 5-1, and 7-1.

5. "The Top 500 in World Banking," *Banker* (London), vol. 133 (June 1983), pp. 177–79.

6. See International Business Information, Inc., *The Japanese City Banks: Moving Toward a Greatly Expanded International Role* (Tokyo: IBI, 1977), p. iii.

7. The one exception to this statement is the Bank of Tokyo: it alone is authorized to join the long-term credit banks in selling debentures. In accordance with its charter as the country's specialized foreign exchange bank, the Bank of Tokyo faces special restrictions on the number of domestic branches it may open, and hence on its ability to generate funding through deposits; as partial compensation, the bank is permitted to raise funds by selling its own bonds. See Hayden, "Internationalizing Japan's Financial System," p. 2.

credit bank and the twenty-first largest bank in the world in 1982, has also become a major force in international finance.[8] The trust banks issue "loan trusts" or medium-term savings certificates, and their strong term deposit base has made them significant participants in the domestic long-term lending market.

—Sixty-three regional banks. In accordance with Ministry of Finance regulations, regional banks' branch networks are typically concentrated in a single prefecture; as these banks have grown in size, however, some have also opened branches in Tokyo or Osaka. Regional banks tend to rely on deposit funding to make short-term loans to small and medium-sized businesses. These banks also frequently on-lend part of their deposits to city banks that are short of funds, and some have recently become active in lending to larger Japanese corporations.

—Seventy-one foreign banks, generally located in Tokyo or Osaka, which operated a total of ninety-six branches in Japan as of March 1982.[9] Foreign banks have traditionally concentrated on wholesale lending to large Japanese corporations and the local subsidiaries of foreign enterprises, as well as on correspondent relationships with Japanese banks. The operations of foreign banks currently account for less than 2 percent of the Japanese banking system's assets.

The Japanese commercial banking sector accounted for approximately 46 percent of the overall banking system's assets at year-end 1982 (see table 5-1), compared with 22 percent in Germany and 52 percent in the United States. Outside of the commercial banking sector, the other most important components of the overall system are government-owned financial institutions (twelve institutions accounting for nearly 9 percent of total system assets); the government-controlled postal savings and loans network (accounting for approximately 15 percent of system assets); small business financial institutions (over 1,000 mutual savings and loan banks, credit associations, and credit cooperatives, with approximately 18 percent of the system's assets); and financial institutions for agriculture and fisheries (over 6,100 cooperatives controlling approximately 12 percent of the system's assets). A more detailed summary of the system is provided in table 5-1.

For purposes of this study, only a few of the financial institutions outside the commercial banking sector are significant; among the most

8. "The Top 500 in World Banking," p. 179.
9. Peat, Marwick, Mitchell and Co., *Banking in Japan* (Tokyo: Peat, Marwick, Mitchell and Co., 1982), p. 27.

Table 5-1. *Structure of the Japanese Banking System, Year-End 1982*

Institution	Number of organi- zations	Assets (billions of dol- lars)	Percent- age of system assets
Commercial banks[a]	157	1,205.7	45.6
City banks	13	603.8	22.9
Regional banks	63	348.9	13.2
Long-term credit banks	3	135.3	5.1
Trust banks	7	70.9	2.7
Foreign banks operating branches	71	46.5	1.8
Government-owned financial institutions	12	232.6[b]	8.8
Export-Import Bank of Japan	1	25.6[b]	1.0
Japan Development Bank	1	26.9[b]	1.0
Others	10	180.1[b]	6.8
Government	2	397.4	15.0
Postal savings	1	314.4[c]	11.9
Postal life insurance and postal annuity	1	83.0	3.1
Small business financial institutions	1,046	484.9	18.4
Mutual savings and loan banks	71	162.9	6.2
Credit associations	456	204.0	7.7
National Federation of Credit Associations	1	18.0	0.7
Shoko Chukin Bank	1	29.3	1.1
Credit cooperatives	468	45.9	1.7
National Federation of Credit Cooperatives	1	5.0	0.2
Labor credit associations	47	16.3	0.6
National Federation of Labor Credit Associations	1	3.5	0.1
Financial institutions for agriculture, etc.	6,131	320.6	12.1
Central Cooperative Bank for Agriculture and Forestry (Norinchukin)	1	59.4	2.2
Credit federations of agriculture cooperatives	47[d]	92.0	3.5
Agriculture cooperatives	4,359[d]	152.6	5.8
Credit federations of fishery cooperatives	35	5.9	0.2
Fishery cooperatives	1,689[e]	10.6[e]	0.4
Total	7,348	2,641.2	100.0

Sources: Asset figures for some categories based on author's estimates from principal accounts found in Bank of Japan, *Economic Statistics Annual, 1982* (Bank of Japan, 1983), pp. 47–106, 156; Bank of Japan, *Economic Statistics Monthly*, no. 430 (January 1983), pp. 49–50; and Peat, Marwick, Mitchell and Co., *Banking in Japan* (Tokyo: Peat, Marwick, Mitchell and Co., 1982), p. 27. Yen converted to U.S. dollars at the rate of $1.00 = 235 yen. Figures are rounded.

a. Excludes assets of Japanese banks' foreign branches and foreign subsidiaries. The assets of branches of foreign banks in Japan are based on a summation of "principal accounts" of those branches. Number of foreign banks operating branches reflects data as of March 1982.

b. Based on summation of "principal accounts" for each government-owned financial institution.

c. Represents balance of postal savings as of September 1982.

d. As of year-end 1981.

e. As of November 1982.

important are the Japan Development Bank and the Export-Import Bank of Japan. The postal savings and loans network is also of considerable relevance because the Ministry of Finance, through its Trust Fund Bureau, has drawn upon the network's vast resources to fund major portions of the activities of the various government-owned financial institutions.[10]

The intermediate degree of concentration in the Japanese banking system invites more in-depth comparisons with both the American and West German systems. In the case of the United States and Japan, the disparity in the total number of commercial banks has already been cited. In addition, however, major differences exist in the scope of their branch networks. The average number of branches per bank for all indigenous commercial banks in Japan was 100 at year-end 1982, compared with 2.6 in the United States. The thirteeen Japanese city banks operated an average of 206 branches per bank throughout the nation during 1981–82.[11] By comparison, the ten largest American banks maintained an average of 262 domestic branches apiece at roughly the same time, but federal and state restrictions confined any one bank's branches generally to a single state and in two cases to a single city.[12] In terms of total domestic assets, the Japanese city banks averaged $46.4 billion at year-end 1982, compared with $37.9 billion for the ten largest American banks, which were operating in a commercial banking sector more than 70 percent larger than the one in Japan.

The German-Japanese comparison is somewhat more complicated but reveals relatively lower concentration in the upper reaches of the banking industry in Japan. As was pointed out earlier, low concentration characterizes the German system overall, with nearly 5,000 separate institutions operating in the country. Nevertheless, a very few large institutions dominate German banking in terms of their influence within the financial system itself, over the German private sector, and vis-à-vis

10. For a detailed discussion, see Eisuke Sakakibara, Robert Feldman, and Yuzo Harada, "Japanese Financial System in Comparative Perspective," prepared as part of the Program on U.S.-Japan Relations of the Center for International Affairs, Harvard University, 1981, pp. 52–55.

11. Bank of Japan, *Economic Statistics Annual, 1982* (Bank of Japan, 1983), p. 156; Board of Governors of the U.S. Federal Reserve System, *69th Annual Report, 1982,* pp. 238–39.

12. Peter Merrill Associates for the American Bankers Association, *The Future Development of U.S. Banking Organizations Abroad* (Washington, D.C.: ABA, 1981), pp. 110–17.

the German federal government. In Japan, by contrast, the thirteen city banks comprise a group four times as large in number as the group at the center of German commercial banking. Further evidence of Japan's relatively lower degree of concentration is the fact that the typical Japanese city bank's branch network in 1982 averaged only one-fifth the size of the average branch network of one of Germany's Big Three banks.[13] Japan's much larger core group of banks controlled an only slightly greater proportion of domestic commercial banking assets (50 percent, versus 39 percent for Germany's Big Three).

The intermediate stage of banking concentration in Japan reflects the measured policy of the Japanese government, which for economic and structural reasons has sought to achieve a balance between the U.S. and European models. The government has wanted to ensure sufficient credit for Japan's small business sector and to maintain a controlled degree of competition within the system. There have been opposing considerations, however. For example, officials of the Ministry of Finance have also been sensitive to the potential benefits of a banking system more responsive to monetary control, a system better positioned to take advantage of economies of scale inherent in banking, and a stronger international banking capability. In recent years, the authorities have implicitly supported modest increases in the prevailing level of concentration through a "very deliberate" policy of authorizing and even stimulating bank mergers, often among institutions in the same region.[14]

The Japanese authorities' endorsement of a medium-sized group of banks at the core of the system carries at least two significant implications:

—As a result of government policy, an elite group of Japanese banks has emerged that is sufficiently small to permit consultation and coordination with the government on important commercial transactions as well as on policy issues.

—Government policy has produced at the same time a core group of banks large enough to preclude a few banks' emergence as a force that

13. For statistics on the scope of German bank branch networks see Deutsche Bundesbank, *Monthly Report,* vol. 35 (March 1983), p. 45. Operations of the Big Three banks and their Berlin subsidiaries have been aggregated. For statistics on Japanese bank networks see Bank of Japan, *Economic Statistics Annual, 1982,* p. 156.

14. For a discussion of arguments both for and against increased concentration in Japanese banking, see Henry C. Wallich and Mable I. Wallich, "Banking and Finance," in Hugh Patrick and Henry Rosovsky, eds., *Asia's New Giant: How the Japanese Economy Works* (Brookings Institution, 1976), pp. 290–93.

could either hold sway over the financial community or consistently challenge government policies.

On balance, the banking structure that the Japanese authorities have settled upon has produced a level of concentration closer to the European (West German) than the U.S. pattern.

Japan's authorities have also favored a banking structure that emphasizes functional specialization. Similar to the American industry but different from the German, the Japanese securities business is separated from commercial banking business; as a result, approximately 220 independent securities companies operate in the country.[15] Other major lines of functional specialization are reflected in the breakdown of the banking system according to institutional type (for example, the division of the commercial sector into city, regional, long-term credit, and trust banks).

The Japanese financial authorities have used functional specialization as a means of augmenting regulatory control over the banking industry. The delineation of the types of business that any single bank can pursue has enabled the Finance Ministry and Bank of Japan (effectively an administrative extension of the ministry) to follow the activities of specific groups of banks and to influence their behavior with often predictable, differentiated effect. For example, especially during the period of Japan's most rapid postwar economic growth (the late 1950s through the early 1970s), the authorities improved their control over the flow of capital to particular industrial sectors by limiting the types and number of banks capable of making long-term loans to major Japanese corporations. Similarly, throughout much of the postwar period, the authorities were able to monitor and control Japan's overseas banking business by designating the Bank of Tokyo as the country's single specialized foreign exchange bank. Japan's competitively oriented banks have intensified their drive in recent years to break out of "the rigid framework of specialization," and the authorities themselves have recognized the need for change.[16] As a consequence, the functional lines separating various types of Japanese financial institutions became progressively less clear-cut during the 1970s and early 1980s. Yet enforced specialization remains a distinctive feature of Japanese banking today and continues to provide an effective instrument of control to the government.

15. Bank of Japan, *Economic Statistics Annual, 1982*, p. 156.
16. See Wallich and Wallich, "Banking and Finance," pp. 278–83, quote on p. 283.

Banking Supervision

If one takes into account the impact of administrative guidance, Japanese banks rank among the most intensely supervised in the non-Communist developed world. The key bureaucracy overseeing the activities of Japanese banks is the Ministry of Finance; its responsibilities, in the words of Stephen Bronte, "incorporate, in U.S. terms, those of the Treasury, Internal Revenue Service, Securities and Exchange Commission, state banking commissions and policy-making responsibilities of the Federal Reserve Board."[17] In a similar vein, a 1977 study by a Tokyo-based consulting firm concluded, ". . . the powers of the Ministry over individual banks are for all intents and purposes absolute."[18]

The principal statutory basis for the Ministry of Finance's supervision of the banking system is the Banking Law, enacted in 1927 and extensively revised for the first time in 1981. (The revisions took effect in April 1982.) Other statutes prescribing specific oversight functions include Japan's Securities and Exchange Law, the Foreign Exchange and Foreign Trade Control Law (amended in 1980), the Temporary Interest Rates Adjustment Law, and the Law on the Reserve Deposit System. In addition, the Ministry of Finance retains broad discretionary authority to issue banking rules, reflecting a de facto delegation of far-reaching policymaking powers by Japan's historically weak Diet.[19] This discretionary authority provides the basis for the ministry's highly effective use of administrative guidance.

The Banking Law (as amended) requires that all banks obtain an operating license from the minister of finance, as well as his approval to open all new branch offices. The law also authorizes the finance minister to demand reports from banks on their business and to inspect them whenever deemed necessary. Furthermore, the finance minister may enjoin a bank "from conducting business in whole or in part, transfer its property to the competent authorities, or take any other necessary

17. Stephen Bronte, "Inside the Tokyo Ministry of Finance: The Most Powerful Men in Japan," *Euromoney* (June 1979), p. 24.

18. IBI, *The Japanese City Banks*, p. 14.

19. For a comparison of the de facto powers of Japanese ministries and the de jure authority of comparable administrative agencies in the United States, see Franklin Strier, "Multipartite Policy Consensus Building in Japan, West Germany, France and the United Kingdom: Analysis and Implications to the United States" (U.S. Department of Commerce, Office of Economic Policy, March 1981), pp. 12–13.

measures'' required in light of a bank's "business situation or financial position." If a bank were to commit "any act harmful to the public interest" or an illegal act, the minister has the authority to revoke the bank's license, among other options.[20] In recent years, the Finance Ministry has supplemented the specific approvals and orders detailed in the Banking Law with administrative guidance of banks' domestic activities, notably regulation of office establishment, large loans, and ancillary business; guidance on financial positions; and supervision of accounting.[21]

In addition to administrative guidance issued directly by the Ministry of Finance, the Bank of Japan has provided extensive guidance to Japanese banks on matters as basic as their lending volume and interest rates. Through "window guidance," the central bank has relied on its informal but potent powers of persuasion to ration commercial credit and enhance official control over the country's money supply.[22] As viewed by Japan's Banking Federation, "This [window] guidance, . . . a sort of moral suasion, presupposes the cooperation of those financial institutions the Bank of Japan deals with."[23] The Bank of Japan, in close coordination with the Finance Ministry, has similarly controlled commercial interest rates in Japan by drawing on a combination of legal authority and moral suasion.[24]

Underlying the Japanese government's influence over the banking

20. See "Banking Law" (unofficial English translation of law as amended by the Diet in May 1981, provided by the Bank of Japan, undated), articles 8, 26, 27.

21. See Federation of Bankers Associations of Japan, *Banking System in Japan, 1982*, 8th ed. (Tokyo: Federation of Bankers Associations of Japan, 1982), pp. 102–07. The revised Banking Law formalized the Ministry of Finance's authority to set limits on large loans to single borrowers. For a more general discussion of administrative guidance, see Gardner Ackley and Hiromitsu Ishi, "Fiscal, Monetary, and Related Policies," in Patrick and Rosovsky, eds., *Asia's New Giant*, pp. 236–39.

22. The Bank of Japan makes its suggestions to the banks on their aggregate lending theoretically as they come to the central bank's "discount window." The Bank of Japan has generally resorted to window guidance only during periods of tight money. See Ackley and Ishi, "Fiscal, Monetary, and Related Policies," p. 202.

23. Federation of Bankers Associations of Japan, *Banking System in Japan, 1982*, 8th ed., p. 87.

24. One example of the considerable informal powers of the authorities in this area has been their influence over the setting of Japan's commercial prime lending rate. Although Japanese commercial banks have not been legally required to tie their prime rate to the Bank of Japan's official discount rate since 1958, changes in the discount rate are still followed within a few days by the commercial banks' voluntary adjustment of their short-term prime. Stephen Bronte, *Japanese Finance: Markets and Institutions* (London: Euromoney Publications, 1982), pp. 16–17.

system is a set of shared values that has drawn together Japan's public- and private-sector financial elites. These common values, in their most general form, have served as a foundation for not only bank-government relations but broader business-government relations as well:

Japan's historical experience and value system have resulted in an economic ideology supportive of close and harmonious government-business relations. One thinks immediately of emphasis on group rather than individual, on cooperation and conciliation aimed at harmony, on national rather than personal welfare. The right of the government to lead, and to interfere where necessary, has substantial basis in ideology as well as in historical experience.[25]

More tangible considerations have also prompted private Japanese banks to accept the government's far-reaching and often informal involvement in their affairs. One of the most effective sanctions that the ministry can employ against uncooperative banks is its power to approve or disapprove new branch openings. At an even more fundamental level, the Banking Law gives the ministry broad discretionary powers to license new banks and to inspect and suspend existing financial institutions. In addition, some observers have argued that the Japanese financial authorities have issued an implied guarantee of the survival of all banks in return for their agreement to detailed supervision. The existence of such a tacit agreement could help to explain why no Japanese bank has failed since the end of World War II.[26] Another cause of Japanese banks' responsiveness to supervision is the practice of "overloan." This term refers to the reliance of the banking system, primarily the city banks, on net borrowings from the Bank of Japan to fund lending. Although "overloan" no longer engenders a sense of outright shame within the banking community as it did during the Meiji era, observers still cite the phenomenon as a source of commercial banks' sense of dependence on and gratitude toward the public authorities. Even those categories of banks not usually caught in the position of overloan still depend indirectly on the Bank of Japan and Ministry of Finance for funding.[27]

25. Hugh Patrick and Henry Rosovsky, "Japan's Economic Performance: An Overview," in Patrick and Rosovsky, eds., *Asia's New Giant*, p. 53.

26. See IBI, *The Japanese City Banks,* p. ii; and Saburo Matsukawa, "Japan: System Heads for Progressive Restructuring," *Financial Times* (London), May 27, 1981.

27. Long-term credit banks and the Bank of Tokyo, for example, maintain their privileged access to Japan's long-term debenture market at the discretion of these authorities, just as the trust banks enjoy the protection by the Finance Ministry of their special right to raise funds through long-term time deposits. On occasion, all of these banks have also effectively become recipients of credit from the Bank of Japan. Yoshio Suzuki, *Money and Banking in Contemporary Japan: The Theoretical Setting and Its*

Japan's financial authorities have derived still another measure of influence over the banking system from their recognized elite status. Finance Ministry officials, often top graduates of the country's best universities, are perceived as a group to be among the most able of Japan's professional talent. These career bureaucrats are respected for their willingness to endure notoriously long working hours and relatively low salaries during their tenure in the Finance Ministry (although to some extent unrivaled power and prestige may compensate officials for the hardships they bear). Upon their retirement from the government, however, many of these elite public officials assume lucrative positions in the private sector. This custom is known as *amakudari,* which translates literally as "descent from heaven." A seasoned official of the Finance Ministry might typically "retire" after thirty years of public service to an influential position within a Japanese bank. The official would bring with him extensive personal contacts within the ministry, and he would probably retain strong ties to it of a broader nature as well. The bank hiring the retiring bureaucrat would hope to develop improved access to other ministry officials and a better awareness of ministry plans and thinking. (*Amakudari* also applies to the retirement of Bank of Japan personnel, and retiring officials may alternatively "descend" to government-owned financial institutions such as the Japan Development Bank or Export-Import Bank.)

Amakudari serves as another link between the financial bureaucracy and the leading banks, enhancing not only the authorities' influence within the private financial community but also the banks' ability to understand and communicate with the government. Many Japanese banks seek to employ at least several former officials of the Finance Ministry and the Bank of Japan at any given time.[28]

Two concluding observations on government supervision of banking in Japan deserve mention. First, observers should be careful in estimating

Application (Yale University Press, 1980), pp. 9, 179. Some observers feel that another factor contributing to the city banks' responsiveness to supervision has been the authorities' ability to restrict wayward city banks' access to the interbank market for funding of domestic loans.

28. Prominent examples of Finance Ministry officials who have retired to banks include Yusuke Kashiwagi, a former vice-minister for international affairs who became president (and subsequently chairman) of the Bank of Tokyo, and Takashi Hosomi, another vice-minister for international affairs, who joined the Industrial Bank of Japan as a senior adviser and later became president of the Japanese government's Overseas Economic Cooperation Fund.

the significance of an apparent trend in Japanese finance toward less regulation. Many of the recent revisions in Japan's Banking Law are indeed liberal in character.[29] Along the same lines, revisions in Japan's Foreign Exchange Law, implemented in December 1980, alter the status of external financial transactions from "prohibited in principle" with occasional exceptions to "free in principle" unless specifically restricted.[30] The revised law thus adopts a laissez-faire stance toward much commercial banking business, similar to that of West Germany's Banking Act. Despite such paper changes, however, Japan's banks remain under the close scrutiny of the Ministry of Finance and the Bank of Japan. A slow, long-term trend may be evolving toward less regulation, but changes in practice will probably occur on the margin and not by abrupt shifts. Moreover, Japanese bank supervision is based fundamentally on operational understandings, not written rules. While bank regulation in Japan may be less intense today than in past years, it is also more precise; as articulated by a Ministry of Finance division director, government involvement in Japanese banking affairs is perhaps not becoming "more active," but it is becoming "more refined."[31]

Second, despite the essentially nonadversarial nature of Japanese bank-government relations, they are still frequently characterized by a mild tension, which stems in large part from the conflict between the financial authorities' restrictive influence and the banking sector's enormous entrepreneurial zeal. Observers from the "Japan, Inc." school have often failed to recognize this tension, perhaps because they have tended to focus exclusively on the conciliatory forces that temper it.[32] Among the most important of these forces is the strong interest that Japan's financial authorities have displayed in Japanese banks' commercial success. Concurrently, a number of important public officials have seemed to feel that whenever public policy is in conflict with bank

29. New provisions in the law allow banks to deal in and make retail sales of public bonds and to increase capital on a prior notification basis instead of through the old approval system. Besides a trend toward somewhat less stringent regulation, the law also reflects an effort to formalize certain major forms of administrative guidance. See "Japan's New Banking Law," in Bank of Tokyo, *Tokyo Financial Review*, vol. 6 (September 1981), pp. 1–3.

30. See Bank of Japan, Foreign Department, *Outline of Foreign Exchange Control in Japan* (Bank of Japan, 1981), p. 1.

31. Interview with official of the International Finance Bureau, Ministry of Finance, Tokyo, February 16, 1981.

32. For a definition of the "Japan, Inc." thesis, see Patrick and Rosovsky, "Japan's Economic Performance," pp. 48–49.

behavior, such dissonance may be a signal that public policy is in conflict with market forces as well, and these may prove far less tractable than the banks.[33] In the end, much truth remains in the observation that "the evolution of Japan's banking system is the history of a continuing struggle between the government, which has a propensity to regulate . . . and institutions bent on an expansionary drive to broaden their markets and functions."[34]

The Government as a Financial Intermediary

Besides supervising Japan's commercial banks, the Japanese government has also functioned as a major coordinator and intermediary in Japanese financial markets. In the words of one senior Japanese commercial banker, the Ministry of Finance has thus acted as the "most powerful merchant bank in Japan."[35] These coordinating and intermediary roles have given the government still another means of mobilizing private-sector financial resources to advance official policy objectives. Some observers have argued, in fact, that the Japanese government has exerted more influence over the financial system's distribution of credit by functioning as a major intermediary than as a regulator or a major borrower.[36]

Through the lending policies of government-owned financial institutions, the Japanese government has sent highly effective signals to private Japanese banks regarding directions it would prefer to see the banks' lending take. The Finance Ministry has exercised considerable influence over this process by serving as a supervisor of all major government-owned banks and by providing a large share of their funding through its Trust Fund Bureau. Other ministries, led by the Ministry of International Trade and Industry (MITI), have also substantially affected the government-owned banks' lending policies.

33. To paraphrase a senior Bank of Japan official on this point: "They [the banks] are not working with us all of the time. But whenever a deviation takes place, it is a warning to us: [Something is wrong] either with us or with the economy [but not with the banks]. While we're annoyed, we still realize this." Interview with senior official of the Bank of Japan, Tokyo, February 18, 1981.

34. Wallich and Wallich, "Banking and Finance," p. 278.

35. Interview with senior official of a Japanese commercial bank, Tokyo, February 13, 1981.

36. Sakakibara, Feldman, and Harada, "Japanese Financial System in Comparative Perspective," pp. 54–55.

A prominent example of the "signaling" effect of government financial intermediation on the rest of the Japanese financial system can be found in the activities of the Japan Development Bank (JDB). Wholly government-owned, this bank was established in 1951 "to supplement and encourage financing by private financial institutions for economic reconstruction and industrial development."[37] Chalmers Johnson has written of the bank's influential role during the early stages of Japanese postwar economic growth:

The JDB itself contributed 22 percent [of total Japanese industrial capital] in 1953 and only 5 percent in 1961, but even as the size of its loans declined relative to the expansion of city-bank funding, the bank retained its power to "guide" capital through the indicative effect of its decisions to support or not support a new industry. A JDB loan, regardless of its size, became MITI's seal of approval on an enterprise, and the company that had received a JDB loan could easily raise whatever else it needed from private resources.[38]

The Ministry of Finance, in addition to MITI, has affected the policies and activities of the JDB by controlling much of its funding (borrowings from the ministry's Trust Fund Bureau provided 70 percent of the JDB's new funds in fiscal 1981), by serving as its supervisory ministry, and by placing retired officials from the ministry and the Bank of Japan on the JDB's loan approval board. The JDB has characteristically undertaken large joint financings with Japanese commercial banks, which invariably are attracted to credits in which the JDB has chosen to participate.[39]

During the period of postwar reconstruction, the JDB focused its lending on strategic industries such as steel, coal mining, shipping, and electric power. Following the 1973 oil crisis the bank began to give energy-related lending special priority; in addition, the bank extended financing to industries that needed to convert excess production facilities as a result of the economic slowdown. During fiscal 1981 JDB lending patterns continued to reflect prevailing official priorities by placing greatest emphasis on Japan's electric power industry, followed by rural

37. Bank of Japan, *The Japanese Financial System*, p. 104.

38. Chalmers Johnson, *MITI and the Japanese Miracle: The Growth of Industrial Policy, 1925–1975* (Stanford University Press, 1982), pp. 210–11.

39. As of 1981, the JDB usually provided 30 percent of the necessary funds for an approved project; a private Japanese banking syndicate provided another 30 percent, and the beneficiary corporation supplied the remaining 40 percent from internal funds. The JDB recorded over $26 billion in outstanding loans as of December 1982 and has directly financed about 4.5 percent of Japanese plant and equipment investment in recent years. Stephen Bronte, "What the Development Bank Develops," *Euromoney* (July 1981), p. 165; and Bank of Japan, *Economic Statistics Annual, 1982*, p. 96.

development, urban development, the coal industry, "improvement of the quality of life," shipping, and the development of new technologies.[40] As Johnson has written, the government-owned financial institutions, particularly the Japan Development Bank, possess "tremendous indicative powers over the whole economy as a result of their decisions to make or refuse 'policy loans.' "[41]

In summary, the Japanese government has regularly operated both as a major force above Japanese financial markets (the supervisor) and as a force in those markets (the coordinator and intermediary). From a comparative perspective, the Japanese government's coordination functions in the financial marketplace are analogous to a role played by the largest private banks themselves in the Federal Republic of Germany. To a degree, this analogy carries implications for the relative roles of banks and government in the economies of these two countries. Whereas many functions of nationwide economic coordination and industrial rationalization have resided de facto with the largest banks in West Germany, a government highly supportive of private-sector interests has performed a number of these functions in Japan. To such a government, the domestic banking system has provided a conduit through which national economic policy could be advanced.

These economic coordination functions have no clear American parallel. The very appropriateness of such central coordination has been challenged in the United States by a traditional economic ideology favoring the "invisible hand" of perfect competition.

Bank-Business Relations

Two essential characteristics of the relationship between business and banking in Japan are important for an understanding of the Japanese banking system. The first is "overborrowing," a term used to describe the unusually heavy indebtedness of many large Japanese corporations to Japanese banks, particularly city banks. (The term should not be confused with "overloan," already discussed.) Japanese business has traditionally relied on bank loans, rather than on other forms of debt (for instance, bonds) or on equity, to fund new investment and growth. As table 5-2 shows, during 1966–70 the average proportion of loan money to total financing for the corporate sector was 49 percent in Japan,

---

40. Bronte, "What the Development Bank Develops," p. 165.
41. Johnson, *MITI and the Japanese Miracle*, p. 200.

Table 5-2. *Financing of the Corporate Sector in Selected Countries, 1966–70*

Percent

Country	External finance			Internal finance
	Borrowed money	Securities issued	Total	
Japan	49.0	11.0	60.0	40.0
West Germany	29.6	7.3	36.9	63.1
France	27.4	7.6	35.0	65.0
United States	12.4	18.2	30.6	69.4
United Kingdom	10.3	38.3	48.6	51.4

Source: Yoshio Suzuki, *Money and Banking in Contemporary Japan: The Theoretical Setting and Its Application* (Yale University Press, 1980), p. 14.

compared with 10 to 30 percent for the United States, West Germany, the United Kingdom, and France. In recent years, the Japanese corporate sector has turned increasingly to the bond and stock markets for funding, and the sector's overall demand for external funds has slackened with the slowdown in Japanese economic growth. Nevertheless, a continued heavy reliance on bank debt has remained a distinctive feature of Japanese corporate finance.

The second characteristic is the group orientation of much of Japanese business. Custom and tradition have greatly influenced this commercial phenomenon. Before World War II, over half of Japan's big businesses were subsidiaries of formal industrial conglomerates called *zaibatsu*.[42] Each *zaibatsu* included a major bank that met the financing needs of other members of the group, but the bank, although powerful, consistently played a subordinate role to the holding company that served as group leader. In postwar Japan, more informal industrial groups, sometimes known as *keiretsu*, have replaced the old *zaibatsu* as a major basis of organization for Japanese big business.[43] Japan's industrial groups today vary considerably in the strength of the centripetal pull of the lead or central firm; similarly, within any given group, the central firm wields more influence over some members than over others. But while the internal cohesiveness of industrial groups has declined since the end of World War II, the relative position of banks within many groups has

42. Kazuo Noda, "Big Business Organization," in Ezra F. Vogel, ed., *Modern Japanese Organization and Decision-Making* (University of California Press, 1975), p. 118.

43. For a discussion from a financial perspective of the structure of modern Japanese industrial groups, see Wallich and Wallich, "Banking and Finance," pp. 293–98.

risen. At least six of the most prominent industrial groups in Japan today have large city banks at or near their centers.[44]

Particularly for the city banks at the core of the banking system, overborrowing has combined with the group orientation of Japanese business to favor the establishment of extremely close bank-business working relationships. Even those large firms that are not members of industrial groups have tended to develop strong ties with a "main bank," while continuing to borrow from a number of banks simultaneously.

An additional factor contributing to strong bank-business ties has been major Japanese banks' tendency to hold sizable blocs of corporate shares. Although the 1977 Anti-Monopoly Act restricts (on a delayed basis) a single bank's investments in equity securities to 5 percent of an invested company's stock, a 1979 survey of over 1,700 publicly listed corporations revealed that a city bank or long-term credit bank ranked as the top shareholder in every sixth firm; in many cases, major banks also served as principal shareholders ranked second or lower. The persistence of these large shareholdings, despite the Anti-Monopoly Act, has further contributed to the ability of the banks to maintain a strong influence over the Japanese corporate sector.[45]

Japanese banks' relationships with client companies often extend well beyond the commercial banking sphere. Banks at the centers of some industrial groups, for example, possess the power to fill senior management positions within group corporations; a bank often uses these positions to reward or retire its own executives or to reinforce its influence over a company in financial difficulty.[46] Japanese banks appear to possess enormously detailed information on the operations of their customers, at least from an American banking perspective. Beyond merely gathering such data, however, the core banks in some industrial groups also perform limited coordinating and planning functions for affiliated companies.[47]

44. The groups in question are the Mitsui, Mitsubishi, Sumitomo, Fuyo, Dai-Ichi Kangin, and Sanwa groups.

45. The survey, conducted by the *Japan Economic Journal (Nihon Keizai Shimbun)*, noted further, "There are also moves among the banks to escape from the restrictions imposed by the new Anti-Monopoly Act by having their subsidiaries possess stocks of enterprises." Tomohisa Yamashita, "Banks Maintain Strong Influence over Big Corporations; Top Stockholder in 257 Firms," *Japan Economic Journal*, May 8, 1979.

46. Wallich and Wallich, "Banking and Finance," p. 295.

47. In addition, as Caves and Uekusa have observed, "One wonders whether banks do not manage somehow to share in the riches when their principal borrowers do particularly well"; these authors note evidence suggesting that city banks' profits have

A brief look at the Mitsubishi group provides an illustration of one aspect of the close relationships that can exist between city banks, in particular, and their corporate clients. The Mitsubishi Bank serves as one of three core members of the group, which includes many of Japan's most important heavy industrial companies and constitutes the most powerful of Japan's modern conglomerates. At the end of fiscal 1978, its 136 affiliated companies generated sales of $111 billion, brought in net profits in excess of $1 billion, and employed 387,000 people worldwide. As of early 1979, the Mitsubishi Bank ranked as the top shareholder in thirty-nine Mitsubishi group firms, possibly making the bank the largest collector of lead shareholder positions of any major Japanese bank.[48] The strong allegiance of Mitsubishi group members to their main bank is evident in the following incident:

When Mitsubishi Bank celebrated its 100th anniversary last year [1980] the group's companies made some $3 billion in "congratulatory" deposits, pushing it up from fourth to second place in the ranking of Japan's city banks. Unfortunately, this upset the [Finance Ministry]; it ordered the bank to give most of the money back, because it constituted unfair competition.[49]

Although Mitsubishi Bank remains their lead bank, Mitsubishi group members also rely on a number of other major domestic banks (as well as foreign banks) for financial services. Thus Mitsubishi Corporation, another core member of the group, showed borrowings in excess of $2.7 billion from seven major Japanese banks during a recent year; Mitsubishi Bank was the largest creditor, but others also provided sizable loans.[50]

Unlike the city banks, the long-term credit banks, as noted earlier, do not possess close affiliations with single industrial groups. Rather, these banks maintain strong working relationships with a number of different groups and are well positioned to acquire extensive knowledge of entire industries. As a result, the long-term credit banks often serve as coordinators and financial advisers to large projects involving multiple industrial groups. Working informally with MITI, these banks are also

been closely related to the growth rates of client enterprises. As a qualification to this argument, the authors also remark, "It is possible, of course, that this seeming equity relation runs solely through shares owned by the banks rather than through the proceeds of loans." Richard E. Caves and Masu Uekusa, "Industrial Organization," in Patrick and Rosovsky, eds., *Asia's New Giant,* p. 480.

48. Stephen Bronte, "The Unique Problems of Mitsubishi's Finances," *Euromoney* (April 1981), p. 105; and Yamashita, "Banks Maintain Strong Influence over Big Corporations."

49. Bronte, "The Unique Problems of Mitsubishi's Finances," p. 106.

50. Ibid., p. 94.

positioned advantageously to assist in periodic strategic planning to
reorganize or rationalize various industrial sectors.

The network of business relationships of the Industrial Bank of Japan
(IBJ) illustrates the long-term credit banks' intricate ties with Japanese
industry. More than 90 percent of Japan's 200 largest firms are clients of
the IBJ, and by its own account, it maintains "close and unbiased
relationships with virtually all of Japan's key industries."[51] According
to one official of the Export-Import Bank of Japan, "IBJ is the only bank
in Japan that has the staff, the funds and the power to bring together all
of the big industrial groups." In 1970, for example, the bank played a
key role in helping to arrange the merger that created the world's largest
steel company, Nippon Steel Corporation.[52]

Finally, while Japan's city banks and long-term credit banks occupy
privileged positions in their dealings with the largest corporations in the
country, the corporations are rarely powerless in these interactions. A
specific relationship may often approach a partnership in which a client's
principal banks carry a heavy burden of responsibility. According to
Japanese custom (although not law), the main bank to a corporation
typically behaves as a subordinated creditor, permitting other lenders to
recover their funds first in the event of the corporation's inability to meet
debt repayments.[53] Similarly, a number of precedents exist for a bankrupt
Japanese corporation's principal banks to use their *own* funds to pay off
other creditors. As a consequence of these and other customs, a mutual
dependence often exists between bank and client.

Japanese International Banking and Foreign Policy

The links between Japanese commercial banking and foreign policy
reflect both a natural extension of domestic economic and political
relationships and an adaptive response to Japan's relative position of
vulnerability in the world. Both considerations have helped to ensure a
significant role for the most internationally active Japanese banks in
limited aspects of their country's foreign policy process.

Domestic determinants have given Japanese foreign economic policy

51. Industrial Bank of Japan, *Annual Report, Fiscal Year 1979* (IBJ, 1980), p. 27.
52. Stephen Bronte, "Ikeura's International Way with IBJ," *Euromoney* (August
1980), p. 36; and Johnson, *MITI and the Japanese Miracle*, pp. 277–78.
53. Wallich and Wallich, "Banking and Finance," p. 273.

an assertiveness normally associated with a country in a more secure international position, one not readily disturbed by external shocks or pressures. Among the most important of these domestic features is a highly centralized state in control of a homogeneous, cohesive people. A broad consensus exists among key elites as to what the basic tenets of Japanese foreign policy should be. Relevant elites in this context have included the official bureaucracy (particularly the Ministries of Finance, International Trade and Industry, and Foreign Affairs); the leadership of the ruling, conservatively oriented Liberal Democratic party; Japanese big business; and the country's largest banks. Drawing on numerous overlapping interests and extensive formal and informal channels of communication, these groups have successfully forged a coherent set of foreign policies concerned foremost with the maintenance of domestic economic growth.

The official bureaucracy has played a remarkably effective role in leading the consensus-building process that underlies Japanese foreign policy. Government ministries have derived their influence over major international policy issues in part from the quality of their career staff and in part from institutional factors that frequently have given the ministries an upper hand in dealing with party politicians on policy questions. For example, political appointees usually hold only the top two positions in government ministries and rarely stay in their posts for more than one year. In contrast, the career officers beneath them might retain and expand their influence within a single ministry over a period of several decades.[54] Largely as a consequence of the career bureaucracy's influence, the foreign policies of the Japanese government have become characterized by continuity over time, internal consistency, and a lack of sensitivity to short-term political and popular pressures.

Strong bureaucratic leadership in forging a conservative consensus behind Japanese foreign policy has not precluded disagreements over individual policy objectives among various elites, even among relevant government ministries. Similarly, those ministries and interest groups proving most influential in shaping one component of foreign policy (such as raw materials procurement policy) frequently have not been the same as those wielding decisive influence over another component (such

54. T. J. Pempel, "Japanese Foreign Economic Policy: The Domestic Bases for International Behavior," in Peter J. Katzenstein, ed., *Between Power and Plenty: Foreign Economic Policies of Advanced Industrial States* (University of Wisconsin Press, 1978), pp. 147–48.

as balance-of-payments policy). But disagreements and differing align-
ments on specific policy issues have tended to occur within a framework
of general accord on broader goals.

Given the high priority attached by relevant Japanese elites to the
economic component of Japan's international interests, Japanese foreign
policy has come to mean foreign economic policy in many important
respects. Japan's foreign economic policy objectives, in turn, are not
easily separable from the goals of domestic economic policy. As T. J.
Pempel has elaborated:

Macro-level economic growth has been the central political goal to which virtually
all other Japanese policies have been subordinated during the postwar period.
Foreign economic policies have been integral to this overall growth. As such,
Japanese foreign economic policy has been neither isolated from, nor contradic-
tory to, domestic economic policies. Nor has it been directed more fundamentally
at achieving security, military, or other external political and noneconomic
aims.[55]

Japan's major commercial banks have acquired a role in the formulation and execution of Japanese foreign economic policy both as
members of the conservative coalition that has helped to shape that
policy and as financial institutions highly responsive to official incentives
and instruction. The interaction between Japanese banks and their
government on international policy issues reveals an official bureaucracy
sensitive to, and in tune with, the international commercial interests of
the banks. Yet in contrast with a country such as West Germany, in
Japan the government is not simply the more equal partner in this
interaction, but rather the overwhelmingly stronger element. To a
significant degree, the government derives its influence over the international activities of Japanese banks from the same factors that underlie
domestic bank-government relations. This influence thus draws, for
instance, upon the government's use of a deliberate structural policy to
enhance control over banking activities; the accepted role of the government as a policeman, coordinator, and influential intermediary in the
financial marketplace; and the high respect that the Japanese financial
community accords officials of the Ministry of Finance, including its
International Finance Bureau.

The significance of the leading banks to Japanese foreign policy also
stems from the banks' role in financing overseas trade and direct
investment. Japan's unique international circumstances have increased

55. Ibid., p. 157.

Table 5-3. *Commodity Composition of Imports for Major Industrial Countries, 1982*

Percent of total imports

Country	Agriculture and raw materials	Fuels	Manufactures
Japan	25	50	25
Italy[a]	20	33	46
Netherlands[a]	20	26	54
West Germany	19	24	58
France	15	27	58
United States	11	27	62
United Kingdom	20	13	67
Canada	12	10	78

Source: Organization for Economic Cooperation and Development, *Monthly Statistics of Foreign Trade* (Paris: OECD, May 1983), pt. 3, pp. 30, 32. Figures are rounded.

a. 1981 data.

the strategic national importance of overseas business, and an awareness of these circumstances has been infused into the thinking and outlooks of the banks.

One of the most distinctive of these international features is Japan's heavy dependence on foreign supplies of fuels, raw materials, and agricultural products. These three items together recently accounted for 75 percent of Japan's imports, the highest percentage for any major industrial country (see table 5-3). In 1981 oil alone accounted for 37 percent of Japan's imports. According to 1980 statistics, Japan depended on external sources to meet almost 85 percent of its total energy requirements, compared with West Germany's 56 percent and the United States' 17 percent.[56] Similarly, Japan lacks any significant supplies of iron ore, bauxite, nickel, manganese, phosphorous ore, copper, and chrome, and in most cases is the leading importer of each among the members of the Organization for Economic Cooperation and Development (OECD).[57] Total Japanese imports are relatively low in comparison to the nation's gross domestic product (GDP): Japan's 1981 import/GDP ratio ranked below that of any other major OECD country except the

56. Keizai Koho Center (Japan Institute for Social and Economic Affairs), *Japan 1982: An International Comparison* (Tokyo: Keizai Koho Center, 1982), p. 48. Degree of dependence on external energy sources is defined as $(B - C)/(A + B - C)$, where A = total domestic energy production, B = energy imports, and C = energy exports.

57. Pempel, "Japanese Foreign Economic Policy," p. 143.

Table 5-4. *Commodity Composition of Exports for Major Industrial Countries, 1982*

Percent of total exports

Country	Nonmanufactures	Manufactures
Japan	2	98
West Germany	11	89
Italy[a]	14	86
France	23	77
United States	29	71
United Kingdom	30	70
Canada	44	56
Netherlands[a]	50	50

Source: OECD, *Monthly Statistics of Foreign Trade* (May 1983), pt. 3, pp. 31, 33.
a. 1981 data.

United States.[58] But the extent of Japan's reliance on foreign natural resources to support its economy is unique among major industrial nations. As a result, in the wording of a Ministry of Foreign Affairs policy statement, ". . . the promotion of constructive and cooperative relations with the resource-rich countries is of vital importance."[59]

A second distinctive feature of Japan's international position, also understood well by the leading banks, is a heavy reliance on exports of manufactures (see table 5-4). Total Japanese exports during 1981 were valued at $151.5 billion, behind only those of the United States and West Germany. Despite their enormous absolute value, exports, like imports, represent only a relatively small percentage of Japan's GDP.[60] But exports have acquired unusual importance for at least two reasons: growing export earnings have been essential in order to cover increasingly costly imports of raw materials, fuels, and foodstuffs; and certain key Japanese industrial sectors have become dependent on foreign demand. In particular, exports represent 30 percent or more of production for a number of Japan's major basic growth industries, several of

58. During 1981 the figure for Japan was 12.6 percent; for the United States, 9.5 percent, and for West Germany 23.8 percent. International Monetary Fund, *International Financial Statistics: Supplement on Trade Statistics,* Supplement Series, no. 4 (Washington, D.C.: IMF, 1982), pp. 52–55.

59. Ministry of Foreign Affairs, *Japan's Foreign Policy: Questions and Answers* (Tokyo: Ministry of Foreign Affairs, 1981), p. 33.

60. In 1981 Japan's exports amounted to 13.5 percent of GDP. Among major industrial countries, only the export/GDP figure for the United States was lower, at 8.1 percent. West Germany's export/GDP ratio was 25.6 percent. IMF, *International Financial Statistics: Supplement on Trade Statistics,* no. 4, pp. 52–53, 118–21.

which have encountered maturing domestic demand over the last decade (for example, steel, shipbuilding and automobiles).[61] Furthermore, in the opinion of some observers, Japanese producers and government planners have relied on exports during periods of pervasive weak demand at home to maintain the country's overall growth objectives.

Given the fundamental importance of exports to Japanese economic health, official policy has sought expanded and more secure overseas markets for Japanese products. In response to growing pressure from the United States and Western Europe to restrict exports of selected manufactures, Japanese policy has also sought to diminish reliance on those markets, in particular, and to reduce the current concentration of exports in a relatively few basic industries.[62]

Geographic circumstances have heightened Japan's (and Japanese bankers') sense of international vulnerability. The great distances that separate Japan from its raw materials sources and most important markets compound the country's dependence on external events. Among major industrial powers, none is so physically removed from other countries at a similar stage of economic development; nor is any other major industrial power so isolated from its allies. Persistent unstable political conditions in East Asia have further intensified the anxieties of many Japanese about their external environment.[63]

Banks in International Finance

By a variety of measures, a select group of private Japanese banks has become increasingly prominent in international finance. In 1961 only six Japanese banks maintained a presence abroad, operating fewer than 30 foreign branches and agencies; by 1979, twenty-three Japanese banks operated 131 branches and agencies, 29 subsidiaries, 93 affiliates, and 158 representative offices overseas. Although they were slow to enter

61. William V. Rapp and Robert A. Feldman, "Japan's Economic Strategy and Prospects," in William J. Barnds, ed., *Japan and the United States: Challenges and Opportunities* (New York University Press for the Council on Foreign Relations, 1979), pp. 112, 118.

62. In support of this thesis, a senior Finance Ministry official cited a desire to develop "secure and expanded overseas markets for our capital goods" as one of the principal motives behind Japan's granting of official development assistance. (Interview with senior official of the Ministry of Finance, Tokyo, February 20, 1981.)

63. Donald C. Hellmann, "Japanese Security and Postwar Japanese Foreign Policy," in Scalapino, ed., *The Foreign Policy of Modern Japan*, p. 325.

the Eurocurrency syndicated loan market in the early 1970s, Japanese banks accounted for over 20 percent of global commercial syndicated lending in both 1978 and 1979.[64] Similarly, Japanese banks' external assets (both yen and foreign currency) more than quadrupled in the five years following year-end 1977 to reach $90.9 billion by December 1982.[65]

Overseas business represents the principal income earner for one of the largest Japanese commercial banks and an increasingly important component of assets and generator of income for the rest. The Bank of Tokyo derived between 60 and 70 percent of its income from international operations during 1980–82.[66] The foreign assets and income of the other leading city banks rose from negligible levels during the early 1970s to an average of 20 to 30 percent of total assets and 10 to 16 percent of income during the early 1980s.[67] With the exception of the Bank of Tokyo, the ratio of international to domestic business for the major Japanese banks is still low in comparison to either the largest American or West German banks, despite the extremely rapid growth in Japanese banks' international business during 1977–79.[68] Japanese banks are likely

64. Diane Page and Neal M. Soss, *Some Evidence on Transnational Banking Structure* (Washington, D.C.: U.S. Office of the Comptroller of the Currency, 1980), pp. 24, 26, 48; Hayden, "Internationalizing Japan's Financial System," pp. 9, 10.

65. Bank for International Settlements (BIS), *International Banking Developments—Second Quarter 1981* (Basle: BIS, 1981), table 1; BIS, *International Banking Developments—Fourth Quarter 1982* (Basle: BIS, 1983), table 1.

66. IBCA Banking Analysis Limited (data service) (London: IBCA, 1982). The Bank of Tokyo, founded in 1880, operated under the name of the Yokohama Specie Bank until the end of World War II. The Japanese emperor owned half of the equity in the original bank. During the postwar occupation, Emperor Hirohito was forced to divest himself of his stake in the bank, and its official ties to the government were thereby severed. Yet even today, in Bronte's view, "The Japanese foreign ministry relies on the bank for up-to-date information on financial and economic developments throughout the world." The Bank of Tokyo has consistently lead-managed more syndicated Eurocurrency and foreign yen loans than any other Japanese bank. Although privately owned, it has also traditionally served as disbursing agent for nearly all Japanese foreign aid, and by its own accounting the bank holds a "substantial" amount of the Finance Ministry's foreign currency reserves. Bank of Tokyo, *The Activities of the Bank of Tokyo Group in the Field of International Financings* (Bank of Tokyo, 1981), pp. 3, 6; Bronte, *Japanese Finance: Markets and Institutions,* pp. 43–44.

67. Data from IBCA Banking Analysis Limited, London, 1982; and Bronte, *Japanese Finance: Markets and Institutions,* pp. 26–27.

68. During the early 1980s, foreign business accounted for 30 to 40 percent of both consolidated assets and income at each of the two largest German banks and 20 to 30 percent at the third and fourth largest. International assets accounted for approximately 35 percent of total assets for the nine largest banks in the United States as of June 1982, and international earnings represented almost half of total earnings for the ten largest

to consolidate their international positions over the remainder of the 1980s, however, and foreign business could account for 30 to 35 percent of all major Japanese banks' assets, and for as much as 30 percent of profits, by 1990.

The Motives for Cooperation

Japanese banks' willingness to engage in international business in accordance with official state objectives stems from many motives, falling roughly into three categories: a natural convergence of major Japanese banks' interests in the international sphere with those of the Japanese government; the responsiveness of the Japanese financial marketplace to governmental signals and incentives; and Japanese banks' deference to administrative guidance as well as formal regulation. Each of these sets of factors deserves closer attention.

CONVERGENCE OF INTERESTS. Prone to take a long-term perspective and to associate their own commercial success with their country's economic health, major Japanese banks are naturally inclined to behave internationally in ways that directly support the home economy. Thus, for reasons reflecting the nature of their own internal decisionmaking and commercial priorities, major Japanese banks are particularly likely to respond to long-term national economic trends and needs. In addition, market forces and existing customer relationships automatically lead Japanese banks toward lending (and deposit-taking) opportunities in countries that are major Japanese trading partners. Not only are banks more likely to learn of potential business in these countries; the banks are also more inclined to accept risks in them because they constitute relatively familiar terrain. To a significant degree, the market mechanism also leads Japanese banks, in combination with their domestic corporate clients, toward commercial opportunities in resource-rich countries. Here it is noteworthy that overseas projects to develop or process natural resources have often been initiated by Japan's private sector, not the government, although MITI has typically become involved in major projects at an early stage.

U.S. banks throughout 1980–82. German bank data from IBCA Banking Analysis Limited, London, 1982. Figure on U.S. banks' international assets from Economic Research Division, Continental Illinois National Bank and Trust Co. of Chicago. Information on U.S. banks' international earnings from Salomon Brothers, Inc., *Bank Weekly* (March 26, 1982); and H. Erich Heinemann, "Third World's $700 Billion Debt Posing a Threat to Richer Nations," *New York Times*, July 5, 1983.

GOVERNMENT INCENTIVES. The Japanese government's incentives to influence commercial banks' international behavior have focused primarily on the fields of export and import credit and the financing of overseas projects undertaken to develop or process natural resources (with a portion of the product usually contracted for export back to Japan). A central intent of the government in this area has been not only to affect the market's allocation of financial resources, but also to spread or socialize the risks associated with large private-sector financial commitments that serve official policy objectives in the international sphere.

One major incentives package is contained in the export insurance scheme administered and underwritten by MITI, which aims to stimulate Japanese exports and overseas direct investment by pooling exceptional risks, political as well as commercial, associated with them. Since its founding in 1950, the insurance program has paid for itself, covering losses from accumulated premium income.[69] It is likely that the value of outstanding MITI export insurance totaled approximately $75 billion as of early 1980, with roughly half of this amount consisting of short-term commitments. During the early 1980s, MITI insurance covered more than 40 percent of all Japanese exports. By comparison, Hermes export credit guarantees covered 9 percent of German exports in 1981. The guarantee and insurance authorizations of the U.S. Export-Import Bank (fiscal 1981) were equivalent to roughly 3 percent of U.S. exports for 1981.[70]

One reason for the MITI program's success to date has been MITI's encouragement of Japanese banks and specific export industries to conclude "global" insurance contracts with the ministry, so that premium income will accrue from relatively riskless as well as risky overseas transactions. The scheme thus seeks to avoid insuring only isolated high-

69. The Japanese government provided the insurance program with initial capital of 6 billion yen (worth approximately $30 million in early 1981). Accumulated profits in the program's premium pool totaled an additional 124 billion yen ($611 million) as of early 1981. Interview with official of the Export Insurance Division, MITI, Tokyo, February 25, 1981.

70. All U.S. Export-Import Bank authorizations (fiscal 1981), including loan authorizations, "supported" U.S. export sales of $18.1 billion, or about 8 percent of U.S. exports for 1981. Hermes Kreditversicherungs-Aktiengesellschaft, *Annual Report for the 64th Business Year Ended 31st December, 1981*, p. 24; Export-Import Bank of the United States, *Fiscal 1981 Annual Report*, p. 1; and Bronte, *Japanese Finance: Markets and Institutions*, p. 162.

risk transactions. A MITI description of the program identifies a central premise behind it as follows:

Revolution and civil war are still liable to occur frequently in certain countries. Political confusion can be expected anywhere. . . . It is wise, therefore, for all concerns engaged in foreign trade to make export insurance a habit. By spreading and sharing common risks through export insurance, the losses sustained by the relative few are readily absorbed by the group and consequently minimized.[71]

Although the MITI program offered nine different kinds of insurance during 1981, four schemes predominated. Three principal schemes, all related to exports, covered preshipment political risk; postshipment risk of nonpayment by the buyer, for political as well as commercial reasons; and essentially all risks incurred by Japanese banks resulting from a foreign buyer's default. MITI insurance has also been generally available to cover Japanese loans and equity purchases associated with overseas direct investments. As an adjunct to this last scheme, insurance covering both political and commercial risks has been specially available to Japanese investors (including banks) lending money to foreign enterprises or governments that will develop natural resources on their own to be exported back to Japan.[72]

Although MITI has sought in principle to run its insurance program on a commercial basis, noncommercial considerations have regularly influenced decisions on the allocation of insurance exposure. Such considerations have included: proposals from various MITI departments and bureaus to give trade or natural resource benefits of a project special weight, the economic condition of the domestic industry in the case of export insurance, Japan's current-account balance, and "diplomatic" concerns.[73] The principal intent of the program has remained the general promotion of Japanese exports and overseas direct investments; nevertheless, MITI decisionmaking has implicitly regarded insurance as a scarce resource and has allocated it in a manner that has taken into account, among other considerations, the political importance to Japan of the country receiving the export or direct investment. An informed MITI official explained that political considerations do not constitute grounds for reducing the availability of insurance to an individual foreign

71. Ministry of International Trade and Industry, "A Brief Introduction to Export Insurance Scheme of Japan," provided by MITI, Tokyo, in February 1981, p. 1.

72. Summary of insurance programs based on ibid., pp. 3–19, and interview with official of the Export Insurance Division, MITI, Tokyo, February 25, 1981.

73. Interview with official of the Export Insurance Division, MITI, Tokyo, February 25, 1981.

country, but they may justify an increase in a country's share over what commercial assessments alone would dictate.[74] Thus MITI export insurance has done more than simply support random exports and foreign investments by Japanese firms; in the words of the same MITI official, "We intend the insurance to influence the flow and direction of financial resources." The insurance scheme has not singled out the interests of Japanese commercial banks for special support; in many cases, Japanese exporters, nonbank investors, and even resident foreign banks have been the policy beneficiaries.

The programs of the Export-Import Bank of Japan provide a second major package of incentives for influencing Japanese commercial banks' international behavior. This government-owned institution, established in 1950, specializes in making loans that supplement and encourage the financing of exports, imports, and overseas investment by private financial institutions. Japan's Export-Import Bank possessed total assets of $23.0 billion at the end of its 1981 fiscal year, making the bank approximately 15 percent smaller than its closest counterpart in West Germany, the government-owned Kreditanstalt für Wiederaufbau (KfW), but more than 40 percent larger than the Export-Import Bank of the United States.[75] In terms of trade-related and foreign loans, however, the Export-Import Bank of Japan was the largest of these three government banks at the end of fiscal 1981, with $22.5 billion in outstanding loans; by contrast, the KfW recorded trade-related and foreign loans outstanding of $13.4 billion, and the U.S. Export-Import Bank reported similar loans of $15.8 billion. Because these three banks do not perform strictly identical functions, comparisons of their relative sizes have only

74. One exception to this statement may be implicit in an unusual limit per transaction on MITI insurance available for Japanese exports to South Africa. As of early 1981 MITI restricted such insurance to a figure "bigger than 6 billion yen" ($30 million) per transaction, and this type of limit apparently applied to South Africa alone. The limit bears a striking resemblance to the unpublicized DM 50 million (approximately $25 million) insurance limit per transaction applied by the German government (through Hermes) to exports to South Africa during the late 1970s and early 1980s.

75. The KfW's total assets at the end of its 1981 fiscal year were $27.1 billion; total assets of the U.S. Eximbank at the end of its 1981 fiscal year were $16.2 billion. Fiscal 1981 for the Export-Import Bank of Japan ended on March 31, 1982; for the KfW on December 31, 1981; and for the Export-Import Bank of the United States on September 30, 1981. (Exchange rates used in calculations were U.S. $1.00 = 247 yen = DM 2.26.) Export-Import Bank of Japan, *Annual Report for Fiscal 1981*, p. 24; Kreditanstalt für Wiederaufbau, *Annual Report for the Year 1981*, unnumbered balance sheet; and Export-Import Bank of the United States, *Fiscal 1981 Annual Report*, p. 18.

limited meaning; still, such comparisons do provide a rough gauge of their respective governments' involvement in extending trade-related and other international credits that supplement loans made by private banks.[76]

A key intent behind the Japanese Export-Import Bank's credit programs has been to stimulate commercial lending patterns that support Japanese international economic and political interests. Most of the bank's lending activities fall into one of two categories: loans to support overseas development of natural resources that will be exported back to Japan, and loans to promote Japanese plant and machinery exports.[77] Export-Import Bank loans commonly take the form of joint financings with Japanese commercial banks. During 1980–81 the Export-Import Bank typically provided funds covering 60 to 70 percent of the financed portion of a given contract or project, while commercial banks provided the remainder of the financed portion. No interministerial committee oversees the Japanese Export-Import Bank's lending activities (like the one that oversees the West German government's Hermes loan guarantee program); nevertheless, informal consultation on a daily basis between the bank and the Ministries of Finance, International Trade and Industry, and Foreign Affairs has ensured that bank activities consistently reflect government policy. The Ministry of Finance, in addition, serves as the formal supervisory ministry of the Export-Import Bank and controls access (through the ministry's Trust Fund Bureau) to one of the bank's most important funding sources, deposits gathered through the nation's huge postal savings system.

The lending programs of the Japanese Export-Import Bank provide a compelling example of the Japanese government's direct use of financial

76. The figures for trade-related and foreign loans cited in the text represent: for the Export-Import Bank of Japan, loans outstanding (consisting of export suppliers' credits, import credits, overseas investment credits, and overseas direct loans) at the end of fiscal 1981; for the KfW, export credits, financial cooperation loans, untied financial loans, and other foreign loans at the end of fiscal 1981; and for the U.S. Export-Import Bank, total loans receivable at the end of fiscal 1981.

77. During the fiscal year ended March 31, 1982, foreign resource development lending—divided evenly between energy resources (particularly natural gas, coal and petroleum) and nonenergy resources (led by wood products)—accounted for 48 percent of the bank's new commitments. Lending in support of Japanese plant and equipment exports accounted for 54 percent. The bank includes certain commitments for plant-related equipment to be used in resource development projects in the figures for both categories. Export-Import Bank of Japan, *Annual Report for Fiscal 1981*, pp. 9, 18–20.

intermediation to influence Japanese commercial bank lending patterns.[78] Lending by the Export-Import Bank, like lending by the JDB and other Japanese governmental financial institutions, serves as a signal to commercial banks of official priorities and objectives. Export-Import Bank participation in a loan syndicate also adds a major element of security for the participating commercial banks: the Japanese government itself has become a party to the loan and will assist in obtaining repayment, if necessary. Thus Export-Import Bank funds act as seed money, encouraging the commercial banking community to provide additional financing. With over $20 billion in trade-related and other international loans outstanding during the early 1980s, the Export-Import Bank has been able to send highly effective messages to Japan's commercial banks. Furthermore, given its ability to provide cheap fixed-rate funds, the Export-Import Bank has frequently succeeded as well in enhancing the competitiveness of overall Japanese financing packages in international markets.

The programs of the Overseas Economic Cooperation Fund (OECF) comprise a third form of incentive that the Japanese government has used to influence commercial banks' international allocation of resources. The OECF is an independent institution whose capital is fully subscribed by the Japanese government and whose funding comes largely from the Trust Fund Bureau of the Finance Ministry.[79] Its main stated role is to contribute to economic growth in developing countries by providing concessional financial assistance that often functions as equity or quasi equity. The OECF's budget totaled $1.9 billion for fiscal 1981, and the institution can be expected to spend approximately $10.7 billion during the fiscal years 1981–85 (half of Japan's projected official development assistance for this period).[80]

78. The following discussion draws upon Sakakibara, Feldman, and Harada, "Japanese Financial System in Comparative Perspective," pp. 52–55.

79. During fiscal 1979 (ended March 31, 1980), the OECF's budget authorized new loans totaling 370.0 billion yen. During the same period, the budget called for the institution to receive funding totaling 230.1 billion yen from the Japanese government's fiscal investment and loan program, which in turn received 82.7 percent of its funding from the Trust Fund Bureau of the Ministry of Finance. Trust Fund Bureau monies thus may have funded as much as 51.4 percent of the new loans extended by the OECF for the year. See ibid.

80. For 1981 budget figure, see Stephen Bronte, "Where Japanese Exports Face Unfair Competition," *Euromoney* (July 1981), p. 151. Approximate OECF expenditures for 1981–85 provided by an official of the OECF, Washington, D.C., November 10, 1981.

A prevailing characteristic of OECF loans and investments is their operation in tandem with other financing from both public and private Japanese sources such as the Export-Import Bank and commercial banks. OECF involvement serves as an even stronger signal than Export-Import Bank participation of the Japanese government's commitment to the success of a particular project (and associated financing). OECF equity participation in an overseas project usually results in its semi-official designation as a "national project." Although this label carries somewhat amorphous connotations, Japan's business and banking communities appear to discern clearly the instances where it applies. As an equity partner in a project through the OECF, the government stands ready to represent the interests of participating Japanese banks and corporations, if necessary, in bilateral discussions with the host country government (which is likely to serve as a joint venture partner in the project as well). Furthermore, in the case of a default or bankruptcy involving the project, the Japanese government, although not formally committed to do so, appears to assume a significant degree of responsibility on behalf of all involved Japanese parties. Thus even a small amount of OECF funding to an overseas project generally assures a major financial contribution to it from private Japanese banks.

These three broad categories of incentives—MITI insurance, Export-Import Bank loans, and OECF concessional loans and equity investments—do not constitute an exhaustive list of means available to the Japanese government for influencing Japanese commercial banks' trade-related and international lending patterns. These particular incentives, however, are among the most effective available to the government. Viewed in combination, they illustrate the remarkable ability of government, business, and the commercial banks to share and hence manage risk when commercial and official international interests overlap.

The Japanese government, in fact, regularly employs the three policy instruments in concert. A typical example of their joint use, in combination with private commercial lending, is the financial structure of a major fertilizer project that Japanese interests began in Indonesia in the late 1970s. As part of an ongoing effort to strengthen relations between Japan and the Association of Southeast Asian Nations (ASEAN), Prime Minister Takeo Fukuda pledged in August 1977 to provide $1 billion in Japanese financial and technical assistance to support several industrial projects in ASEAN countries. The first project to move forward was the fertilizer plant, and during the course of 1979 the Japanese and Indonesian

Figure 5-1. *Financing for $300 Million Indonesian Fertilizer Plant, 1979*
Millions of dollars

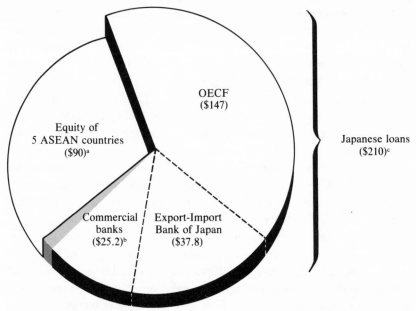

Sources: Japan External Trade Organization, *Economic Cooperation of Japan, 1979* (JETRO, 1980), p. 56; "Japan Will Foot 70% of Cost of Building Indonesia Urea Plant," *Japan Economic Journal*, May 1, 1979; and information provided by the Embassy of the Republic of Indonesia, Washington, D.C. Cost figures are approximate.

a. Equity breakdown among ASEAN member governments: Indonesia ($54 million); Malaysia ($11.7 million); Philippines ($11.7 million); Thailand ($11.7 million); and Singapore ($0.9 million). Their $90 million in equity covered 30 percent of the project's original cost.

b. Shaded area represents $2.5 million of the commercial banks' loans not insured by the Ministry of International Trade and Industry.

c. The $210 million in Japanese loans covered 70 percent of the project's original cost.

governments agreed to fund the bulk of this $300 million undertaking along the lines shown in figure 5-1. The OECF, Japanese Export-Import Bank, and a consortium of Japanese commercial banks extended credit directly to the Indonesian government, which had become the controlling partner in a joint venture company established by the five ASEAN states to own the plant. MITI insured 90 percent of the loans by commercial banks, leaving them with a modest $2.5 million in uncovered Indonesian risk. While commercial bank participants presumably extended their loans at market rates and terms, the OECF and Export-Import Bank loans were concessional, resulting in a below-market blended rate and terms for the overall financing package. The Japanese loan package was not officially tied to Japanese exports; nevertheless, the Indonesian government awarded the principal contract for the project to a Japanese firm. The general format of this financing has been a common one for many Japanese overseas projects; the Japanese commercial banks' share in such financings, however, has often been considerably larger in both percentage and absolute terms.

DEFERENCE TO REGULATION. Japanese commercial banks' deference to legally mandated regulation and administrative guidance is a third category of motives prompting the banks to align their business pursuits with government objectives. The Ministry of Finance, in a manner similar to its approach to domestic banking, has preferred to supervise Japanese international banking through a flexible system of guidelines rather than through codified rules. Reflecting this preference, as well as the liberalization of the bureaucracy's legal framework for regulating international banking, informal administrative guidance acquired enhanced importance as an external policy tool beginning in the late 1970s.

From the vantage point of the Finance Ministry, Japan's commercial banks appear "cognizant of the official character of their work" in the international field.[81] Significantly, this has been the case even as the leading Japanese banks have remained zealously competitive in their dealings both with one another and in overseas financial markets. More than any other policy instrument, administrative guidance, in all of its semi-institutionalized forms, has assured the financial authorities of the ability to persuade Japanese commercial banks to conform with a wide range of official objectives. During the late 1970s and early 1980s the principal forums available to the authorities for providing commercial banks guidance on international issues included both quarterly and monthly meetings.

In the first of these two forums, officials from the Finance Ministry's International Finance Bureau and the Bank of Japan have met as a group every third month with senior representatives from the international departments of the approximately twenty-three Japanese commercial banks that actively pursue overseas business. Topics regularly discussed at these rather formal meetings have included monetary market trends, the volume of international syndicated lending by Japanese banks and their share of the global market, the interest spreads charged overseas by Japanese banks and their degree of success in managing Eurocredit syndications, the current status of Japan's balance of payments, and "quarterly statistics and general problems." These meetings have been

81. Interview with senior official of the Ministry of Finance, Tokyo, February 20, 1981.

a key forum for interaction on international policy issues between Japanese banks and their government, as the financial authorities have frequently used the meetings to obtain suggestions from the banks as well as to present policy.[82]

The monthly meetings, also known as *Nissuikai* or the "Second Wednesday Club," have permitted International Finance Bureau officials to engage in more detailed discussion of international issues with representatives from a smaller number of major Japanese commercial banks. According to a participating bureau official, only the fourteen banks most active internationally attended these meetings during early 1981. Issues addressed at *Nissuikai* meetings have included trends in Japan's balance of payments, Japanese economic growth, commercial banks' accrual of foreign deposits, and their overseas lending in yen.[83] In July 1979, as reported by one published source, the Finance Ministry used a *Nissuikai* session to inform Japanese banks of its intention to impose major restrictions on their overseas lending activities.[84]

In addition to the above regular group discussions, Finance Ministry officials have provided guidance on international business matters to Japanese banks on an individual basis. Every commercial bank must submit a program of its proposed international lending to the director of the International Finance Bureau's short-term capital division twice a year; the director might then make suggestions to a particular bank to increase or decrease its overseas lending.[85] In addition, as of 1980–81 exchanges took place almost daily on an individual basis between International Finance Bureau officials and representatives of the international departments of major Japanese commercial banks. One ministry official described these meetings as "informal and at random."[86] Both

82. Discussion topics at quarterly meetings were compiled from interviews with an official of the Ministry of Finance (Tokyo, February 16, 1981) and with the managing director of a major city bank (Tokyo, February 10, 1981). Both of these individuals regularly attended the meetings.

83. Discussion topics at monthly meetings were compiled from interviews with a senior official of the Ministry of Finance (Tokyo, February 19, 1981) and with two officers of a major city bank (Tokyo, February 10, 1981). The ministry official and at least one of the two bank officers regularly attended the meetings.

84. At the same meeting, the ministry also requested the attending banks to submit suggestions as to what the specifics of the restrictions should be. Stephen Bronte, "The Dilemma of Japan's City Banks," *Euromoney* (September 1979), pp. 28–30.

85. Interview with senior official of the Ministry of Finance, Tokyo, February 23, 1981.

86. Interview with official of the Ministry of Finance, Tokyo, February 16, 1981.

bankers and ministry officials appear to regard their substance as highly confidential; as a consequence, it is impossible for an outsider to state categorically what is discussed at these ad hoc sessions. Given their frequency, however, it appears highly likely that pending individual international transactions are considered. Still, a number of bureau officials denied for the record any official interest in individual commercial transactions.

Frequent contacts between the Finance Ministry and Japanese commercial banks have established an ongoing basis for information exchange and coordination on international financial matters. In the words of one ministry official, a key goal of the International Finance Bureau has been to develop "not written rules but operational understandings" with Japan's commercial banks regarding their international business activities.[87] Similarly, another ministry official emphasized the importance of "confidence" between banks and government as the underpinning to administrative guidance's effectiveness. More precisely, just as much of the Finance Ministry's influence over commercial banks is determined and exercised by individuals, the issue of confidence is "really a personal matter, a man-to-man problem."[88] Given the importance of interpersonal trust in the ministry's working relationships with commercial banks, it is not surprising that the International Finance Bureau has avoided rotating its officers quickly through assignments; even younger career officials have tended to remain in the bureau for years.

Although sixty Japanese banks maintained at least correspondent banking relationships abroad in early 1981,[89] only the approximately twenty-three commercial banks that attended the Finance Ministry's quarterly meetings on international policy issues operated branches or subsidiaries overseas and engaged in significant amounts of overseas business. In early 1981 these twenty-three banks included the Bank of Tokyo and the twelve other city banks, the three long-term credit banks, six trust banks, and one regional bank.[90] The existence of this core group

87. Interview with senior official of the Ministry of Finance, Tokyo, February 20, 1981.
88. Interview with senior official of the Ministry of Finance, Tokyo, February 23, 1981.
89. Interview with senior official of the Ministry of Finance, Tokyo, February 19, 1981.
90. Interview with two senior officials of a major city bank, Tokyo, February 10, 1981.

in international finance is consistent with the financial authorities' dual desires to maintain an intermediate number of major Japanese banks and to encourage functional specialization within the system. With specific regard to international banking, the active involvement of a limited number of banks has enhanced the government's ability to supervise and coordinate Japanese-sourced international finance. At the same time, government policy (as realized, for instance, through the International Finance Bureau's monitoring of each bank's aggregate international lending program) has ensured that no international financial behemoth could emerge within the private banking sector.[91]

Under Japan's amended Foreign Exchange and Foreign Trade Control Law, which went into effect in December 1980, the bureaucracy's formal regulatory powers over commercial banks are reduced from previous levels, but they remain substantial. Under the previous exchange control system, operative from the end of World War II through the mid-1970s, capital transactions with the rest of the world were specifically controlled, and no loan could be made into or out of Japan without permission.[92] The new system, while rendering all transactions free in principle, retains many basic features of the old system. The Finance Ministry continues to be able to designate "authorized foreign exchange banks," and only these banks may conduct foreign business; similarly, the ministry must still approve all new overseas offices opened by a Japanese bank.[93]

Nor has the government's framework for imposing controls on capital transactions been disbanded. All liberalization can be overridden, and any capital transactions brought back within formal government control,

91. This group of 23 banks compares with 12 West German banks that maintained overseas branches and agencies as of 1978, reflecting the greater concentration characteristic of the upper reaches of the German banking system, and 136 such U.S. banks, reflecting significantly lower banking concentration in the United States. Page and Soss, *Some Evidence on Transnational Banking Structure*, p. 26.

92. Andreas R. Prindl, "Tokyo's Foreign Exchange Law: Japan Is Liberalizing the Wrong Things," *Euromoney* (March 1980), p. 96.

93. See Ministry of Finance, International Finance Bureau, *Foreign Exchange and Foreign Trade Control Law*, as amended by Law No. 65, dated December 18, 1979 (Japanese Ministry of Finance, 1980), articles 10 and 71. Furthermore, according to Eric W. Hayden, the Ministry of Finance during the late 1970s "deliberately restricted overseas expansion to one branch every three years [per major bank] and one representative office every year. In an effort to push the internationalization of the Japanese banks, the Ministry of Finance in early 1980 altered the regulations, permitting each city bank to open one overseas branch every two years and two overseas rep offices annually." Hayden, "Internationalizing Japan's Financial System," p. 9.

if (1) the foreign exchange market is volatile; (2) balance-of-payments problems develop in the form of either large deficits or surpluses; or (3) "financial confusion" occurs.[94] As Andreas R. Prindl noted in early 1980, "One or more of the three types of loophole conditions has existed ever since 1971. In late 1979, Japan had a chaotic exchange market, a deteriorating balance of payments and financial confusion all at one time."[95] As of mid-1983, the Ministry of Finance had not yet imposed any of the emergency capital restrictions provided for in the law, although officials apparently had already considered such action.

Although the formal legal authority of the Ministry of Finance over Japanese commercial banking remains substantial, the changes in the Foreign Exchange Law appear to have given new impetus to administrative guidance as a means of supervising the banks' international behavior. A primary effect of the law may be to require that the Finance Ministry, in one observer's words, "be more subtle in monitoring Japanese lending of both yen and dollars overseas." To another observer, interpretation and enforcement of the new law will constitute "the private preserve" of the Ministry's International Finance Bureau.[96] For reasons already cited, Japanese commercial banks, while highly entrepreneurial in outlook, pay careful heed to administrative guidance; from the perspective of both the financial authorities' intentions and the impact of the guidance on the banks, the line separating guidance from formal regulation can be vague. Thus, despite the freeing of international capital transactions in principle, the International Finance Bureau will almost certainly be able to continue to require Japanese commercial banks to provide prior notification of all major overseas yen and dollar loans. By the same token, the formal freeing of international capital transactions should not affect the Finance Ministry's demonstrated ability to set unofficial but rigid quotas on Japanese banks' collective participation in dollar-syndicated loans abroad.[97]

94. See Prindl, "Tokyo's Foreign Exchange Law," p. 96, and Richard Hanson, "Controls Relaxed under New Legislation," *Financial Times* (London), December 3, 1980. The formal wording of the exceptions is in article 23 of the law.

95. Prindl, "Tokyo's Foreign Exchange Law," p. 96.

96. Hanson, "Controls Relaxed under New Legislation"; and Bronte, *Japanese Finance: Markets and Institutions*, p. 226.

97. See Stephen Bronte, "The Japanese Revel in Their Freedom To Invest Abroad," *Euromoney* (March 1981), p. 91. During the second half of 1980 and through the first half of 1981, the Ministry of Finance limited aggregate Japanese bank participations in overseas dollar-denominated syndicated loans to 20 percent of the total amount of any given loan; this limit was relaxed only under exceptional circumstances. The Ministry's

Conclusion

The conformity of the leading Japanese banks' international behavior with the policy objectives of the Japanese government has represented a natural extension of domestic bank-government relations. In both overseas and domestic dealings, the banks have been conscious of an official bureaucracy above them, one not fully convinced of the efficacy or usefulness to Japan of free market competition as a resource-allocating mechanism. Yet even as domestic institutional relationships have paved the way for the banks' pursuit of international business within parameters adjusted by the financial authorities, the process of economic policy formulation in Japan has also recognized the banks' international interests as legitimate concerns worthy of official advancement. Tokyo's financial community has constituted an important member of the coalition that has built Japanese foreign economic policy over the last thirty years, along with big business, the Liberal Democratic party and the career bureaucracy of government. In Japan's relatively centralized political and economic system, therefore, the major banks have provided both input for the design and support for the execution of foreign economic policy.

As the cases that follow will illustrate, the banks have regularly supported Japanese foreign policy objectives for commercial reasons, and they have at least occasionally sought to manipulate official Japanese policies to their own advantage. To a remarkable degree, however, the banks have also pursued trade-related and other international business in response to official signals and incentives and to official supervision and guidance. Administrative guidance, in particular, has given the government a highly effective means of informally influencing Japanese banks' overseas business behavior.

International Finance Bureau also applied informal limits on the share of total global syndicated lending that Japanese banks collectively could acquire. During 1981 this limit was set at roughly 10 percent, a figure corresponding to Japan's share of GNP within the OECD. See Hayden, "Internationalizing Japan's Financial System," p. 11; and "The Worrying Japanese Interest in Syndicated Loans," *Euromoney* (September 1981), p. 65.

CHAPTER SIX

Bank-Government Relations

A CENTRAL THEME implicit in the earlier analysis of the Federal Republic of Germany was that most West German commercial international
banking transactions are either irrelevant to or inherently consistent
with Germany's trade-oriented foreign policy. As a result, most
transactions stimulate little or no direct bank-government interaction,
in keeping with Germany's laissez-faire financial traditions. Under
exceptional circumstances, however, where the foreign policy relevance
of a particular loan is quite high and bankers have not accommodated
the German government's interests of their own accord, an array of
mechanisms available for effecting bank-government coordination is
brought into action.

The relations of Japanese banks and their government on international
policy issues must be characterized in a different way. The heavy use of
administrative guidance by Japan's financial authorities is itself sufficient
to create the possibility of official involvement in virtually all major
overseas transactions by Japanese commercial banks. In many instances, the precise impact of the Japanese authorities on the banks may
be impossible to identify because of Japan's consensus-oriented style of
decisionmaking. Even the substance of administrative guidance may
frequently be the product of consultations in which the banks themselves
provided important input.

Cases exemplifying several major international objectives of the
Tokyo government that Japanese banks have helped to advance will
consequently be discussed in this chapter. The government has sought
in recent years, for example, to harness Japanese international banking
capabilities to offset politically problematic current-account surpluses
and deficits; to encourage commercial lending to finance foreign projects

135

that would help make supplies of natural resources more secure; and to promote financial relations with countries of special economic or political significance to Japan. While serving the objectives of Japanese foreign policy, the banks have shown an uncanny ability to serve their own commercial interests simultaneously. The banking transactions considered below are illustrative; there are numerous additional instances of commercial bank behavior supporting the same (and other) official policy objectives.

Overseas Lending by the Bank of Tokyo, 1975–81

Entrepreneurial considerations have been a strong determinant in the distribution of overseas loans by Japan's principal city and long-term credit banks. During the late 1970s, for example, these banks tended to lend to those foreign borrowers that were successful in generating the greatest demand for credit in international markets and were perceived as offering high quality and low risk. One logically would expect such behavior from financial institutions of any nationality that were eager to increase their international market share. Yet universally applicable commercial criteria have not been the entire story behind Japanese banks' international lending patterns. The influence of national considerations peculiar to Japan can also be detected, most notably:

—The importance of the borrower's country as a real or potential source of fuels, raw materials, and foodstuffs for Japan;

—The importance of the borrower's country as a real or potential market for Japanese exports;

—The relevance of the borrower or its country to other Japanese official interests, such as the strengthening of bilateral ties in the East Asian region or the execution of global responsibilities increasingly incumbent upon Japan as a leading industrial power.

It is often difficult, if not impossible, for an observer to determine the means through which such considerations influence a given international lending decision by a Japanese bank. As discussed, market forces themselves may naturally lead Japanese banks toward business opportunities in countries that are important trading partners or sources of raw materials. Signals, incentives, and guidance from the Japanese government undoubtedly also play a role. It is somewhat easier, however, to detect the *effect* of these considerations on lending patterns.

A discussion of the major foreign loans managed by the Bank of Tokyo, Japan's leading international bank, during three nine-month intervals between 1975 and 1981 will illustrate the impact of a variety of political and strategic influences on banking practices.[1] The three intervals were selected because of their diversity in terms of both the government's prevailing attitudes toward overseas lending and the banking community's readiness to extend such credit. During the first period, the first three quarters of 1975, the Ministry of Finance maintained extensive restrictions on overseas lending, reflecting in large part the authorities' desire, for balance-of-payments reasons, to discourage capital outflows. At the time, Japanese banks, not yet major lenders in the Euromarket, possessed a limited capability to extend international credit. During the second period, the first three quarters of 1979, the Japanese government generally encouraged international lending by the leading Japanese banks; this positive official attitude stemmed partly from the fact that Japan had enjoyed large current-account surpluses over the preceding two years and continued to show a modest surplus during the first months of the period. By the beginning of this period, the banks had become more experienced at international lending and were extremely eager to undertake new financial commitments abroad. During the final period, the fourth quarter of 1979 through the first two quarters of 1980, the Japanese government virtually suspended the banks' international lending, mainly because the Japanese current account had again moved into deficit, reflecting the impact of the second oil shock. This time the government's actions pulled the banks out of a market in which they had become major participants.

1. Information on these loans is from Bank of Tokyo, Ltd., *The Activities of the Bank of Tokyo Group in the Field of International Financings* (Bank of Tokyo, Ltd., 1981); supplementary information was also provided directly by the bank. This case focuses on the volume of syndicated credits managed by the Bank of Tokyo, not on the amounts lent by the bank. Most large banks, including the Bank of Tokyo, generally do not make public their figures on actual loan participations and country exposure. However, the amounts that the Bank of Tokyo has managed on behalf of various countries should provide an acceptable surrogate and give a reasonably accurate indication, at minimum, of which countries the bank has been most willing to assist in obtaining funds in international financial markets. Also, it is likely that the Bank of Tokyo retained for its own portfolio a significant share of most credits that it managed.

Restrictions on Overseas Lending

During the first three quarters of 1975 the Bank of Tokyo managed very few syndicated foreign currency credits on behalf of foreign borrowers. The bank lead-managed a single $150 million term credit for the government of Indonesia in which four other Japanese banks also served as managers, and a Bank of Tokyo affiliate served as a manager in two additional Eurocredits, one to a private-sector borrower in Indonesia (for $85 million) and the other to the central bank of Iraq (for $500 million).[2]

During this period of officially restricted international lending activity by Japanese banks, Indonesia and Iraq both were of considerable strategic importance to Japan. Both members of the Organization of Petroleum Exporting Countries (OPEC), they provided 13 percent of Japan's oil imports in 1975, and their combined share would increase to 21 percent within four years.[3] Indonesia was also important as a major provider of numerous other raw materials needed by Japan, as an influential member of the Association of Southeast Asian Nations (ASEAN), and as a country bordering all major sea lanes linking Japan with the Middle East.

The few publicly known details of the $150 million term credit to Indonesia, in fact, do suggest the influence of the Japanese government. The Bank of Tokyo extended the loan at a time when Indonesia was experiencing serious debt-servicing difficulties as a result of the financial collapse of Pertamina, the state oil company. Indirect evidence of the Japanese government's encouragement of the loan is contained in a 1975 editorial:

In early May Japanese bankers began to complain of pressures being exerted by the U.S. authorities on the Japanese Government. According to these bankers, the U.S. wanted Japan to participate in a major aid package for Indonesia. . . . The U.S. was worried about the political situation deteriorating and, according to bankers in Tokyo, it told the Japanese Government that it must give Indonesia all the assistance it could.

Reluctantly, the Japanese agreed to help. In mid-May loans and aid totalling over $1 billion to Indonesia were announced, some of them in the form of syndicated loans from Japanese banks at commercial spreads, but the bulk from

2. World Bank, "Eurocurrency Credits by Borrowing Country: Annual List—1975" (computerized data base) (Washington, D.C.: World Bank).

3. Keizai Koho Center (Japan Institute for Social and Economic Affairs), *Japan 1982: An International Comparison* (Tokyo: Keizai Koho Center, 1982), p. 52.

the World Bank and the Asian Development Bank. Directly and indirectly, the Japanese Government's share of these is thought to be more than $400 million.[4]

At least sixty-seven countries raised Eurocurrency credits during 1975, including thirty non-oil-exporting developing countries, nineteen industrial countries, ten oil exporters, and eight Communist countries.[5] Yet the only countries for which the Bank of Tokyo managed loans during the nine months in question were two major oil-exporting countries. Although both Indonesia and Iraq ranked among the most active international borrowers during 1975, neither country represented an exceptionally attractive credit risk compared with numerous other borrowers in the market; Indonesia was actually on the brink of default. Furthermore, Indonesia's high level of overall activity was due at least in part to loans from Japanese sources.[6]

The Bank of Tokyo refrained from lead-managing any syndicated yen credits to foreign borrowers during the first three quarters of 1975. Interestingly enough, however, the bank did manage one such credit during the remainder of the year: a seven-year loan to the Indonesian central bank for 15 billion yen (about $50 million at the time).[7]

Expanded International Lending

Major Japanese banks, including the Bank of Tokyo, lent aggressively to overseas borrowers during the first three quarters of 1979, a consequence of the banks' expanding international capabilities as well as apparent encouragement from the Tokyo authorities. Because the Japanese government lifted most restrictions on overseas lending during these months, commercial criteria logically should have played a greater role in the banks' decisionmaking at this time than they did in 1975. Indeed, this seems to have been the case for the Bank of Tokyo. Of the thirty-three countries on whose behalf the bank managed syndicated foreign currency credits, sixteen were among the twenty highest-volume borrowers in the market at the time, and ten numbered among the twenty

4. "The Pertamina Affair" (editorial), *Euromoney* (June 1975), p. 3.

5. "Publicized Eurocurrency Credits by Country," *Euromoney* (March 1976), pp. 40–41.

6. A September 1975 press report identified "over $1.5 billion of credits to Indonesian entities from Japanese sources already in the metaphorical pipeline." Rothschild Intercontinental Bank, "Medium-term Eurocredits: Spate of Borrowers," *Euromoney* (September 1975), p. 190.

7. Bank of Tokyo, *The Activities of the Bank of Tokyo Group*, p. 8.

countries perceived as the most creditworthy in the Euromarket during 1979.

At the same time, however, the Bank of Tokyo's international lending patterns reflected strategic Japanese interests in a subdued form. The most remarkable overseas loan arranged by the bank during the period was a $2.0 billion syndicated term credit to the People's Republic of China, touted by the Japanese as "the world's first commercial loan to China with no governmental interest subsidy."[8] The loan, which followed the conclusion of a long-term Sino-Japanese trade agreement, was seen at the time as a major step in strengthening economic relations between the two Asian states. The $2 billion all-Japanese-bank loan, along with a related $6 billion short-term trade facility for China that the Bank of Tokyo syndicated among some thirty Japanese banks, was specifically intended to finance Japanese exports under the trade agreement.

Although the Japanese government did not become openly involved in the negotiations between the Bank of China and the Bank of Tokyo, the Ministry of Finance "was desirous of seeing a satisfactory conclusion of [a loan] agreement," in the words of a senior officer of the Bank of Tokyo.[9] According to the general manager of a participating Japanese trust bank, "We were urged to get the business." His bank fully realized that a failure to join in the credits carried certain commercial risks (in the form of foreclosed future business opportunities), but at the same time, "the Ministry of Finance watched and suggested regarding [the] banks' attitudes."[10] The Chinese were intensely concerned about the term credit's pricing, because it would set a precedent for future Chinese borrowings in the Euromarket. They therefore must have been quite satisfied with the pricing finally agreed upon: 0.5 percent over the London interbank offered rate (LIBOR), with no fees. A Bank of Tokyo officer described the pricing as the "bare minimum."[11]

The Bank of Tokyo managed syndicated foreign currency credits with an aggregate value of at least $500 million for each of eleven countries during the period (see table 6-1). They include four countries that were

8. "Private Banks Reach Agreement with China on Terms of Syndicate Loan," *Japan Economic Journal,* April 3, 1979.

9. Interview with senior official of the Bank of Tokyo, Tokyo, February 25, 1981.

10. Interview with general manager for international banking of a major trust bank, Tokyo, February 13, 1981.

11. Interview with senior official of the Bank of Tokyo, Tokyo, February 25, 1981.

Table 6-1. *Major Bank of Tokyo Overseas Borrowers, January–September 1979, Ranked by Volume of Borrowing and Perceived Creditworthiness in Euromarket*
Amounts in millions of dollars

Country[a]	Amount managed by Bank of Tokyo	Total borrowed in Euromarket	Rank among 20 highest-volume borrowing countries[b]	Rank among 20 most credit-worthy countries[c]
Mexico	4,685	5,738	1	...
People's Republic of China	2,000	2,975	3	6
Italy	1,100	2,467	4	19
South Korea	1,050	1,691	8	...
USSR	850	1,095[d]	14	9
Philippines	707	1,407	10	...
Hong Kong	660	749	...	...
Colombia	634	769	...	...
Poland	622	752	...	...
Denmark	600	1,121	13	14
Ecuador	540	921	18	...

Sources: Bank of Tokyo, *The Activities of the Bank of Tokyo Group in the Field of International Financings* (Bank of Tokyo, 1981), pp. 19–21; World Bank, *Borrowing in International Capital Markets: Foreign and International Bond Issues, Publicized Eurocurrency Credits, Fourth Quarter 1979*, EC-181/794 (Washington, D.C.: World Bank, 1980), pp. 22–24, 29–73; and "The Country Risk League Table," *Euromoney* (February 1980), pp. 40–48.

a. Countries for which Bank of Tokyo managed at least $500 million in syndicated foreign currency credits during first nine months of 1979. The vast majority of individual borrowers of record in these countries were sovereign or government-guaranteed entities.

b. Based on total Eurocurrency credits raised by both public- and private-sector borrowers in each country during first nine months of 1979.

c. Rankings reflect perceived creditworthiness of all borrowing countries in Euromarket. Based on average weighted spreads, taking into account volume of borrowings and maturity structure, obtained on floating-rate U.S. dollar and deutsche mark syndicated loans signed during all of 1979. Excludes all fixed-rate loans and loans denominated in other currencies, and covers only loans arranged for sovereign and sovereign-guaranteed entities. See "The Country Risk League Table," p. 48.

d. Borrowings of the International Investment Bank, Moscow, have been aggregated with those of the Soviet Union.

both high-volume borrowers and perceived as highly creditworthy by the Euromarket at the time: China, Italy, the Soviet Union, and Denmark. Because of their enviable credit standing and the sizable lending opportunities they afforded, these countries numbered among the most commercially attractive customers for large banks everywhere during the period. It is therefore probably significant that the Bank of Tokyo acted as a manager for loans adding up to a remarkably large share of the total volume of credit raised by two of them: China (67 percent) and the Soviet Union (78 percent), both countries of major consequence to Japan largely because of their proximity and natural resources. Of the remaining seven countries favored by the Bank of Tokyo, five were of decided strategic economic or political importance to Japan: South Korea, the Philippines, and Hong Kong (neighbors and trading partners of Japan), and Mexico and Ecuador (both rich in natural resources).

The Bank of Tokyo also managed syndicated yen credits on behalf of ten overseas borrowers during the period. The two largest of these credits, each for 70 billion yen (approximately $290 million at the time), went to the World Bank, whose international development work the Japanese government has actively supported, and to Canada, another Pacific Basin country rich in natural resources. South Korea received the third largest yen credit, for 28 billion yen (about $115 million). The remaining seven recipients were all sovereign or government-guaranteed borrowers, and they included at least three countries of strategic economic or political significance to Japan: Brazil (an important source of raw materials and a major target of Japanese direct investment), Argentina (an important Latin American trading partner and a potentially significant supplier of foodstuffs to Japan), and the Philippines.

A Return to Restrictions

Because of the Japanese authorities' severe curtailment of international lending by Japanese banks during the fourth quarter of 1979 through the first two quarters of 1980, the Bank of Tokyo managed syndicated foreign currency credits for only sixteen countries, compared with thirty-three during the preceding nine months. The Ministry of Finance maintained a relatively open policy during this final period of favoring commercial loans tied to overseas natural resource development, Japanese trade, or the programs of international agencies.[12] As a consequence, one might expect that commercial criteria would have played a lesser role in the banks' selection of overseas borrowers, compared with the preceding period. The available evidence suggests, however, that the Bank of Tokyo still weighed commercial criteria to a significant degree. Twelve of the sixteen borrowing countries selected by the bank (and approved by the Ministry of Finance) ranked among the twenty highest-volume borrowers in the Euromarket during the

12. Eric W. Hayden, "Internationalizing Japan's Financial System," An Occasional Paper of the Northeast Asia–United States Forum on International Policy (Stanford University, 1980), p. 11.

Table 6-2. *Major Bank of Tokyo Overseas Borrowers,*
October 1979–June 1980, Ranked by Volume of Borrowing
and Perceived Creditworthiness in Euromarket
Amounts in millions of dollars

Country[a]	Amount managed by Bank of Tokyo	Total borrowed in Euro-market	Rank among 20 highest-volume borrowing countries[b]	Rank among 20 most credit-worthy countries[c]
Brazil	1,550	2,411	5	. . .
Canada	1,250	2,084	7	8
Belgium	1,200	2,200	6	8
Mexico	650	3,807	2	20
South Korea	637	1,870	10	. . .
Malaysia	550	1,050	16	5
Greece	500	1,544	11	12
Italy	500	2,558	3	. . .

Sources: Bank of Tokyo, *Activities of the Bank of Tokyo Group*, pp. 21–22; World Bank, *Borrowing in International Capital Markets, Fourth Quarter 1979*, pp. 22–24; World Bank, *Borrowing in International Capital Markets: Foreign and International Bond Issues, Publicized Eurocurrency Credits, First Half 1980*, EC-181/801 (Washington, D.C.: World Bank, 1980), pp. 13–15; and "The Country Risk League Table," *Euromoney* (October 1980), pp. 26–40.

a. Countries for which Bank of Tokyo managed at least $500 million in syndicated foreign currency credits during October 1979–June 1980. The vast majority of individual borrowers of record in these countries were sovereign or government-guaranteed entities.

b. Based on total Eurocurrency credits raised by both public- and private-sector borrowers in each country during October 1979–June 1980.

c. Rankings reflect perceived creditworthiness of all borrowing countries in Euromarket. Based on average weighted spreads, taking into account volume of borrowings and maturity structure, obtained on floating-rate syndicated loans signed during the first seven months of 1980. Covers only loans arranged for sovereign and sovereign-guaranteed entities. See "The Country Risk League Table," pp. 26, 38–40.

period, and six of the sixteen ranked among the twenty countries perceived to be the most creditworthy in the market during January–July 1980.

The bank managed syndicated foreign currency credits aggregating more than $500 million for each of eight countries, down from eleven countries during the preceding period (see table 6-2). Surprisingly, compared with the previous period, an even higher proportion of these countries numbered among the most commercially attractive customers for large banks anywhere. Five of the eight countries were both high-volume borrowers and looked upon as highly creditworthy by the Euromarket at the time, compared with the previous period, when only four out of the eleven countries fell in this category. Thus, rather than making the bank's Euromarket activity more politicized, the official restriction of Japanese overseas lending that accompanied the second oil shock actually may have made that activity more conservative. (The Bank of Tokyo itself also may have experienced a heightened aversion to risk during the period.)

The Bank of Tokyo nevertheless remained sensitive to broader Japanese strategic interests during this last period, in keeping with the Ministry of Finance's lending guidelines. Of the five high-volume and high-quality countries favored by the bank, at least three (Canada, Mexico, and Malaysia) were countries of special strategic importance to Japan. Of the remaining three favored countries that did *not* rank among both the high-volume and high-quality borrowers in the market, two (Brazil and South Korea) were of major strategic significance to Japan. Interestingly, the Bank of Tokyo helped to manage more than 60 percent of the total volume of credit raised by two of the eight countries that received at least $500 million in bank-managed credits: Brazil and Canada, both countries of established strategic importance.

The Bank of Tokyo managed only three syndicated yen credits to overseas borrowers during this period. The three recipients of the loans— the World Bank, the Indonesian central bank, and a major government-owned bank in Argentina—were all considered commercially viable credit risks at the time. Yet each of the three was also a borrower of strategic economic or political significance to Japan. The World Bank received by far the largest loan, for 55 billion yen (approximately $230 million).[13] Indonesia received a loan of 11.7 billion yen (approximately $50 million), while the Argentine loan was for only 5 billion yen ($21 million).

In summary, the Bank of Tokyo showed a consistent concern for its entrepreneurial position during the three periods under scrutiny between 1975 and 1981. Non-Japanese banks active in global syndicated lending could have made, and did make, many of the same credit decisions. Yet a large portion of the Bank of Tokyo's loans still flowed to countries of specific strategic value to Japan.

Official Japanese policy frequently encouraged the Japanese banks' pursuit of lending opportunities in these particular countries; the Ministry of Finance's policy of favoring loans to develop overseas natural

13. The Japanese authorities were especially eager to promote loans to the World Bank at the time because of growing criticism that Japan was failing to meet its full responsibilities to the developing world. The restrictions on Japanese banks' overseas lending, in particular, had all but eliminated a major source of commercial finance to developing countries.

resources during late 1979 and early 1980 is but one example. At minimum, official policy reinforced commercial considerations in guiding the banks toward overseas customers of strategic significance. A corollary observation is that the government has naturally restricted commercial overseas lending most severely during periods when Japan's sense of international vulnerability has been greatest (such as after the first and second oil shocks). During these periods, the innate conservatism of Japan's financial elites in both the public and private sectors has been pronounced, tempering their willingness to use Japanese international banking capabilities for strategic economic or political ends.

Commercial Banking as an Offset to Current-Account Disequilibria

On numerous occasions from 1970 through 1980 the Japanese government utilized aggregate international lending and deposit-taking by Japanese commercial banks to offset surpluses and deficits in Japan's current-account position. Throughout this period current-account disequilibria posed recurring economic and political problems for Japan, exacerbated by the fact that fluctuations in the current account tended to provoke parallel movements in the value of the yen.[14] Twice during the 1970s, sharp rises in imported oil costs helped to generate large current-account deficits, which in turn contributed to a depreciation of the yen that increased the effective cost of imports and raised domestic rates of inflation. At other times, surpluses placed undesired upward pressure on the yen's value and stimulated growing international demands that Japan restrict exports and assume a greater role in fostering third world development.

During times of current-account deficit, Japan's financial authorities, eager to promote net capital inflows, severely restricted international lending by Japanese banks. (During such a time after the second oil shock, the authorities also encouraged the banks' solicitation of foreign deposits and overseas sales of Japanese government bonds.) Resulting reductions in overseas lending in yen by Japanese banks directly assisted

14. For a concise discussion of the relation between the effective value of the yen and changes in Japan's current-account balance, see Morgan Guaranty Trust Company of New York, *World Financial Markets* (March 1981), pp. 6–7.

the government's efforts to stem net capital outflows. Insofar as Japanese banks funded their foreign currency lending through Japanese sources (for example, through swaps of yen for dollars or through "hidden" foreign currency reserves deposited with the banks by the Ministry of Finance), reductions in foreign currency lending also helped to reduce net capital outflows.

During times of current-account surplus, the Japanese government's relaxation of restrictions on commercial overseas lending, combined with the imposition of strict incremental reserve requirements on "free yen" deposits placed in Japan by foreign investors, helped to stimulate net capital outflows. The resulting reinvestment of accumulated dollars out of the country helped to counter undesired upward pressure on the yen as well as to restrain foreign demands on Japan to do more to promote North-South economic cooperation and share in the burden of petrodollar recycling.

Bank Responsiveness to Swings in the Current-Account Position

The sequence of shifts in the level of Japanese bank activity in international markets during 1970–80 provides evidence of the Japanese authorities' acumen in harnessing that activity to support the balance-of-payments objectives of Japanese foreign economic policy. During the first years of the decade, the combination of Japanese trade surpluses and growing official reserves figured decisively in the government's decision to encourage major Japanese banks to lend in the Euromarket.[15] From 1970 to 1973 the financial authorities liberalized restrictions on the export of capital from Japan, and many types of international financial transactions took place in Tokyo for the first time, including foreign currency–denominated medium- and long-term loans by Japanese financial institutions to foreign borrowers.[16] The Japanese government also

15. The country's current account registered a surplus of more than $6.6 billion during 1972 alone. Japan Economic and Foreign Affairs Research Association, *Statistical Survey of Japan's Economy, 1981* (Tokyo: The Association, 1981), p. 75.

16. In this regard, Wilbur Monroe has observed, "Of course, it was no secret that the Japanese authorities still carefully controlled these new developments and sanctioned their occurrence, *precisely* because of Japan's strong external payments situation and the attendant desire to mitigate as much as possible the rapid buildup in official foreign exchange reserves." Wilbur F. Monroe, "The Rise of Tokyo as an International Financial Center," *Journal of World Trade Law*, vol. 8 (November–December 1974), p. 659.

placed large amounts of accumulated foreign currency reserves with Japanese commercial banks from at least May 1972 until November 1973, a period when a number of them first began to develop their Euroloan portfolios.[17] The arrangement permitted Japanese banks to minimize their reliance on the overseas interbank market for foreign currency funding, while at the same time enabling the government to trim excess official reserves and stimulate a capital outflow to offset Japan's swelling current-account surplus.[18]

From late 1973 through 1975 Japan's current account swung into deficit, reflecting the impact of sharply higher imported oil costs. (The deficit peaked at $4.7 billion for 1974, then fell to $0.7 billion for 1975.)[19] To check capital outflows throughout this period, Japanese financial authorities severely restricted all new medium- and long-term loans to foreigners denominated in foreign currencies (offshore loans in yen were still minimal at the time).[20] Concurrently, the government provided Japanese commercial banks with major new incentives to bring capital into the country in the form of free yen deposits (convertible deposits

17. The Japanese government adopted a seven-point "international economic countermeasures emergency program" in May 1972 that provided for the redepositing of official reserves in authorized Japanese foreign exchange banks, according to Krause and Sekiguchi, "to help repay foreign liabilities." In November 1973, as Japan's current account swung into deficit, Japanese financial authorities recalled about $650 million of these deposits from Japanese commercial banks, thereby forcing the banks to increase significantly their borrowings from the Euromarket to fund their foreign currency loan portfolios. See Lawrence B. Krause and Sueo Sekiguchi, "Japan and the World Economy," in Hugh Patrick and Henry Rosovsky, eds., *Asia's New Giant: How the Japanese Economy Works* (Brookings Institution, 1976), p. 457; and International CD Market Association, "London Dollar CDs: Markets Bear Up in Spite of Gloom," *Euromoney* (January 1974), p. 85.

18. See Rothschild Intercontinental Bank, "Medium-term Eurocredits: Japanese Banks to Move into Interbank Market?" *Euromoney* (January 1974), pp. 83–85.

19. Keizai Koho Center, *Japan 1982*, p. 37.

20. Other adverse circumstances also caused Japanese financial authorities to discourage Japanese banks' offshore lending during this period. Sharply increased short-term borrowings by Japanese banks in international markets, combined with general nervousness in the Euromarket following the collapse of West Germany's Bankhaus Herstatt in mid-1974, contributed to the emergence of the "Japan rate," which forced Japanese banks to pay sizable premiums for Euromarket borrowings. As a consequence, Japanese financial authorities became seriously concerned about many Japanese banks' ability to fund themselves. See Hayden, "Internationalizing Japan's Financial System," p. 10; and Eiichi Matsumoto, "The Developing Role of the Japanese Banks in the International Capital Markets," speech at conference sponsored by the *Financial Times* (London), Amsterdam, December 9, 1980, pp. 5–6.

held by nonresidents).[21] By the end of the period, the financial authorities' seesaw approach to the development and expansion of Japanese international banking activities was well established. The authorities' approach remained quite consistent from a balance-of-payments perspective, however.

From 1976 through 1978 Japan's current account moved back into surplus, climbing to $10.9 billion during 1977 and peaking at $16.5 billion during 1978.[22] Largely in response to this swing, the authorities relaxed restrictions on overseas lending by Japanese banks in both foreign currencies and yen in July 1977.[23] From then through mid-1979, Japanese banks ranked among the most aggressive lenders in the Euromarket. Scarcely active during 1976–77, Japanese banks accounted for 41 percent of total new medium-term syndicated lending in the market during the first five months of 1979.[24] Interestingly, this rapid increase in foreign currency lending by Japanese banks occurred as the government began to move huge foreign currency deposits (drawn from official reserves) back to them. By November 1978 the outstanding balance of these "hidden reserves" had reached at least $10 billion; as of the same date, outstanding offshore medium- and long-term dollar loans of Japanese banks amounted to approximately $20 billion, having more than doubled in less than a year.[25] Simultaneously, with clear official encouragement, Japanese banks also engaged in substantial yen-denominated syndicated lending to foreign borrowers for the first time; these loans reached the equivalent of $4.1 billion by year-end 1978 and $6.0 billion by May 1979. As another part of its overall plan to promote net capital outflows, the Ministry of Finance reinstituted in 1978 a program of disincentives, in

21. Monroe, "The Rise of Tokyo as an International Financial Center," p. 660.

22. Keizai Koho Center, *Japan 1982*, p. 37.

23. Tracy Dahlby, "Banking: The Good News from Tokyo," *Far Eastern Economic Review* (October 10, 1980), p. 80.

24. Stephen Bronte, "Destined to be the World's No. 3—Despite the MoF," *Far Eastern Economic Review* (December 14, 1979), p. 59.

25. See "How Japan's Ministry of Finance Explains Its 'Friendly Advice' to the Banks," *Euromoney* (December 1978), pp. 65, 68. This article notes that Masazumi Kawaguchi (deputy chief manager of the International Division of Mitsubishi Bank) "rejected out of hand the suggestion of any direct link between the dollar deposits made by the Ministry with the commercial banks, and the increase in the banks' international lending." It quotes Kawaguchi: "The deposits are linked to import financing. They tend to decrease the cost of import financing, and encourage the import of goods into Japan. They are not to be used to fund medium and long-term international loans." However, it continues, "In private conversations, some Japanese bankers say that to some extent the Ministry deposits are being used to fund international loans."

the form of strict incremental reserve requirements, to reverse the banks' accumulation of free yen deposits.[26]

Hurt by the massive OPEC price hikes of 1979, Japan's current account registered a deficit of $8.8 billion for that year, nearly twice as large as the 1974 oil-induced deficit.[27] Once again, the Japanese financial authorities faced the need to generate a large capital inflow, and once again they looked to the country's commercial banking system. To the chagrin of many Japanese banks as well as overseas borrowers, the Ministry of Finance's International Finance Bureau moved in October 1979 to suspend virtually all new offshore lending in yen and to restrict offshore foreign currency loans.[28]

According to widely broadcast reports at the time, the Ministry announced to the Japanese banking community its intention to give priority to lending linked with Japanese trade, natural resource projects (particularly those related to oil), and international agencies such as the World Bank.[29] Furthermore, as described in one published report, "The ministry has decided to implement a policy of scrutinising each loan on a case-by-case basis, often chopping the Japanese participation in the loans by as much as two thirds."[30] The Bank of Japan simultaneously drew down its hidden foreign currency reserves with Japanese commercial banks, thereby forcing them once again to rely more heavily on external sources for foreign currency funding.[31]

Concurrently, the financial authorities provided special incentives to

26. Stephen Bronte, "The Dilemma of Japan's City Banks," *Euromoney* (September 1979), p. 30; and Bronte, "Destined to be the World's No. 3—Despite the MoF," p. 62.

27. Keizai Koho Center, *Japan 1982*, p. 37.

28. Officials were responding to at least three factors besides a renewed current-account deficit and downward pressure on the yen. First, the extremely aggressive lending practices of Japanese banks in the Euromarket over the previous two years had provoked considerable foreign pressure on the Japanese government to restrain the banks' overseas lending. Second, particularly after the fall of the shah of Iran, the Ministry of Finance and Bank of Japan had become concerned about Japanese banks' ability to assess country risk. Third, Japanese financial authorities were fearful that growing uncertainties in the Euromarket and tightening U.S. monetary policy could confront Japanese banks with renewed foreign currency funding problems, similar to those associated with the "Japan rate" of 1974. See Hayden, "Internationalizing Japan's Financial System," pp. 10–11.

29. Ibid., p. 11.

30. Bronte, "Destined to be the World's No. 3—Despite the MoF," p. 59.

31. Tracy Dahlby, "Banking: Getting Back into the Game," *Far Eastern Economic Review* (April 18, 1980), p. 59.

the banks to attract OPEC financial surpluses to Japan. In March 1980 the Finance Ministry authorized Japanese banks to pay whatever interest rates they desired on free yen deposits from foreign governments and international institutions. This reform allowed the banks to raise interest rates on these deposits from the 5.5 percent ceiling previously enforced by the ministry to the much higher Euroyen rates prevailing at the time (which tend to move with Eurodollar rates). In conjunction with this action, the Finance Ministry also waived withholding taxes that foreign governments and international institutions might have to pay on interest earned on bank deposits in Japan.[32] As assessed in a special report of the *Middle East Economic Digest*, "With yields finally competitive, such deposits with Japanese banks from Middle East central banks soared." The *Financial Times* additionally reported, "To attract individual 'rich sheiks', as one banker put it, the banks were given an additional special quota for bringing in Euroyen deposits [into Japan by converting them into free yen deposits]."[33] These combined measures led to large inflows of oil funds; during the second quarter alone, free yen deposits increased by $6.4 billion, or 130 percent.[34]

The Japanese government supplemented its offering of market incentives with diplomatic efforts to persuade Arab governments to place their funds in Japan.[35] At the same time, Japanese banks geared up to handle their officially sanctioned new business with a rush to establish offices in the Middle East, generally in Bahrain.[36] The Finance Ministry

32. Stephen Bronte, "Banking: Petrodollar Sophistication Grows," in *Japan and the Middle East: A Middle East Economic Digest Special Report* (December 1980), p. 10; Richard Hanson, "Growing Force in World Markets," *Financial Times* (London), December 3, 1980; and Adrian Dicks, "Bigger Role This Time Round," *Financial Times* (London), December 3, 1980.

33. Bronte, "Banking: Petrodollar Sophistication Grows," p. 10; and Hanson, "Growing Force in World Markets."

34. Bank for International Settlements, *Fifty-First Annual Report, 1st April 1980–31st March 1981* (Basle: BIS, 1981), p. 119.

35. Dicks, "Bigger Role This Time Round."

36. The interest of Japanese banks in obtaining surplus funds from the Middle East throughout 1980–81 reflected more than simply a desire to increase their nonresident yen-denominated liabilities. In comparison to their behavior following the first oil crisis, Japanese banks became far more active in recycling petrodollars to third countries following the second crisis of 1979. The more dollar funding that Japanese banks could obtain directly from Middle East sources, the less dependent those banks would be on foreign banks to fund these dollar loans. Additionally, Japanese banks were eager to acquire OPEC dollars in order to pay for Japan's own oil imports, billed in dollars. See Bronte, "Banking: Petrodollar Sophistication Grows," p. 10.

relaxed restrictions on the opening of foreign offices by Japanese banks in April 1980, and shortly thereafter ten Japanese banks sought and obtained licenses from the Bahrain Monetary Agency to operate representative offices in the emirate, joining three other Japanese banks already there.

Some volume of Middle Eastern financial resources would have flowed into yen-denominated assets during 1980 regardless of specific actions taken by the Japanese government, banks, and other Japanese financial intermediaries. As 1980 began, many Middle Eastern investors were probably eager to lessen their dependence on the dollar and American banks following the U.S. government's freezing of Iranian assets in November 1979. Investing in yen-denominated financial instruments constituted a potentially attractive alternative, not only because of the small existing role of the yen in Arab portfolios (approximately 5 percent), but also because of the perceived basic strength of the Japanese economy and the yen's rising value throughout 1980. Japanese government actions during 1980 nevertheless served as a distinct catalyst to the flow of OPEC financial resources into the country.

To assure the result that it desired, the Finance Ministry supplemented its actions in the market with direct consultations with various Middle Eastern governments during the period and apparently also gave administrative guidance to Japanese banks. Through their close cooperation, the Finance Ministry and the banks probably generated a faster, greater flow of OPEC financial resources into Japan than would have otherwise occurred, particularly during the first through third quarters of 1980. The result served both Japanese strategic economic interests and the commercial interests of the banks.

Finally, as Japan's current account showed signs of improvement during the course of 1980, the Ministry of Finance slowly eased restrictions on overseas lending. First, restrictions on offshore foreign currency lending (expressed through administrative guidance) were relaxed in June.[37] Then late in the year, the authorities also "made it clear that they regard the improvement in the payments position and the recovery of the yen to around 200–210 yen to the dollar as the occasion for some liberalisation in yen lending abroad." They "also let it be known to the banks and securities houses that they wish to see the limited volume of funds available [for overseas syndicated yen loans and yen bond issues]

37. Matsumoto, "The Developing Role of the Japanese Banks," pp. 5, 7.

steered in the direction either of prime names or of borrowers whose purposes suit the ends of Japanese foreign policy."[38]

The ministry's deployment of authorized foreign exchange banks to move large amounts of capital into and out of Japan during the 1970s in response to its balance-of-payments circumstances is remarkable because it happened with such regularity and produced extreme shifts in the banks' international lending and deposit-taking activities. Certainly governments of other major capital-exporting countries, including the United States and West Germany, have perceived a linkage between their countries' balance-of-payments accounts and their banks' overseas lending and deposit-taking activities. Faced with large balance-of-payments deficits, these other governments have also placed limits on banking activities.[39] In West Germany as well as the United States, however, such official efforts to harness international banking flows to balance-of-payments ends have been exceptional since the end of World War II; furthermore, these efforts have overwhelmingly emphasized restraints on the activities of banks rather than direct, positive encouragement to undertake increased lending or deposit-taking.

Official policies in Japan, while successfully drawing on Japanese international banking capabilities to achieve a series of important macro objectives of Japanese foreign economic policy, were not pursued without cost. Japanese government actions unquestionably retarded both the growth of Japanese banks' influence in international finance and Tokyo's maturation into a world-class financial center along the lines of London or New York. The slowness of Tokyo's growth into such a center has disappointed Japanese commercial banks, overseas borrowers, and even many foreign lenders, among others. The Japanese government itself has taken an ambivalent stance toward this growth. While Japanese financial authorities profess to welcome the expansion of Japanese commercial international banking, they have also appeared loath to give up any more of their control over Japanese monetary and

38. Adrian Dicks, "Lending Abroad Has Yet to Match Potential," *Financial Times* (London), December 3, 1980.

39. For instance, the U.S. government instituted an unusual Voluntary Foreign Credit Restraint program in 1965 that restricted American bank lending abroad as a means of limiting the outflow of capital. Similarly, the German Bundesbank obtained the agreement of leading German commercial banks in December 1980 to refrain from granting loans denominated in deutsche marks to foreigners through March 1981. This "gentlemen's agreement" covered domestically booked loans with a term of four years or more.

credit policy, a step that any major expansion of Tokyo as an international financial center would entail.

Samurai Leasing to Reduce a Current-Account Surplus

From 1970 through 1980 Japanese commercial banks contributed to their government's efforts to counter current-account surpluses and deficits primarily by promoting offsetting capital flows. From approximately March 1978 through June 1979, however, the banks helped to ease Japan's balance-of-payments problems in an additional and highly interesting way.

At least one large Japanese commercial bank assisted MITI with the design of an unusual international leasing plan, primarily intended to produce a largely cosmetic reduction in Japan's swelling current-account surplus, but also envisioned as a means of fostering Japanese ties with developing countries. Following formal endorsement of the plan by the Japanese government, a larger number of major Japanese banks helped to implement it. Before the plan's termination, participating banks and leasing companies effected an improvement in Japan's statistical balance of payments, not only by stimulating capital outflows from the country, but also by *reducing* its current-account surplus by nearly $1 billion through the promotion of imports. For their efforts, the banks and leasing companies earned extraordinary profits.[40] The evolution of the plan, sometimes known as the "samurai lease" aircraft financing scheme, reveals much about the interaction between major Japanese commercial banks and the foreign economic policy machinery of the Japanese government during this period.

Japan's current account, as previously noted, experienced a growing surplus from 1976 through early 1979. The $10.9 billion surplus during 1977 was nearly triple that of 1976, reflecting an expanding gap between Japan's merchandise exports and imports.[41] Simultaneously, the country's international reserves climbed to unprecedented levels: having totaled less than $5 billion at the end of 1970, they would peak at more than $33 billion in January 1979.[42] From 1977 through early 1979, as

40. A senior official at one involved Japanese bank maintains that "Big profit [was] not the original aim [of the plan], but did result in the end." Written comments by senior official of a Japanese commercial bank on samurai plan, August 1982.

41. Keizai Koho Center, *Japan 1982*, p. 37.

42. Bank of Japan, *Economic Statistics Annual, 1981*, p. 249; and "Exchange Reserves Fell to $28.8 Billion at March-end," *Japan Economic Journal*, April 10, 1979.

foreign sales of Japanese manufactures surged, the governments of the United States and various European Community countries, among others, placed mounting pressure on Japan to balance its trade account, by either curtailing exports to their economies or stepping up imports. Indicating its own heightened concern, the Japanese government adopted a major eight-point program aimed at reducing the growing balance-of-payments surplus in December 1977.[43]

The *Japan Economic Journal,* the English-language weekly edition of Japan's leading financial daily, first mentioned the possibility of creating an international leasing scheme to ease Japan's balance-of-payments problems on March 14, 1978. According to two separate reports on that date, "Concrete measures for reducing the balance of payments, such as import of airbuses under a 'leasing formula,' will be swiftly studied and enforced"; and "government ministries *and others* now were said to be investigating [a leasing scheme's] feasibility."[44] Almost certainly before these press references, perhaps as early as late 1977, informal discussions began between officials of MITI and one of Japan's leading international commercial banks regarding the feasibility of such a scheme.[45] Officials of that bank appear to have supplied the initial idea and passed it informally to colleagues in MITI's Industrial Policy Bureau. Before the scheme's official sanctioning, in an effort to build interest within the Japanese government, officials of the same bank also obtained the support of "close friends" working with Nobuhiko Ushiba, state minister in charge of external economic affairs and special trade representative for Prime Minister Fukuda. While this first bank worked with MITI to develop the leasing plan's details, a second major Japanese bank, also one of Japan's most internationally active, may have provided supplementary assistance in the design of the scheme at an early stage.[46]

43. Included in the program were an "emergency import schedule" promoting the stockpiling and prepayment of imports and a plan to expand the Japanese Export-Import Bank's foreign-currency financing of imports. See Yoshinori Ikeda, "Gov't Decides Eight-Point External Economic Policy," *Japan Economic Journal,* December 13, 1977.

44. Ryuzo Morohoshi, "Government Will Mobilize All Means to Spur Business"; and "Import-Lease System Is Explored As New Way to Cut Payments Surplus," *Japan Economic Journal,* March 14, 1978. Emphasis added.

45. The description of the involvement of one major commercial bank in particular in formulating the samurai lease scheme is based primarily on two extended interviews with a senior official of the bank in question, Tokyo, February 20, 1981, and February 25, 1981.

46. The first bank disputes this possibility, claiming that it alone helped the government to design the lease plan.

From its conception, the samurai plan called for Japanese-based financial institutions to provide lease financing for sales of high-priced equipment, primarily aircraft, between parties in foreign countries. As lessor in any given transaction, a Japanese leasing company would acquire title to the equipment, causing it to appear as an import in Japan's trade statistics. Even though the overseas lessee, usually a government-owned airline, would receive immediate use of the equipment (which might never enter Japan), each transaction was designed so that no corresponding export entry in Japan's trade statistics would result; thus a net reduction in Japan's recorded trade surplus would occur. Crucial to both the intent and success of the arrangement was maintaining the fiction that neither lessor nor lessee planned to transfer the equipment's title through the financing. Thus Japanese leasing companies accounted for each transaction as an operating rather than a financing lease.[47] As a result, each transaction appeared as a means of providing an overseas lessee temporary use of equipment, in return for rental payments, rather than as a means of financing the equipment's ultimate sale to the lessee. In fact, however, overseas airline lessees typically signed lease-*purchase* agreements that gave them the option of taking formal ownership of the aircraft at the end of the lease term for a token sum, perhaps $1.[48]

The actual financial arrangements behind each samurai lease were as elliptical as the lease accounting just described. First, a Japanese bank or leasing company would identify the prospective sale of a foreign aircraft to a foreign airline. The bank and associated Japanese leasing interests next would seek Japanese government approval, granted through the Japanese Export-Import Bank, of the pending financing as a qualified transaction under the government's foreign currency lending program for urgent imports (part of the eight-point program announced in December 1977). If government approval followed, the Export-Import Bank

47. See, for example, Orient Leasing Co., Ltd. (Tokyo), *Annual Report 1980,* p. 10.

48. A hypothetical example would be the acquisition by Thai Airways International of a new Boeing 747. The aircraft would appear as an import from the United States in Japanese trade and current-account statistics, valued at perhaps $50 million. Although Thai Airways would take possession of the plane, Japan would not record an export in its balance of payments until the plane's title passed from Japan to Thailand at the end of the lease period, that is, after ten years. An export of perhaps $1 would then be shown, corresponding to the token purchase price paid by Thai Airways and also the plane's depreciated value on paper. The Japanese payment to Boeing for the aircraft would be recorded immediately as a Japanese net capital outflow of $50 million, offsetting the merchandise import entry. See William Schwartz, "Foreign Banks Take a Lease on Samurai Plan," *Asian Wall Street Journal,* March 30, 1979; also Stephen Bronte, "Groping in the Grey Areas," *Euromoney* (June 1979), p. 31.

would obtain sufficient foreign currency reserves from the Finance Ministry to pay for the aircraft and on-lend these funds to the Japanese lessor at a concessional rate of 6 percent for ten years. The lessor would remit the funds to the foreign party selling the aircraft, while the foreign airline lessee would take possession of it, paying the lessor a fixed annual rental fee of 8.25 percent in accordance with the terms of the lease-purchase agreement between lessor and lessee.[49] The Export-Import Bank required that its funding risk be guaranteed by the participating Japanese commercial bank; in return, the commercial bank could draw attractive fees (0.20 to 0.25 percent a year) from the lessor's own sizable gross interest spread of 2.25 percent.[50]

Several implications of the arrangement merit explicit mention. First, the scheme required the Japanese government (particularly the Ministry of Finance) to adopt an extremely liberal interpretation of the Export-Import Bank of Japan law. That law restricts the bank's import financing to "goods including equipment which are necessary for the sound development of the national economy";[51] under the samurai lease program, however, Japan's Export-Import Bank found itself providing "import financing" to fund the sale of U.S. and European aircraft to countries such as Iceland and Papua New Guinea.

Second, because major Japanese commercial banks assumed all of the Export-Import Bank's risk, the government did not need to worry about credit quality when deciding whether to approve particular aircraft lease transactions for inclusion in the emergency import program. Third,

49. Because MITI wanted the entire Japanese leasing industry to share any windfall profits derived through the scheme, a syndicate of leasing companies usually served as lessor. The lessor's 6 percent cost of funds and lessee's rental fee of 8.25 percent remained in effect until April 1979, when the Ministry of Finance raised both rates.

50. Information from interview with official of major Japanese leasing company involved in samurai lease financings, Tokyo, February 6, 1981; and from internal memorandum provided by a foreign bank active in Japan, dated August 15, 1978. Late in the period during which the samurai program was operational, Japanese authorities also permitted *foreign* banks to guarantee the Japanese Export-Import Bank's risk in several of the lease transactions. Chase Manhattan and Citibank, in particular, structured and participated in at least six samurai leases. However, formalization of the first lease involving a foreign bank did not occur until March 30, 1979, less than a week before the Japanese government announced the termination of the program. See Schwartz, "Foreign Banks Take a Lease on Samurai Plan."

51. "Using Foreign Exch. Reserve for Import Financing is Being Studied," *Japan Economic Journal,* November 22, 1977. See also Export-Import Bank of Japan, *The Export-Import Bank of Japan Law* (Export-Import Bank of Japan, September 1978), chap. 3, article 18(4), p. 5.

the lease scheme enabled the government not only to create the appearance of an increase in net imports but also to draw down its record-level foreign currency reserves—at a time when overseas criticism of the growing surplus and the level of reserves was acquiring new intensity.

Fourth, the Japanese government consciously ran the leasing program on a basis that afforded Japanese banks and leasing companies extremely attractive profits. The Ministry of Finance directly controlled the interest rate at which the Export-Import Bank on-lent the government's reserves to Japanese leasing companies, and through administrative guidance the ministry informally controlled both the 8.25 percent interest rate charged lessees and the fee income earned by Japanese banks. Ultimately, Japanese financial institutions received considerable business, because the government operated the samurai program at below-market rates. Specifically, during the summer of 1978, when a foreign airline could obtain financing for 8.25 percent (including all fees) through a samurai lease, a prime-rated U.S. airline would have paid 9 to 9⅛ percent for similar equipment trust financing in the United States. Late the following winter, when samurai lease financing was still available to foreign airlines at 8.25 percent, U.S. leasing firms were charging between 10 and 14 percent for similar financing.[52] Finally, the samurai program also provided selected foreign airlines and their owner governments the equivalent of Japanese foreign aid in the form of subsidized aircraft financing.

Following the Japanese press reports on the lease scheme in early March 1978, a major bureaucratic struggle ensued within the Japanese government over the scheme's desirability.[53] On the one hand, officials of MITI and several other government ministries strongly supported the proposed plan, fearing that Japanese exports would be hurt if Japan could not demonstrate to foreign critics that it was doing everything possible to purchase more imports from other industrial countries. On the other hand, many senior officials of the Ministry of Finance were "furious" over the proposal, and their displeasure was felt not only in MITI but also in the commercial banks that had corroborated in its

52. Information contained in internal memorandum provided by a foreign bank active in Japan, dated August 15, 1978; and "U.S. Seeks Exim Bank Loans for Also [sic] American Airline Companies," *Japan Economic Journal*, March 13, 1979. During approximately the summer of 1978, a non-U.S. airline purchasing a new Boeing 747 would have paid a blended fixed rate of around 9 percent (*plus* fees) for ten-year joint financing from the U.S. Export-Import Bank and U.S. commercial banks.

53. For a rather indirect discussion of this struggle, see "Import-Lease Idea Dims After Much 'Hullabaloo,' " *Japan Economic Journal*, March 28, 1978.

development.[54] The mere fact that its arch-rival ministry had proposed the samurai lease plan made the plan objectionable to the Finance Ministry. In addition, however, the ministry's opposition focused on the opportunity cost, and possible outright expense, that the government would have to incur to support the scheme's concessional interest rates; the fact that it would show favoritism to certain sectors of the economy (particularly the leasing sector); and the reality that its impact on the Japanese trade surplus was purely cosmetic.

Although the scheme was controversial even within the principal commercial bank that had promoted its design, the prevailing mood within Japan's internationally active commercial banks was naturally supportive. On balance, leading Japanese bankers shared MITI's fears that a continued inability to stimulate imports from other industrial countries would lead to the imposition of export curbs, and these would hamper the banks' commercial interests. In addition, samurai leasing promised the banks windfall income through equity participations in major leasing companies as well as through finder's fees and loan guarantees. The intensity of the debate between the Ministry of Finance and MITI over the merits of the scheme eventually forced the decision on whether to implement it to the highest levels of the Japanese government. According to officials in one major commercial bank, Prime Minister Fukuda himself appeared responsible for the final go-ahead.[55]

Even before the leasing plan received final authorization, MITI officials began to explore possible political uses for it beyond pacifying Japan's trade critics in other industrial countries. In early April 1978 MITI began sounding out various Southeast Asian nations on their interest in leasing aircraft from Japan at cut rates; in response to these inquiries, which the Bank of Tokyo and a Japanese trading company helped MITI to make, many of the nations in the region, among them the Philippines and Thailand, expressed an early desire to participate in any program.[56]

From this period through the first months of the plan's implementation, MITI officials also displayed an interest in restricting lessees to govern-

54. Interviews with senior official of a Japanese bank involved in development of the leasing proposal, Tokyo, February 20, 1981, and February 25, 1981.

55. Interview with senior official of a Japanese commercial bank, Tokyo, February 25, 1981.

56. "MITI Quizzes SEA Nations on 'Import-Lease' Chances," *Japan Economic Journal*, April 11, 1978.

ment-owned air carriers from developing countries. Hopes of using samurai leases to allocate foreign aid to countries of political or strategic economic interest received a setback, however, when Japanese commercial banks balked at issuing guarantees to the Export-Import Bank of Japan on behalf of countries that they did not regard as creditworthy. Countries rejected by the banks included Pakistan, Bangladesh, and Vietnam. In the end, according to an official of the Japanese leasing industry, "the authorities understood."[57] The government's hopes of using the lease program to improve Japanese bilateral ties in the region were further dampened during the summer of 1978 when the governments of South Korea, the Philippines, and other Southeast Asian nations reassessed their positions and declined involvement.[58]

While some elements of the Japanese government, particularly within MITI, sought to obtain international political benefits from the lease program, other elements, led largely by officials of the more conservative Ministry of Finance, remained consistently sensitive to potential political embarrassments that the program might create. Such sensitivity became apparent in early 1979, for example, after a Japanese leasing company approached the Japanese Export-Import Bank for approval to use a samurai lease to finance delivery of an aircraft manufactured by the Grumman Corporation of the United States to Pemex, the Mexican state oil company. The Export-Import Bank granted preliminary approval, but subsequently a Japanese parliamentary investigation began to uncover details of a political scandal involving kickbacks from Grumman to Japanese government officials. The Export-Import Bank then quietly reversed its earlier authorization, adding that no Grumman aircraft sales whatever could be financed with samurai leases.[59]

Japanese authorities encountered a potentially far larger problem when the U.S. government asserted through diplomatic channels in early March 1979 that Japanese implementation of the samurai lease plan had shown favoritism to East Asian and European air carriers.

57. Interview with official of a major Japanese leasing company involved in samurai lease financings, Tokyo, February 6, 1981.
58. "Seoul Government Junks Plan to Lease 3 Big Airliners from Japan," *Japan Economic Journal*, August 1, 1978.
59. Henry Scott-Stokes, "Japanese Kills Himself in Plane Scandal Case," *New York Times*, February 2, 1979; Judith Miller, "Grumman: 'No Evidence' of Any Japan Payment," *New York Times*, February 9, 1979; and interview with official of a major Japanese leasing company involved in samurai lease financings, Tokyo, February 6, 1981.

Requesting "nondiscriminatory application" of the plan, U.S. officials sought the Japanese government's agreement to offer identical subsidized lease financing to U.S. airlines. Once again an intense debate over the samurai program flared within the Japanese government: the Ministry of Foreign Affairs openly joined MITI in seeking the program's expansion, while the Finance Ministry continued to lead the opposition.[60] MITI saw the offering of samurai leases to U.S. carriers as "a trump card in reducing [Japan's current-account] surplus," estimating that Japanese leasing of American planes back to American airlines could reduce the surplus by $800 million during fiscal 1979 alone.[61] Finance officials argued, however, that the artificiality of such a "U.S.-U.S. formula" as a means of generating net imports for Japanese trade statistics would be apparent to all, and that the technique would fail. The intensity of the MITI-Finance debate once again forced a decision to at least the cabinet level, in the assessment of informed observers. But this time the view of the Ministry of Finance prevailed, and in early April 1979 the Japanese government decided in principle to terminate the entire samurai program.[62]

In the end, a combination of three factors probably ensured the samurai lease plan's demise. First, the U.S. government's demand that Japan offer leases to U.S. airlines would have subjected the Japanese government to potentially enormous political embarrassment if it had continued the scheme. To deny the U.S. request while continuing to offer samurai leases to other foreign carriers would have led to irrefutable charges of Japanese trade discrimination, while inclusion of U.S. carriers would have rendered the scheme ludicrous as a means of improving Japan's trade balance, which was, after all, its primary intent. Second, the International Monetary Fund had announced stricter standards in 1977 (to take effect on January 1, 1979) for the accounting of international lease transactions in balance-of-payments statistics. The new standards, which Japanese government officials had been aware of for many months before their activation, clearly prohibited the recording of samurai-leased aircraft as net Japanese imports.[63] Finally, Japan's

60. "U.S. Seeks Exim Bank Loans for Also [sic] American Airline Companies."

61. "MITI Hopes for Bigger Aircraft Import-Leasing," *Japan Economic Journal*, March 27, 1979.

62. "Government Decides to Terminate Import-Lease of Foreign Aircraft," *Japan Economic Journal*, April 10, 1979.

63. International Monetary Fund, *Balance of Payments Manual, Fourth Edition* (Washington, D.C.: IMF, 1977), pp. 76–77.

current-account surplus was shrinking of its own accord during the early months of 1979, and thus the samurai lease scheme's raison d'être eventually ceased to exist.

The Japanese government continued to operate the samurai lease program and to account for aircraft leased under it as Japanese imports through June 1979, three months after the end of the government's prior fiscal year and six months after formal activation of the IMF's new accounting standards. A total of thirty-one aircraft valued at $990 million were leased to third countries and recorded as Japanese imports under the scheme; the bulk of these transactions actually occurred during January–June 1979.[64] To the presumed satisfaction of MITI and the Ministry of Foreign Affairs, East Asian countries that received subsidized aircraft financing under the program included Singapore, Thailand, and Papua New Guinea. In light of the Japanese banks' preference for quality debtors, however, other countries benefiting from the program's below-market rates and terms ironically included Canada, France, Great Britain, Iceland, and the Netherlands.

Although the samurai lease program does not provide a good example of Japanese foreign economic policy in either its most farsighted or candid form, it does illustrate the extensive role that Japanese banks can play in both the shaping and implementation of that policy. Vigorous yet tortuous negotiations marked the samurai lease plan's long evolution, contradicting the notion of some outsiders that consensus-building in Japan is always easy and harmonious. At the same time, the samurai case reveals an interaction between Japanese government officials and bankers in which distinctions between the public and private sectors seem muted. The government bureaucracy was clearly prepared to use its country's leading financial institutions to achieve international political and economic objectives. Highly committed corporate entrepreneurs in the financial institutions were striving to advance their own commercial interests, yet were keenly aware of the need to work with the Japanese government to do so.

Thus, even as the banks served as important tools of Japanese foreign economic policy in the program, the content reflected in large part the

64. MITI officials met with Japanese leasing company representatives on August 8, 1978, and informed them of the impending change in IMF accounting standards. Because of the change, the MITI officials asserted at the time, leasing companies would have to consummate all samurai leases before December 31, 1978, in order to receive government approval. Internal memorandum of foreign bank active in Japan, dated August 9, 1978.

commercial objectives of those banks that helped to design it. Government policy accommodated the banks' interests by providing highly attractive income for them, and the government also acquiesced in the banks' decision not to undertake politically desirable lease financing that they considered commercially unsound.

Finally, the leasing program's chronology underscores the limits that can sometimes characterize the consensus supporting foreign policy in Japan. Although all relevant government ministries, private financial institutions, and other parties normally participating in that consensus could agree on the political need to stimulate Japanese imports between 1977 and early 1979, major bickering continued among these parties throughout the period as to the efficacy of samurai leasing as a means of achieving that goal.

Lending to Secure Natural Resources Abroad

Throughout the 1970s Japanese banks joined with Japanese industrial consortia and the government to pursue a variety of overseas projects intended to develop natural resources for export back to Japan. The general pattern of government-industry-bank cooperation in these instances roughly parallels that illustrated by the Japanese government's 1979 agreement to provide Indonesia with a major fertilizer plant, discussed in chapter 5. (In that particular case, however, ASEAN member countries planned to consume most of the plant's output themselves.) In essence, this general pattern has called for private Japanese industry to execute a given overseas project, relying on the Japanese government and a syndicate of Japanese commercial banks to provide a major share of the necessary financing. Sources in the host country (normally its government but in some cases private interests) have typically provided supplementary loans or equity.

The Japanese government has used a variety of means to mobilize Japanese private financial resources to support foreign resource development ventures. One of the most effective official incentives has been MITI insurance, which has generally covered political risk on 90 percent of private Japanese financing in such instances. In addition, an important measure of implied support has consisted of the government's direct financial involvement in many projects, usually in the form of loans extended by the Japanese Export-Import Bank and, more significantly, the Overseas Economic Cooperation Fund (OECF).

One common feature of overseas resource development projects has been the involvement of both Japanese and host country equity in a joint venture company established to oversee a given project. A number of Japanese industrial interests and the Japanese government might contribute equity, but they have usually organized themselves into a single joint venture partner by forming an all-Japanese investment company. A further distinctive financial characteristic, as Terutomo Ozawa writes, has been the "use of [official Japanese] assistance as an internal aid to the overseas investment activities of Japanese industry in large-scale resource development ventures." Ozawa elaborates:

Once an overseas venture is designated as "a national project," government aid takes the form of participation by the [OECF], Japan's official aid agency, as the major stockholder of a Japanese investment company set up by the consortium involved in such a project. The Japanese government also provides low-interest loans both to the Japanese partner and to the host government from the Export-Import Bank of Japan, loans often to be used as equity capital by both parties.

This new form of economic assistance—a simultaneous aid to both the host country and Japanese [industrial] consortia . . . is now known as "the Asahan formula." This formula was originally worked out in connection with a regional development project in Indonesia. It has come to take the characteristic of being a national project entailing a political commitment of the Japanese government, and has set a precedent for Japan's resource-related ventures in other host countries.[65]

A syndicate of Japanese commercial banks normally participates in the Japanese Export-Import Bank loans. In the case of the Asahan project, Japanese commercial banks assumed 30 or 40 percent shares in all major Export-Import Bank loans, and these loans covered approximately 60 percent of the project's cost, estimated in 1978 to exceed $2 billion.[66]

65. Terutomo Ozawa, "Japan's New Resource Diplomacy: Government-Backed Group Investment," *Journal of World Trade Law,* vol. 14 (January–February 1980), pp. 3–4.

66. According to the financial plan for Asahan as restructured in 1978, the Export-Import Bank directly funded the remaining share of its own loans. The OECF provided additional soft loans and equity, and the government-owned Japan International Co-operation Agency (JICA) extended further credit jointly with Japanese commercial banks. Japanese public and private sources together accounted for 87 percent of the financing for the project, and the Indonesian government provided the remaining 13 percent. Japan External Trade Organization, *Economic Cooperation of Japan, 1979* (Tokyo: JETRO, 1980), p. 55; and interviews with officials of OECF, Tokyo, February 17 and 23, 1981.

The Japanese private sector, in many cases, has initiated Japanese participation in individual foreign resource development ventures, although MITI inevitably has become involved at an early stage in a coordinating role, on both an intra- and interproject basis. The activities of Japanese banks in the resource development area characteristically have reflected both a concern for their own financial gain and a keen sense of Japan's strategic economic interests. The official bureaucracy has typically relied on the banks to obtain and pass on information (for example, on potential resource development opportunities, project feasibility, and compatibility of simultaneous projects). The bureaucracy has also counted on the banks to join in providing financial support for those ventures deemed collectively by Japanese business, the banks, and the government to be economically sound and to advance specific government policies.

The remainder of this chapter will focus primarily on the attempt of one large Japanese bank to procure Mexican oil for Japan. A discussion of that topic, however, must be preceded by a brief consideration of one other overseas resource development effort involving Japanese banks.

Failure in Iran

The $3.2 billion petrochemical complex at Bandar Khomeini in Iran has been both the largest and most problematic Japanese overseas investment to date. Already well under way by the mid-1970s, the project markedly influenced the context in which Japanese interests began to seek access to Mexican oil in 1978.

Based on feasibility studies begun in the late 1960s, the Iranian project was designed to provide Japan with long-term supplies of liquid petroleum gas and a range of petrochemical feedstocks for industrial use. (Iran and other countries were to benefit from the project's output as well.) Initial financing for the project came principally through loans from the Export-Import Bank of Japan, the Iranian Ministry of Finance, and a syndicate of private Japanese banks led by the Industrial Bank of Japan (which also did substantial feasibility work), Mitsui Bank, and the Bank of Tokyo. These three private banks alone had lent an estimated $200 million to the project as of 1978.[67] Under a complicated financial arrangement, the bulk of the Japanese-sourced loans was guaranteed by

67. International Business Information, Inc., *Japan's Economic Interests in Iran and the Implications of the Current Crisis* (Tokyo: IBI, 1979), pp. 30, 39.

the principal Japanese coinvestors in the project, led by Mitsui and Co. and composed predominantly of members of the Mitsui industrial group. These firms acquired MITI export insurance generally covering 90 percent of their exposure.[68] (Whether Mitsui and other Japanese firms could legitimately file insurance claims, however, if they voluntarily withdrew from the Iranian project became a point of legal and political contention in Tokyo during 1980–82.)

Following the overthrow of the shah's regime during the early months of 1979 and the disruption of construction work at Bandar Khomeini in March of that year, the Japanese government granted the project "national" status and made additional investments in it through the OECF. (The project was 85 percent completed by this time.) But even this major new commitment proved insufficient to enable the project to overcome the mounting obstacles it faced. The Iranian-Iraqi war, which began in September 1980, led to repeated bombing of the construction site, and many observers subsequently concluded that even if the complex were completed it could never be profitably operated.[69] Although it seems probable that Japanese interests will suffer a major loss at Bandar Khomeini, perhaps approaching $1 billion, continued Japanese participation in the petrochemical complex, in an effort to complete it, appeared increasingly likely during 1982–83.[70]

By late 1978 both the Japanese public and private sectors had already begun to focus intently on the Mitsui group's overexposed and deteriorating position in Iran. To many influential Japanese, the faltering Iranian project underscored anew the need to diversify Japan's natural resource

68. Ibid., pp. 33, 37–40. See also Stephen Bronte, "Tokyo: Exeunt, Pursued by Ayatollah," *Euromoney* (February 1979), p. 143. For investments made after the beginning of the Iranian revolution, the percentage of insurance coverage was somewhat lower.

69. "Mitsui Head Says Japanese May Pull out from Iran-Japan Project," *Japan Economic Journal*, August 18, 1981.

70. As of mid-1983, Mitsui reported a 49 percent equity interest in Iran Chemical Development Co. (ICDC), the Japanese joint-venture partner in the project. The ICDC, in turn, owned 50 percent of Iran-Japan Petrochemical Co. (IJPC), the Iranian joint-venture company charged with carrying out the project; the remainder of the IJPC was owned by Iran's national oil company. Significantly, according to a preliminary Japanese-Iranian agreement reached during 1983, Iran would bear all additional costs of the project until completion, rescheduled for around 1986. The arrangement would gradually increase Iran's equity share in the project to at least 70 percent, and Mitsui officials hoped that Iranian equity might yet reach 100 percent. As of mid-1983 the petrochemical complex continued to be located in the middle of a war zone. Equity information provided by finance section, Mitsui and Co., Tokyo, July 1983.

supplies away from the volatile Middle East. The project also drew attention to the need to seek a wider sharing of risks in future overseas projects. Resource development ventures should be pursued jointly by several industrial groups rather than by one group alone, and whenever possible, more host- and even third-country participation should be elicited. Finally, the Mitsui experience in Iran caused many Japanese to question the wisdom of making such sizable direct investments in foreign countries to develop natural resources.

Mixed Results in Mexico

Late in 1978, amid the growing controversy over Japan's investment experience in Iran, the Industrial Bank of Japan began to advance a highly innovative proposal to obtain long-term oil supplies from Mexico. The primary mover behind the scheme was the bank's president, Kisaburo Ikeura. In some quarters he became "almost a national hero" as a consequence of his efforts to procure Mexican oil for Japan;[71] to others, however, the plan was an ill-advised, even naive, attempt by one Japanese bank to promote its own commercial interests.

Although the IBJ and Pemex, the Mexican state oil company, may have discussed the feasibility of some form of loan-for-oil "swap" as early as the summer of 1978, the main impetus behind the IBJ's Mexican oil plan probably derived from a visit by Ikeura to Mexico in October 1978.[72] "An influential Mexican" proposed to Ikeura during that visit the possibility of swapping Japanese "economic cooperation" for stable, long-term supplies of Mexican crude.[73] Apparently the Mexican suggestion was carefully timed and planned; although the oil swap scheme soon became uniquely associated with Ikeura's bank, at least one other major Japanese bank has claimed privately that Mexican officials approached

71. Stephen Bronte, "Ikeura's International Way with IBJ," *Euromoney* (August 1980), p. 37.
72. The talks during the summer of 1978 apparently considered a three-way arrangement whereby the IBJ would lend money to Mexico, Mexico would sell crude to the United States (which had an existing pipeline connection with Mexico), and the United States would provide Alaskan crude to Japan. However, this three-way concept was abandoned, perhaps before the end of 1978, because of U.S. legal barriers and the heavy quality and hence limited attractiveness to Japan of Alaskan crude.
73. "IBJ and Traders Seek Big Oil Deal with Mexico," *Japan Economic Journal,* December 19, 1978.

it with the same offer (which it declined) at approximately the same time.[74]

The general Mexican proposal, as phrased by one Japanese banker, was: "We have 100,000 barrels per day (bpd) to offer, if you can offer attractive terms and conditions."[75] (Despite the enormous interest that this proposal generated in Japan, 100,000 bpd represented less than 2 percent of Japanese imported oil requirements at the time.) As of late 1978, the discussions between the IBJ and Mexican authorities centered on roughly $500 million of Japanese assistance to build a 300-kilometer pipeline from Mexico's rich southeast oil fields to the Pacific harbor town of Salina Cruz and to expand the port facilities there. In return for this assistance, Mexico would agree to sell 100,000 bpd of oil to Japan on a long-term basis, shipping the crude through the new facilities at Salina Cruz.[76]

The IBJ saw the plan as a means of securing for Japan fixed supplies of crude from a potentially major Pacific Basin oil producer for as long as ten years. From a Japanese strategic perspective, the attractiveness of obtaining oil from Mexico was enhanced by the country's location, its non-OPEC status, and reports that Mexican oil reserves might surpass all but those of Saudi Arabia.[77] The IBJ also had more immediate commercial objectives in mind, however. At minimum, the swap would permit the IBJ to become the agent and lead-manager for a loan of approximately $500 million to a major international borrower considered an attractive risk at the time. Moreover, it soon became evident that the IBJ hoped to use the swap to become involved in Japan's oil-importing business, an activity in which no Japanese bank had previously engaged.

Under Japan's Petroleum Industry Law, enforced by MITI, the importing of oil into Japan is limited principally to oil refining companies. In addition, the Mitsubishi Corporation has been allowed to import oil because it engaged in the business before the law's implementation in 1962, and other trading companies have also been permitted to do so

74. Interview with senior official of a Japanese commercial bank, Tokyo, February 25, 1981.

75. Ibid.

76. "IBJ and Traders Seek Big Oil Deal with Mexico"; and "Gov't Plans to Reach Accord with Mexico on Oil Import," *Japan Economic Journal*, June 26, 1979. During this early phase of the discussion, it is possible that the IBJ in fact sought an agreement covering 200,000 bpd.

77. "Gov't Plans to Reach Accord with Mexico on Oil Import."

only if domestic refining firms entrust such activity to them.[78] Well aware
of the special status of the Mitsubishi Corporation in particular and of
other trading companies in Japan's oil-importing business, Ikeura approached the presidents of both Mitsubishi and Mitsui sometime between
October and mid-December 1978, suggesting their companies' involvement in the swap plan. Both presidents accepted Ikeura's invitation.[79]

Although Ikeura's precise intentions are not known, several apparent
reasons existed for drawing two of Japan's largest trading companies
into the plan. As of December 1978 Mitsubishi was the only Japanese
firm to have concluded even a modest oil purchase contract with Pemex.
By asking both the Mitsubishi and Mitsui trading companies, but no
other parties, to join in the scheme, the IBJ could promote a monopoly
over Japanese importation of Mexican crude. The IBJ plan accounted
for all of the Mexican oil that would have been available to Japan for
some time. Furthermore, the IBJ could possibly enter the importing
business indirectly by establishing an overseas oil-importing affiliate,
for instance, one jointly owned with Mitsubishi, Mitsui, and Pemex.[80]
In extending invitations to the trading companies, Ikeura and the IBJ
could also create broader private-sector sponsorship for the swap plan,
thereby increasing the likelihood of MITI support, and also involve in
the plan companies that could actually orchestrate the pipeline and
harbor construction work sought by the Mexicans.

Initial reaction to the IBJ plan from parties other than the bank's
chosen partners was extremely negative. Japanese oil refiners balked at
the higher total price (including shipping charges) they would have to
pay for Mexican crude relative to Middle Eastern crude. In addition,
both the Japanese government and the oil refining industry felt "that it
was unwise . . . that IBJ and the two traders went out to make their
proposal to Mexico without informing others that would be affected by
the Mexican oil," for example, the oil refiners that the proposal effectively cut out of the market.[81] Furthermore, MITI officials, while pleased

78. "MITI Moves Further to Tighten Crude Oil Check," *Japan Economic Journal,*
January 1, 1980.

79. According to one account, "Ikeura is said to have suggested such major economic
cooperation to the presidents of the two general traders, and the three then are reported
to have agreed jointly to realize the plan. . . . [Ikeura stated,] 'Other interests, such as
traders, most likely will be allowed to join the project as soon as it begins to harden.' "
"IBJ and Traders Seek Big Oil Deal with Mexico."

80. Interview with officials of MITI, Tokyo, February 24, 1981; written comments
by senior official of a Japanese commercial bank on Mexican oil plan, June 1982.

81. " 'Advance Payment' for Mexico Oil Is Proposed by IBJ and Two Traders,"
Japan Economic Journal, June 12, 1979.

with the IBJ's efforts to make a loan in order to secure oil supplies for Japan, were not happy at all with the IBJ's attempt to enter into the oil-importing business, even indirectly.[82]

A senior Japanese banker identified other reasons behind MITI's concern and also elaborated the reactions of the Japanese refineries and trading companies:

[MITI's] Agency of Natural Resources and Energy, which holds sole administrative authority over the petroleum industry, was furious by the fact that IBJ was developing a newly conceived structure to import crude oil without any prior consultation with them. They were worried that such a tied loan . . . (in this case under unusually soft terms) for the purchase of crude oil . . . would have an overwhelming ripple on other oil exporting countries such as Indonesia and China, if not on the rich Middle East oil countries. They considered that it could create a problem for Japan of how to face and avert subsequent requests for similar financing from other sources.

The refineries, the actual users of the oil, were surprised at the fact that negotiations for crude oil import should be undertaken without their involvement and under the leadership of a bank. . . .

The reaction of the [trading] companies not directly involved was various, but even Mitsui and Mitsubishi were faced with the contradiction of hoping to obtain monopolistic privileges and wishing not to hurt their relationships with the refineries.[83]

The Ministry of Finance, upon learning of the plan somewhat later than MITI, expressed still more objections, based on entirely different reasons and interests. Another apparent facet of the IBJ's strategy was to fund the $500 million Mexican loan with cheap, fixed-rate dollars obtained from official Japanese reserves, which, as previously noted, were embarrassingly large in late 1978 and early 1979. In light of the Finance Ministry's commitment at the time to provide dollar reserves to fund MITI's aircraft lease program, the IBJ's funding calculations were not altogether unreasonable. But the Finance Ministry had never been comfortable with the use of surplus official reserves in the lease scheme, and it was reluctant in early 1979 to relinquish still further reserves to subsidize a separate commercial loan to Mexico (in effect, at Japanese taxpayers' expense).[84]

In the face of opposition from all these sources, the Mexican oil plan lay dormant through the early months of 1979. The revolution in Iran

82. Interview with officials of MITI, Tokyo, February 24, 1981.

83. Written comments on Mexican oil plan by senior official of a Japanese commercial bank, June 1982.

84. Interview with senior official of a Japanese commercial bank, Tokyo, February 25, 1981.

(then Japan's third largest oil supplier) took place during this period, however, and construction work at the Japanese-sponsored petrochemical project at Bandar Khomeini ground to a halt. By late spring, Japanese refiners' resistance to Mexican crude on the basis of its higher price dissipated. In the space of a few months, Mexican oil had achieved a new aura of attractiveness.[85]

Under these changed circumstances, the IBJ attempted to revive its loan-for-oil plan late in the second quarter of 1979. The plan, as now structured, approximated a barter arrangement, with an IBJ-led syndicate granting Mexico a long-term credit and receiving repayment in the form of contracted oil shipments over a multiyear period. (The IBJ, Mitsubishi Corporation, and Mitsui and Co. would sell the oil they acquired to Japanese refiners, whose cash payments would repay the loan syndicate.) IBJ officials envisioned that the amount of oil initially covered by the swap would still be 100,000 bpd, but they hoped to raise this amount to 250,000 bpd within a short period.[86]

By this time, however, Japanese refiners were eager to acquire Mexican oil on their own. Implicitly seeking to block any attempt by the IBJ to control the market, the top executives of six major Japanese-owned oil refining companies, led by Masami Ishida of Idemitsu Kosan Co., agreed in late May to set up a joint council to "serve as a window" for Mexican crude oil imports. Ishida, who was also chairman of the influential Petroleum Association of Japan, quickly obtained informal agreement to the council plan from both MITI Minister Masumi Esaki and the chairman of Japan's Federation of Economic Organizations (*Keidanren*). In mid-June, still another Japanese group, led by Nippon Oil Co., announced its intention of seeking to import large quantities of Mexican oil on a long-term contract basis. With three consortia all fighting to win Pemex's favor simultaneously, the *Japan Economic Journal* could predict conservatively that "the race for Mexican crude oil is likely to grow complex and fierce."[87]

No group feared the consequences of intense competition among Japanese firms to secure Mexican oil more than officials of MITI. While

85. "Nippon Oil Envisages Securing Mexican Oil through Caltex," *Japan Economic Journal,* June 19, 1979.

86. " 'Advance Payment' for Mexico Oil Is Proposed by IBJ and Two Traders."

87. "Six Oil Firms Will Form Council to Promote Importation of Mexico Oil," *Japan Economic Journal,* May 29, 1979; and "Nippon Oil Envisages Securing Mexican Oil through Caltex."

MITI continued to oppose any attempt by the IBJ to become actively involved in the oil-importing business or to corner the Mexican oil trade with Japan, the ministry was also concerned that excessive competition among Japanese oil importers would lead to unnecessary increases in the price that Japan would have to pay for Mexican crude. Beginning perhaps as early as late 1978, MITI officials had encouraged cooperation between proponents of the IBJ plan and Japanese oil refiners in the hope that a united negotiating position would emerge within Japan's private sector. By late June 1979, however, no such united front appeared likely to evolve of its own accord, and Japanese interest in Mexican oil was reaching unprecedented levels.

In late June the Japanese government intervened directly in the negotiating process between the Japanese private sector and Mexican authorities, substituting a plan to import Mexican oil on a government-to-government basis. In shedding its official role of silent observer, the Japanese government, and specifically MITI, adopted essentially the same negotiating objectives previously advanced by the IBJ and other private Japanese firms: the procurement of an initial import volume of 100,000 bpd and a long-term contract (approximately ten years). Ideally, MITI also wanted the import volume to rise to an average of 200,000 bpd to 300,000 bpd over the entire contract period.[88] As the MITI plan developed, it called for a consortium (consisting eventually of twenty-four refiners, nine trading companies, and three banks, including the IBJ) to establish a joint venture company, tentatively named the Mexican Crude Oil Import Co. (MEP), that would deal exclusively in the Mexican oil trade for Japan once government-to-government negotiations produced a contract.[89] The MITI plan also adopted the basic loan-for-oil concept that the IBJ had originally championed. The concept now evolved into a $500 million financing involving both the Japanese Export-Import Bank and a syndicate of private Japanese banks, with the IBJ serving as agent and as lead-manager. However, the barter aspects of the arrangement that had surfaced in the Japanese press in early June quietly disappeared, probably reflecting the evolving preferences of both Mexican and Japanese authorities. Any Japanese loans to Mexico and Mexican oil sales to Japan would now constitute parallel but separate transactions.

88. "Gov't Plans to Reach Accord with Mexico on Oil Import."
89. "New Japan-Mexico Ties Loom: With Oil Deal as Starting Point," *Japan Economic Journal*, October 16, 1979.

Finally in possession of a unified negotiating stance and prepared to offer a $500 million combined public- and private-sector loan as a "sweetener," Foreign Minister Sunao Sonoda and MITI Minister Esaki visited Mexico City during the week of August 13, 1979, in an effort to negotiate a long-term Japanese-Mexican oil contract. The pressure on the two Japanese ministers was enormous; as one senior Japanese banker commented wryly afterwards, their mission was to "get 100,000 barrels per day or commit hara-kiri." The same banker also recounted that Esaki and Sonoda "had a hell of a time" accomplishing their task.[90] Based on preliminary discussions, their expectations upon arriving in Mexico City were that their $500 million loan offer would be sufficient to ensure 100,000 bpd of Mexican oil for Japan over a ten-year period and that the oil flow could increase to as much as 300,000 bpd within three years if Japan offered Mexico further economic cooperation. During their meetings in the Mexican capital, however, Esaki and Sonoda apparently learned that the contemplated loan would procure a flow of only 50,000 bpd, and that supplementary economic assistance would have to be provided forthwith, as well as the loan, in order to obtain the desired 100,000 bpd.[91]

Under these adverse conditions, the Japanese ministers finally agreed to grant Mexico a package that included:

1. A $500 million, ten-year loan denominated in dollars and priced at a highly favorable fixed rate of 8 percent. According to a Japanese press report, the loan would finance "development of Pemex's petroleum-related facilities"; more specifically, according to sources in the IBJ, the loan was intended to cover the harbor and associated pipeline construction at Salina Cruz that the original IBJ loan of 1978 would have financed.[92] Japan's Export-Import Bank would provide 70 percent of the total amount, while a syndicate of twenty-two private Japanese banks, led by the IBJ, would provide the remaining 30 percent ($150 million).

90. Interview with senior official of a Japanese commercial bank, Tokyo, February 25, 1981.

91. "Setting up of Joint Company Is Eyed for Import of Mexico Oil," *Japan Economic Journal,* August 14, 1979; interview with senior official of a Japanese commercial bank, Tokyo, February 25, 1981.

92. "Mexican Gov't Agrees to Export Oil to Japan under 10-Yr Accord," *Japan Economic Journal,* August 21, 1979; and interview with officials of the Industrial Bank of Japan, Tokyo, February 24, 1981.

At the time, the market rate for similar fixed-rate dollar loans was approximately 10 percent.[93]

2. A soft loan of approximately $150 million, extended by the OECF and denominated in yen. Terms and conditions for this loan, intended to finance part of Mexico's massive Sicartsa steel mill project at Lazaro Cardenas on the Pacific coast, included a concessionary interest rate of "about 4 percent" and a twenty-five-year repayment term.[94]

In return for these *two* credits, Mexico at last consented to export 100,000 barrels of crude oil daily to Japan (through the MEP consortium) under a ten-year contract.

The immediate reaction in Japan to the deal was favorable. Japanese banks, which particularly benefited from the loan's complicated financial structure,[95] appeared generally pleased with the arrangement, even if some competitors of the IBJ possibly resented its achievement of a public relations coup through the loan.

Over the longer run, however, the results of the loan-for-oil exchange must be regarded as mixed from a Japanese perspective. On the positive side, the IBJ loan plan did enhance considerably the attractiveness to Mexico of selling oil to Japan. The $500 million financing that was actually concluded was also one of a series of major transactions that enabled Japan to emerge as the Mexican public sector's chief source of

93. Interview with senior official of a Japanese commercial bank, Tokyo, February 25, 1981.

94. "Government Decides to Extend Loan to Mexico out of OECF," *Japan Economic Journal,* September 4, 1979; and Alan Riding, "Japan Fails to Increase Mexico Oil," *New York Times,* May 5, 1980.

95. The loan's convoluted structure illustrates the striking ability of the Japanese public and private sectors to share (and disperse) the commercial risk associated with large projects deemed in the national interest. Both the Export-Import Bank of Japan and the private Japanese banking syndicate advanced their share of funds in yen to MEP, which then on-lent to Pemex in dollars. Japanese banks, including the Export-Import Bank, thus acquired exposure primarily to Japanese oil refiners through the arrangement, not to Pemex. Private Japanese banks received from MEP the equivalent of Japan's long-term prime rate on their portion of the credit, fixed at the time of disbursement (between 8 and 9 percent), while the Export-Import Bank received a fixed interest rate of 6.25 percent from MEP. MEP (that is, primarily the Japanese refiners) was forced to absorb any foreign exchange risk associated with the credit, but presumably could pass on any costs it incurred to Japanese consumers in the form of higher retail prices for oil. Finally, it is probable that MITI insurance covered most of the MEP loan to Mexico. Interview with officials of the Industrial Bank of Japan, Tokyo, February 24, 1981.

foreign credit during 1979.[96] Such heavy Japanese lending to the Mexican government and its state-owned corporations necessarily generated a degree of official Mexican good will toward Japan at a time when Japan, for highly pragmatic reasons, sought closer ties with Mexico at all levels. Japanese banks additionally obtained a somewhat improved position in the Mexican market, which they assiduously sought at the time. At least until the advent of the Mexican financial crisis late in the summer of 1982, the banks probably accrued reasonable profits from the overall deal.

On the negative side, however, the agreement that Esaki and Sonoda thought they had concluded with Mexican authorities in August 1979 did not produce a rapid increase in Mexican oil sales to Japan. Those sales rose to a mere 22,000 bpd by April 1980, and did not reach 100,000 bpd until March 1981.[97] Throughout the 1979–80 period, the Japanese found the Mexicans to be unexpectedly shrewd negotiators, continuously raising their demands for financial and economic assistance while offering shrinking increments of oil in return. The Mexicans did not find the Japanese to be easy business partners, either. As one Mexican diplomat observed shortly after Prime Minister Masayoshi Ohira's generally unsuccessful oil procurement mission to Mexico City in May 1980, "Japan is always just about to get deeply involved here, but execution of the project [for instance, the Sicartsa steel mill] always seems to be delayed. We want to tie them down before releasing any more oil."[98]

The IBJ's efforts to secure Mexican oil during 1978–79 constitute a unique episode in the general involvement of major Japanese banks in developing and procuring foreign natural resources for the Japanese domestic market. With the growing turmoil in Iran during the period, Japanese interests (including MITI, various trading companies, and banks) became increasingly concerned about obtaining oil supplies outside of the Middle East and reducing the amount of direct single-project investment in developing countries required to obtain natural resources. Kisaburo Ikeura's loan-for-oil swap was a plan tailored to Japan's needs at the moment. A factor certainly impeding realization of the plan, however, was the IBJ's attempt to use it to obtain extraordinary

96. Alan Riding, "Ohira Seeking More Oil from Mexico," *New York Times,* May 3, 1980.

97. Ibid.; and "Mexico Will Get All-Out Help," *Japan Economic Journal,* April 7, 1981.

98. Riding, "Japan Fails to Increase Mexico Oil."

commercial gain at the expense of other well-organized Japanese corporate interests (for instance, the Japanese refining companies, whose bureaucratic patron is MITI), and possibly also at the expense of the Ministry of Finance.

The original IBJ loan-for-oil concept influenced greatly the final package that MITI Minister Esaki and Foreign Minister Sonoda offered the Mexicans in August 1979. After implicitly helping to define the Japanese government's negotiating position, the IBJ played almost as prominent a role in implementing the final agreement. At least until the summer of 1982, the IBJ found commercially attractive business in financings associated with the Japanese acquisition of Mexican oil, even if the level of profits and market position were not what it may have hoped for. At the same time, the entrepreneurial zeal, combined with an awareness of national priorities, of the IBJ (and other Japanese firms) helped Japan to achieve a limited diversification of its oil supplies.

Conclusion

Japan's leading banks, although concerned primarily with commercial gain, have functioned internationally in support of broader Japanese strategic objectives and in response to official influence. The banks have of necessity recognized the dominant role of the state in the Japanese financial system, and they have deferred to official wishes as a matter of sound business judgment. Japan's international financial bureaucracy, for its part, has seen the banks' tremendous competitive drive as a force that, if properly harnessed and directed, could be especially useful in helping to carry out official policies. At the same time, the bureaucracy has remained consistently sensitive to the commercial advancement of the banks.

Domestic preferences and institutional relationships have combined with Japan's extreme dependence on distant raw materials sources and markets to promote foreign economic policy to the forefront of Japanese foreign policy. Under these circumstances, Japan's financial community, through its selective pursuit of international business, has been able to play a particularly useful role in advancing the foreign policy objectives of the state.

The relationship between the banks and the country's foreign policy apparatus has relied heavily on informal understandings. In the process of building bank-government consensus, individual banks and bureaucratic factions have often competed with one another to further their own narrow causes. Bank-government disagreements on specific policy issues have tended to occur within a framework of accord on broader political, economic, and commercial goals, however. In the end, a value structure and economic ideology supportive of harmonious business-government relations, combined with highly regularized communication, personal trust, and a convergence of self-interests, have facilitated efforts by senior Japanese bankers and government officials to reach agreements.

PART THREE

The United States

CHAPTER SEVEN

Inferences and Conclusions

AMONG the world's democracies, the Federal Republic of Germany and Japan trail only the United States in the size of their economies and the volume of their international trade. These two economic giants are now also playing increasingly prominent roles in international politics, although this is in part an unavoidable consequence of their newfound economic stature.

Germany and Japan have concurrently emerged as two of the world's leading possessors of international banking resources. Drawing on the strength of their national currencies and the remarkable domestic and international expansion of their countries' economies throughout the postwar period, large commercial banks in Germany and Japan have joined a handful of other world-class banking institutions capable of offering a broad range of financial services on a global scale. All these leading banks, regardless of country of origin, have pursued vastly expanded cross-border financial relations, often with sovereign entities, and in so doing have created both problems and opportunities for their home governments. Especially in light of the growing entanglement between the commercial banking pursuits and foreign policy concerns of most industrial countries, Germany and Japan offer provocative examples of the coordination that can exist between a nation's financial expertise and political power in the international sphere.

The close links between commercial banking and foreign policy prevailing in Germany differ markedly from those found in Japan. Bank-government relations in Germany have been influenced heavily by the existence of a strong liberal banking tradition and a historically centralized, activist public sector. Amid the thousands of private institutions operating in Germany's relatively laissez-faire financial environment, a

179

very few large banks have emerged as preeminent in German finance. These big banks, with their extensive ties to German industry and throughout the broader economy, have been uniquely positioned to assist the German government on selected financial, economic, and industrial policy issues. Major power centers in their own right, these banks have even overseen much of their own regulation. Significantly, in keeping with the credit-based, bank-dominated character of the financial system, Germany's industrial growth and adjustment strategies over much of the last eighty years have reflected a process of negotiated change, in which both banks and government have played a decisive role.[1]

The predominantly export-led nature of German economic growth has helped create a natural convergence of interests among German big banks, industry, and government on international matters. Formal consultations between Germany's foreign policy bureaucracy and big banks need rarely occur, given their general agreement on the major goals of German foreign policy, including foreign economic policy, and on the utility of employing German-sourced international finance to advance their country's interests. Still, the government has developed a range of highly effective policy instruments for influencing the international behavior of German banks in cases where they have not accommodated official policy objectives entirely of their own accord. These instruments include the provision of Hermes trade credit guarantees (usually granted or withheld on economic and commercial grounds, but sometimes on political grounds as well); the involvement of the Kreditanstalt für Wiederaufbau (KfW), a government-owned financial institution, in syndicated financings as a means of supplementing and encouraging private bank participation; and the Ministry of Finance's direct guaranteeing of "untied" credits by commercial banks, such as a large balance-of-payments financing to Portugal in 1978. In cases involving high political stakes where these indirect means have proved insufficient, or their employment potentially too embarrassing, the government has also resorted to direct negotiations with Germany's core banking elite in an effort to effect officially desired outcomes. One of the most prominent recent examples was the government's prodding of German banks to extend a DM 1.2 billion term loan to Poland during 1980.

1. John Zysman, *Governments, Markets, and Growth: Financial Systems and the Politics of Industrial Change* (Cornell University Press, 1983), pp. 251–65, 286–87.

The German authorities' influence over German international banking does know absolute limits. The banks, committed to protecting their own commercial interests, have become increasingly tough negotiators vis-à-vis the German government in recent years, as illustrated by communications between the Deutsche Bank and the German Finance Ministry during February 1980 over Turkey's financial problems, and by German banks' public refusal to lend further sums to Poland without a government guarantee in December 1981.[2] But the prevalent pattern of interaction between large German banks and their government on matters of mutual international concern has been one of quiet consensus, enhanced by official sensitivity to the banks' financial interests and the banks' responsiveness to government incentives and suasion.

Japan, in keeping with the credit-based, price-administered character of its financial system, has followed a state-led pattern of industrial adjustment.[3] In contrast to Germany's laissez-faire banking principles, the Japanese banking community has traditionally accepted the right of government to lead and interfere in the operations of financial markets. Japan's official financial authorities have shaped the country's banking system and affected the allocation of its resources through a broad range of signals, incentives, legally mandated supervision, and administrative guidance. Partly as a result of the authorities' conscious structural policy for the financial system, no "Big Three" banks have come to dominate Japanese finance. Rather, the thirteen city banks at the core of Japan's commercial banking system constitute a group small enough to facilitate coordination with the government on policy issues, yet sufficiently large to preclude the emergence of one or two banks as centers of concentrated financial and economic power that might rival the official bureaucracy. The largest private Japanese banks wield enormous influence within the Japanese economy, but that influence falls far short of the domestic economic leverage exercised by Germany's premier banking houses. Compared with the largest German banks, those of Japan appear more responsive to official bureaucratic leadership in guiding the allocation of their financial resources, while considerably less prone to assume responsibility for coordinating domestic economic growth, even on a basis of implicitly delegated authority from the government.

2. John Tagliabue, "German Banks Seek Bonn Pledge on Poland," *New York Times*, December 21, 1981.

3. Zysman, *Governments, Markets, and Growth*, pp. 234–51, 286–87.

Japanese bank-government relations, as well as those in Germany, have benefited from a natural convergence of interests. Indigenous traits of each country—such as a homogeneous people and a set of coherent foreign economic policy objectives actively supported by the domestic financial community—have helped to produce this convergence. For example, banks, government, and industry in both countries have rallied together to support the cause of exports and to help develop foreign natural resources required by the home economy. But in Japan, unlike Germany, the links between commercial banking and foreign policy have operated across the full spectrum of international banking transactions. Although both the German and the Japanese governments have employed signals and incentives to influence the allocation of financial resources abroad by their countries' private sectors, the Japanese authorities have clearly done so more systematically and more vigorously. Instruments at their disposal have included the Japanese Export-Import Bank's highly focused lending policies, the Ministry of International Trade and Industry's $75 billion export insurance program, the ability to designate overseas "national projects," and the occasional provision of official foreign currency reserves to fund commercial transactions. Beyond such indirect means, Japan's financial authorities have also drawn on both legislatively mandated and assumed supervisory powers to affect Japanese commercial international banking patterns. Administrative guidance, through its encouragement of an extensive, ongoing dialogue between Japanese international bankers and bureaucrats, has greatly enhanced the potential for coordination between these two groups. Compared with Germany's financial authorities, those in Japan possess far more detailed information about the banks' international financial dealings, pending as well as consummated. This comprehensive information base has further contributed to the ability of the Ministry of Finance to harness Japanese commercial international banking resources to support official policy objectives.

In Japan, "the economy is not administered but the government seeks to act to affect the terms of competition in order to create the outcomes it favors. In essence, the state is another powerful economic player shaping market development. . . . Finance is a vital instrument . . . in the government's repertoire of domestic policies."[4] Compared with their

4. Ibid., pp. 250–51.

counterparts in Germany, Japan's financial authorities, drawing on unique social and institutional traditions, have developed a wider and more potent set of mechanisms for influencing the commercial behavior of banks, both domestically and internationally. Furthermore, Japan's financial bureaucrats, unhindered by the German government's public adherence to such principles as economic liberalism and the separation of politics from international commerce,[5] have demonstrated a much greater willingness to employ such mechanisms. Direct coordination and consultation between large banks and their government on matters of foreign policy have occurred periodically in Germany, but have been commonplace in Japan.

As in Germany, the ability of Japan's government to use indigenously sourced international banking as a tool of foreign policy has experienced definite limits. Although more difficult to observe, the existence of these limits in Japan can be discerned, for instance, in the refusal of Japanese banks to guarantee samurai aircraft leases to poorer developing countries, contrary to government preferences. The process of achieving coordination between internationally active Japanese banks and the bureaucracy has invariably reflected vigorous tugging and pulling among banks and various ministries, each eager to advance its own viewpoint or interests; in the end, a compromise solution has usually emerged. This process of compromise has been aided by acceptance within both the Japanese public and private sectors of the need for cooperation and the need on occasion to pool or socialize risks associated with large financial undertakings deemed to advance specific policy objectives.

In many ways, the interaction of commercial banking and foreign policy interests in Germany bears only limited resemblance to the same interaction in Japan. But these two relationships acquire pronounced similarities when juxtaposed with their counterpart in the United States. A history of adversarial bank-government dealings has limited the extent to which large American commercial banks communicate with the central government on foreign policy–related issues. Compared with those in the United States, the highly sophisticated relations that have evolved

5. See, for example, Peter Hermes, "Foreign Policy and Foreign Trade Interests," *Aussenpolitik (German Foreign Affairs Review)*, vol. 27, no. 3 (1976), pp. 247–56; and Peter J. Katzenstein, "Conclusion: Domestic Structures and Strategies of Foreign Economic Policy," in Katzenstein, ed., *Between Power and Plenty: Foreign Economic Policies of Advanced Industrial States* (University of Wisconsin Press, 1978), p. 316.

Table 7-1. *Structure of the U.S. Banking System, Year-End 1982*

Category	Number of organizations	Total assets (billions of dollars)	Percentage of system assets
Commercial banks	15,165	2,071.0[a]	51.6
Top ten banks	10	378.8[b]	9.4
Top twenty banks	20	519.8[b]	12.9
Members of Federal Reserve System	5,619	1,398.8	34.8
National	4,579	1,070.0	26.6
State member	1,040	328.8	8.2
Nonmember insured banks	8,821	462.4	11.5
Noninsured banks	525	2.1[c]	0.1
Foreign banks operating branches and agencies	200	207.7	5.2
Government-affiliated financial institutions	11	443.4	11.0
Export-Import Bank of the United States[d]	1	17.3	0.4
Federally sponsored credit agencies[e]	6	247.6	6.2
Federally sponsored mortgage pools[f]	4	178.5	4.4
Private nonbank financial institutions[g]	24,226	1,502.6	37.4
Savings and loan associations	3,833	706.0	17.6
Mutual savings banks	418	174.2	4.3
Credit unions	16,435[h]	88.6	2.2
Finance companies	2,775[i]	229.6	5.7
Real estate investment trusts	120[j]	7.7	0.2
Open-end investment companies (mutual funds)	486[j]	89.9	2.2
Money market mutual funds	159[j]	206.6	5.1
Total	39,402	4,017.0	100.0

Sources: Board of Governors of the Federal Reserve System, *Federal Reserve Bulletin*, vol. 69 (April 1983), pp. A74–79; Board of Governors, *69th Annual Report, 1982*, pp. 238–39; Board of Governors, "Sector Statements of Financial Assets and Liabilities, Year-End Outstandings, 1971–82" (computerized data, May 31, 1983); Board of Governors, "Structure Data for U.S. Offices of Foreign Banks by Country of Foreign Bank" (computer run, May 3, 1983); Board of Governors, *Introduction to Flow of Funds* (The Board, June 1980), pp. 34–35; National Association of Real Estate Investment Trusts, *REIT Fact Book, 1981* (Washington, D.C.: The Association, 1982), p. 8; Investment Company Institute, *1982 Mutual Fund Fact Book* (Washington, D.C.: The Institute, 1982), pp. 51, 74; National Credit Union Administration, "1982 Year End Statistics" (Washington, D.C.: NCUA, 1983), pp. 1, 27; and the staffs of the Board of Governors, Federal Deposit Insurance Corporation, and United States League of Savings Associations. Figures are rounded.

a. Excludes assets of U.S. banks' branches in foreign countries and in U.S. territories and possessions, subsidiaries in foreign countries, and all offices of Edge Act and Agreement corporations wherever located. The data include assets of international banking facilities (IBFs) established by U.S. commercial banks; however, the assets of IBFs established by Edge Act and Agreement subsidiaries of U.S. commercial banks are excluded.

b. Total domestic assets of these banks as reported to the Federal Reserve. Figures do not reflect consolidated assets of bank holding companies.

c. Includes both banks of deposit and nondeposit trust companies; probably somewhat understates total assets of all noninsured banks.

d. As of September 30, 1982.

e. As defined by the Flow of Funds Section of the Board of Governors of the Federal Reserve System. Data reflect total financial assets only.

f. As defined by the Flow of Funds Section.

g. As defined by the Flow of Funds Section, except that life insurance companies, private pension funds, state and local government employee retirement funds, other insurance companies, and security brokers and dealers are excluded. The figures represent total financial assets for all institutional categories except money market mutual funds, where total assets are measured.

h. Includes federal credit unions and federally insured state credit unions, except for corporate central credit unions.

i. As of mid-1980.

j. As of year-end 1981.

between commercial banking and foreign policy in both Germany and Japan appear less antagonistic, more coordinated, and more consistently oriented toward the achievement of mutually accepted goals.

The Growth of U.S. International Banking

The American banking system is characterized by an extremely large number of operating institutions, combined with a noteworthy concentration of assets in a few banks (see table 7-1). The commercial component of the system, excluding branches of foreign banks, consisted of 14,965 banks with total domestic assets of $1,863 billion as of year-end 1982. On that same date, the commercial component of the German banking system included 182 domestic banks (possessing roughly $229 billion in domestic assets), while only 86 domestic commercial banks operated in Japan (with assets of $1,159 billion).

The ten largest American banks accounted for 18 percent of the U.S. commercial banking sector's domestic assets at year-end 1982, and the twenty largest American banks possessed 25 percent of these assets. These shares must be regarded as significant in absolute terms, although they remain well below the proportion of similar assets held by either Germany's Big Three banks (39 percent) or Japan's thirteen city banks (50 percent). These U.S. shares also fall considerably short of the percentage of commercial banking assets controlled by the leading banks in most other major industrial countries.[6] In terms of their share of domestic deposits, the largest German, Japanese, and American banks occupy the same relative positions within their respective banking systems. The German and Japanese systems thus exhibited somewhat higher levels of deposit concentration at year-end 1982, with the Big Three banks claiming roughly 40 percent of commercial banking deposits in Germany and the thirteen city banks accounting for 55 percent of similar deposits in Japan.[7] By comparison, the ten largest American banks held 15 percent of their own system's commercial banking deposits

6. C. Stewart Goddin and Steven J. Weiss, *U.S. Banks' Loss of Global Standing* (Washington, D.C.: U.S. Office of the Comptroller of the Currency, 1980), p. 26.

7. Derived from Deutsche Bundesbank, *Monthly Report*, vol. 35 (March 1983), pp. 34–35; Bank of Japan, *Economic Statistics Annual, 1982* (Bank of Japan, 1983), pp. 52, 58; and Bank of Japan, *Economic Statistics Monthly*, no. 430 (January 1983), pp. 49–50. The percentage for Germany is based on borrowing by banks as well as deposits with them, as Bundesbank statistics do not distinguish between these two liability items.

at year-end 1982.[8] In summary, despite the existence of roughly 15,000 commercial banks in the United States, a small number of them have achieved positions of clear prominence within the domestic commercial banking sector.

Although documentary evidence exists of a U.S. banking presence in foreign financial markets as early as the late nineteenth century, national banks were not allowed to establish foreign branches until passage of the Federal Reserve Act in 1913.[9] Even then, the growth of American international banking remained unspectacular for another five decades. The most important expansion of American international banking to date occurred during the decade following 1965, as shown in table 7-2; although only 13 Federal Reserve member banks operated a total of 211 foreign branches in 1965, 126 such banks operated 762 branches abroad ten years later. By the late 1970s nearly 140 American banks operated foreign branches, more than five times as many banks as from any other country.[10] At the same time, however, as few as twelve banks have conducted 75 percent of U.S.-sourced international banking activity in recent years.[11] The very largest American banks have thus accounted for an even greater share of the nation's international banking capability than their strong position within the domestic commercial banking sector might suggest.

Multiple factors, led by restrictive changes in the U.S. domestic bank regulatory environment, prompted American banks to expand their overseas networks beginning in the mid-1960s. These factors were summarized cogently in a 1979 congressional study:

As the supply of dollars in the Eurocurrency market increased, so did the demand. Instead of borrowing in the United States, European subsidiaries of

8. The one hundred largest American banks (as opposed to bank holding companies) held 37 percent of deposits on the same date. (On a consolidated holding company basis, this figure would probably approach 50 percent.) Based on an analysis of Federal Reserve call data for the one hundred largest commercial banks in the United States, year-end 1982 (Continental Illinois National Bank and Trust Co. of Chicago); and Board of Governors of the Federal Reserve System, *Federal Reserve Bulletin*, vol. 69 (April 1983), pp. A74–A77.

9. Christopher M. Korth, "The Evolving Role of U.S. Banks in International Finance," *Bankers Magazine* (Boston), vol. 163 (July–August 1980), p. 68.

10. Diane Page and Neal M. Soss, *Some Evidence on Transnational Banking Structure* (Washington, D.C.: U.S. Office of the Comptroller of the Currency, 1980), p. 26.

11. *Financial Institutions and the Nation's Economy: Compendium of Papers Prepared for the FINE Study*, Committee Print, House Committee on Banking, Currency and Housing, 94 Cong. 2 sess. (Government Printing Office, 1976), bk. 2, pt. 4, p. 885.

Table 7-2. *Foreign Branches of U.S. Banks, Selected Years, 1950–82*

Year	U.S. banks with foreign branches	Number of foreign branches	Total assets of foreign branches (billions of dollars)	
			Gross	Net[a]
1950	7	95	. . .	. . .
1960	8	131	3.5	. . .
1965	13	211	8.9	. . .
1967	15	295	15.7	. . .
1969	53	460	41.1	. . .
1970	79	532	52.6	. . .
1971	91	577	67.1	55.1
1972	107	627	77.4	72.1
1973	125	699	118.0	108.8
1974	125	732	140.5	127.3
1975	126	762	162.7	145.3
1976	126	723	193.9	174.5
1977	130	730	227.9	205.0
1978	137	761	257.6	232.0
1979	139	789	312.9	279.5
1980	159	787	343.5	310.5
1981	159	841	390.9	343.3
1982	162	900	388.5	341.3

Sources: Staff, Board of Governors of the Federal Reserve System, Washington, D.C. (1960–82 data); Peter Merrill Associates for the American Bankers Association, *The Future Development of U.S. Banking Organizations Abroad* (Washington, D.C.: ABA, 1981), p. 6 (1950 data). Data cover foreign branches of Federal Reserve member banks only.

a. Net of claims on other foreign branches of the same bank.

U.S. multinational corporations found it convenient (and often cheaper) to augment their capital through local borrowings in Eurodollars. Policies adopted by the U.S. Government also contributed to this trend. One major factor was Regulation Q of the Federal Reserve System [imposed in 1969] which limits rates of interest paid on [domestic] time deposits. This regulation led investors to seek dollar denominated assets abroad for their higher interest rates. . . .

A series of other U.S. government controls fostered the growth of the dollar portion of the Eurocurrency market. . . . Although the purpose of these controls was to reduce U.S. payments imbalances by decreasing dollar flows abroad, their net effect was to turn those seeking dollars to sources outside of the United States [including foreign branches of American banks].[12]

Other major factors contributing to the growth in the banks' international

12. *The Operations of U.S. Banks in the International Capital Markets*, Committee Print 98-8, House Committee on Banking, Finance and Urban Affairs, 96 Cong. 1 sess. (GPO, 1979), p. 8.

networks that began in the mid-1960s included the expansion of U.S. corporations' overseas operations (and financing needs) and the growth of U.S. foreign trade.[13]

Just as the number of American banks running foreign branches increased dramatically in the years following 1965, so did the volume of assets those branches controlled. These assets rose by a factor of over eighteen between 1965 and 1975, from $9 billion to $163 billion, and then more than doubled again to reach $390 billion during 1981–82 (see table 7-2). The oil price hikes of the 1970s contributed still further to the growing supply of dollars held outside the United States, and the associated petrodollar recycling process, whereby oil-importing countries borrowed heavily in the Eurocurrency market, became a principal cause of the tremendous growth in American banks' foreign branch assets from 1973 onward.

Bank-Government Relations

The existence of approximately 15,000 U.S.-chartered commercial banks, and the presence of over 160 of them in overseas markets as of year-end 1982, are both testament to a tradition of opposition in the United States to major concentrations of financial power. This tradition has proved instrumental in shaping American bank-government relations, even though a few large American banks have achieved positions of great strength in both domestic and international financial markets.

From at least the time of Andrew Jackson's veto of the recharter of the second Bank of the United States in 1832, the history of American bank-government relations has reflected both a popular reluctance to see banking power centered in any one city or region, and similar opposition to any highly centralized supervisory structure for overseeing banks.[14] The first of these two factors was a major cause of the demise

13. For a more comprehensive summary of the origins of the Euromarket (a phenomenon closely related to the expansion of American banks' international branch networks), see Marilyn J. Seiber, *Developing Countries in the Eurocurrency Market: A Debt Overhang Escalator,* U.S. Department of Commerce, Bureau of International Economic Policy and Research (Department of Commerce, 1977), pp. 6–9.

14. Still earlier evidence of antibanking sentiment in the United States can be found in a pervasive agrarian distrust of banks and paper money during the 1780s and 1790s, and in the writings of founding fathers such as Thomas Jefferson and John Adams. For a definitive history of early American bank-government relations, see Bray Hammond, *Banks and Politics in America: From the Revolution to the Civil War* (Princeton University Press, 1957). See pp. 111 and 352 regarding Jackson's veto.

of the second Bank of the United States, a hybrid commercial-central bank authorized to operate interstate branches and headquartered in the country's then-principal financial center, Philadelphia.[15] A combination of the two factors nearly blocked establishment of a national banking system in the 1860s, and both factors remain at least partly responsible for the assortment of overlapping bank supervisory authorities that exists today, including the Comptroller of the Currency, the Federal Reserve System, the Federal Deposit Insurance Corporation, and fifty state supervisory agencies. In a more general sense, the traditional American suspicion of both banking power and centralized control over banks has reflected an American aversion to concentrations of power in either the public or private sectors.

At the same time, this popular American suspicion of large commercial banks has long worked against any movement to bring about a close dialogue between the government and those banks. In the early 1900s, prominent public figures as diverse as William Jennings Bryan and Carter Glass, a congressman and later senator whose influence on the American banking system has known few rivals in this century, attacked the concentration of financial power on Wall Street and its perceived control of the nation's credit resources. Two decades later, when the banking system's failure to withstand stress helped to aggravate the Great Depression, the public blamed commercial banks in general, and big banks especially, for the country's disastrous economic downturn.[16]

A number of key pieces of federal legislation, reflecting widespread distrust of big banks and the effectiveness of "the astonishingly influential small-bank lobby,"[17] imposed broad restrictions on the ability of big banks to grow throughout the postwar period. The Glass-Steagall Act (1933) prohibited commercial banks from engaging in most securities-underwriting business. (Japan has an analogous law, the Securities and Exchange Law, which was modeled during the postwar occupation after Glass-Steagall; Germany's universal banking practice, however,

15. Hammond has written of the forces that brought about the collapse of the second Bank in ibid., pp. 329, 354.

16. Ross M. Robertson, *The Comptroller and Bank Supervision: A Historical Appraisal* (McCall Printing Company for the U.S. Office of the Comptroller of the Currency, 1968), pp. 88–89, 118. Robertson, writing of the economic collapse of 1929–33, has observed, "A large part of the electorate, not realizing that it was the duty of the central bank to provide liquidity for the commercial banks, laid the entire blame on commercial bankers. In the whole history of our country, no single group had been so bitterly castigated."

17. Ibid., p. 132.

calls for no such separation of commercial banking and securities underwriting.) Similarly, the 1927 McFadden Act, as amended in 1933, effectively checked American banks from expanding their branch networks across state boundaries, and at least twenty-nine states maintained substantial additional restrictions on branching within their borders as of 1981.[18] (In contrast, the large banks comprising the cores of both the German and Japanese commercial banking systems have enjoyed nationwide banking privileges.) The McFadden Act, in combination with the individual states' additional restrictions on branch banking, has been a primary reason for the continued existence of so many thousands of commercial banks.[19] In a fundamental sense, both McFadden and Glass-Steagall have helped to decentralize power within the American private financial sector.

One of the most salient features of modern U.S. bank-government relations is their fragmented, arm's-length character. Those relations have been significantly weakened by the structure of the financial system itself, the framework of American banking supervision, and an ethic of separateness in U.S. business-government relations in general. Each of these three factors, because of its enormous impact on overall U.S. bank-government relations and hence indirectly on those relations in the international sphere, deserves somewhat more attention.

The American financial system, as noted earlier, can be classified as capital market–oriented and price-competitive.[20] Because the system is

18. See Eisuke Sakakibara, Robert Feldman, and Yuzo Harada, "Japanese Financial System in Comparative Perspective," prepared as part of the Program on U.S.-Japan Relations of the Center for International Affairs, Harvard University, 1981, app. 1. Section 3(d) of the Bank Holding Company Act of 1956, known as the Douglas amendment, also prohibited multibank holding companies from acquiring a bank in another state, unless that state's law affirmatively provided for such entry.

19. For a comprehensive discussion of U.S. branch banking policy, see Report of the President (Carter), *Geographic Restrictions on Commercial Banking in the United States* (Washington, D.C.: Department of the Treasury, 1981). The report's conclusions, presented as the official view of the Carter administration, included the following: "That fragmentation [characteristic of the U.S. financial system] is a product of neither historic accident nor unencumbered market forces; rather, today's balkanized financial system is largely a result of deeply held beliefs which have been codified in Federal policy. . . . [The federal statutory framework] is an outgrowth of long-standing fear of an undue concentration of financial power in the hands of banking institutions." Ibid., p. 1.

20. The following discussion draws on Zysman's model of the U.S. financial system, developed as part of his comparative analysis of bank-government relations on issues of industrial policy in several industrialized countries. See Zysman, *Governments, Markets, and Growth*, pp. 266–81.

not based primarily on bank credit, as are the systems of Germany and Japan, banks collectively do not possess the same degree of financial influence that they hold in the other two countries. Furthermore, in the United States, corporate access to the securities markets, the predominant financial markets, "is arranged for the most part by nonbank intermediaries such as brokerage houses—a fact that limits company dependence on banks for external funds."[21] Within the commercial banking component of the U.S. financial system, power is still further diffused as a result of the extraordinarily large number of operating institutions.

In similar fashion, the government's ability to influence or coordinate with banks is fragmented and dispersed. Official intervention in the financial system to regulate banks or to execute monetary policy has, by and large, not disrupted the system's market-driven character. In this regard, the intricate and overlapping regulatory structure has helped "to insulate the system from executive interference and discretion."[22] Distinctive features of U.S. banking supervision in this context include the two-tiered structure of federal and state regulation, and the division of federal oversight responsibilities among the Federal Reserve, the Comptroller of the Currency, and the Federal Deposit Insurance Corporation. Coordination among all of these regulatory bodies has not always come easily.

A final influence on U.S. bank-government relations has been the tradition of distance in dealings between business and government, reinforced by an American penchant for litigation and the judicial process. Factors contributing to this tradition have included the formal and legalistic character of U.S. bank regulation; the long-standing popular distrust of concentrations of financial power in this country; and a concomitant emphasis on transparency in relationships between the government and private parties, including banks. Recent manifestations of this doctrine of transparency have included the passage of various "sunshine" and freedom-of-information statutes. The forcing of bank-government dealings into the light of day may complicate them for bankers and government officials alike, limiting the willingness of either

21. Ibid., p. 270. Again, this arrangement, mandated by the Glass-Steagall Act, contrasts markedly with the intermediary function of universal banks in German capital markets. Japanese banks do not control corporate access to Japan's securities markets, but those markets only recently emerged as an important source of corporate funding in Japan.

22. Ibid., p. 271.

side to become involved. Most bankers, given the nature of their work, tend to place a premium on confidentiality in business relationships. Even from government's perspective, there may be certain decisions or arrangements that may be legal but not politically acceptable if publicized.[23] Observations by John Zysman on the impact of legal constraints and litigation on business-state relations bear relevance because of their special applicability to bank-government relations:

Finally, there exists a wide range of explicit constraints on what government can do with business and on the arrangements firms may make between themselves. These limits can be lifted by particular legislation, but this process is also time-consuming and generates a great deal of publicity. . . . Significantly, the system of trial by legal combat gives an adversarial character to business-state relations, since litigation—using the courts to block the opponent—is a readily available alternative to negotiation.[24]

The resulting U.S. pattern of bank-government exchanges, conducted under the scrutiny of the public eye and in the shadow of the courts, contrasts markedly with the German reliance on achieving quiet agreement between banks and government, often out of public view. The U.S. pattern differs still more emphatically from the Japanese approach, which has encouraged an exclusive, continuous dialogue between the financial authorities and bankers. One of the key official instruments for achieving bank-government coordination in Japan, administrative guidance, frequently may not even result in written documentation of bank-government agreements, let alone public announcement of them.

In summary, a variety of quintessentially American characteristics has combined to weaken the ability of the country's large commercial banks and central government to coordinate with one another. The United States' multicentered financial system "was shaped by politics to fit the preferred economic system. A role for financial institutions in industrial management [in America] was explicitly blocked by legislation aimed at keeping business and banks apart. The result is a system of company-led industrial change."[25] In a broader sense, at issue is the accepted role of the federal government in the American economy. Government in the United States has been charged essentially with regulating the private sector in an effort to ensure that the country's market economy functions with maximum efficiency. The market mech-

23. Ibid., p. 268.
24. Ibid., pp. 268–69.
25. Ibid., p. 281.

anism itself has served as the principal distributor of goods and services and as the principal determinant of the course of the country's economic growth. Observations that Andrew Shonfield offered on the American system in the mid-1960s still hold validity:

Among the Americans there is a general commitment to the view, shared by both political parties, of the natural predominance of private enterprise in the economic sphere and of the subordinate role of public initiative in any situation other than a manifest national emergency.

. . . Yet that does not mean that in practice private enterprise has it entirely its own way. Indeed, coming from Europe and observing the behaviour of people in industry and commerce, one may well be struck by the way in which it seems to be accepted that it is part of the lot of businessmen to be pushed around intermittently by one Federal agency or another.[26]

The U.S. government has approached the U.S. commercial banking community far more as a sector requiring regulation than as a source of input for policy formulation or a tool for policy implementation. On a comparative basis, in fact, American banks appear subject to many more restrictions than Germany's liberal financial regulatory structure imposes on German banks; in a similar vein, *statutory* banking regulations in the United States are more extensive in both scope and stringency than in Japan.[27]

American International Banking and Foreign Policy

The links between U.S. commercial international banking and U.S. foreign policy have evolved within the context of a multicentered, relatively weak relationship between the executive and the financial system. Nonetheless, some degree of dialogue has unquestionably existed for decades between the U.S. financial community and government on foreign policy issues.

In the 1920s, during the relatively early days of American international banking, leaders of the New York financial establishment, such as

26. Andrew Shonfield, *Modern Capitalism: The Changing Balance of Public and Private Power* (Oxford University Press for the Royal Institute of International Affairs, 1965), pp. 298–99.

27. Sakakibara, Feldman, and Harada, "Japanese Financial System in Comparative Perspective," p. 26. It should be recalled that Japanese bank supervision has relied primarily on informal, operational understandings rather than written rules; furthermore, the evolution of these understandings has required an ongoing dialogue between Japanese banks and the government's highly centralized bureaucracy.

Thomas W. Lamont, Paul M. Warburg, and Alexander Hemphill, helped
to found the Council on Foreign Relations, a private institution that has
subsequently served as a forum for off-the-record foreign policy discussions among American businessmen, academics, government officials,
bankers, and others.[28] Similarly, the Dawes Plan of 1924, intended to
stabilize the faltering economies of Europe, constitutes an early but
clear example of the ability of American foreign policy officials and
bankers to work together in an effort to advance complementary interests. Since the end of World War II, the movement of a few prominent
persons between New York City's investment and commercial banks,
in particular, and high-ranking international posts in government has
continued to facilitate communication between bankers and foreign
policy officials.[29] Beginning in the early 1970s, David Rockefeller of the
Chase Manhattan Bank came to symbolize the ability of the American
financial community to influence U.S. foreign policy, an influence
popularly believed to be great both in the United States and abroad. Past
and present senior U.S. officials, including George P. Shultz, Henry
Kissinger, and Alexander Haig, have also served at one time or another
on the directing boards or international advisory councils of major
American commercial banks.[30]

Still, the essential features of today's dialogue between America's
international bankers and foreign policy officials continue to reflect the
arm's-length nature of U.S. bank-government relations. Interviews
conducted with senior American bankers and U.S. foreign policy officials
in late 1982 suggest that this dialogue has retained an episodic quality: it
has tended to develop on an ad hoc basis, after crises have already
begun. Furthermore, with each new crisis, often a set of different players
gathers to begin the necessary bank-government exchanges. Observed

28. Laurence H. Shoup and William Minter, *Imperial Brain Trust: The Council on
Foreign Relations and United States Foreign Policy* (New York: Monthly Review Press,
1977), pp. 14–16, 105, 108.

29. Americans who have moved between the worlds of private finance and foreign
policy during this period include John J. McCloy, W. Averell Harriman, Robert V.
Roosa, George W. Ball, Peter G. Peterson, and Robert D. Hormats. It should be noted,
however, that this talent flow has primarily involved New York's investment and private
banking houses, rather than the large commercial banks that have become the leaders
in U.S. international finance.

30. The appointment of A. W. Clausen, president and chief executive officer of the
Bank of America, to head the World Bank in 1980 provides additional, although probably
less direct, evidence of the links between American foreign policy and commercial
banking.

one official: "The players must be known to one another, so you can sit down without [having to conduct] an extensive feeling out. . . . You can't start from scratch each time, and we do."[31] This situation contrasts markedly with that in either Germany or Japan, where key international bankers and government officials frequently know one another and appear to meet informally and regularly.

The U.S. dialogue has also tended to involve a handful of key U.S. banks, but by no means all those with significant international operations. One example of the exclusion of several major American banks is contained in the bank-government exchanges that apparently preceded the U.S. freezing of Iranian assets in November 1979. According to an article in *Foreign Policy,* Citibank chairman Walter Wriston was not consulted on the freeze, but he indicated "there was a conversation" with the Treasury Department. However, the White House announcement came as a surprise for certain other major banks. "The most negative reaction came from banks such as Chemical or Security Pacific National Bank which, unlike Chase or Citibank, had large loans to Iran but few or no offsetting deposits."[32]

Another factor hampering an effective U.S. bank-government dialogue on international policy issues has been the emergence of regional banks as more aggressive international lenders, beginning in the late 1970s. As a result, international lending activity has become increasingly dispersed across the country. By December 1982 regional and smaller U.S. banks, generally headquartered outside New York City, accounted for 42 percent of all U.S. commercial bank lending abroad, up from approximately 32 percent at year-end 1977.[33] While the nine largest

31. Interview with senior official of the Federal Reserve Bank of New York, New York City, November 29, 1982.

32. Karin Lissakers, "Money and Manipulation," *Foreign Policy,* no. 44 (Fall 1981), p. 114. Citibank was almost certainly not the only large bank to benefit from conversations with U.S. officials before the freeze. A top officer at another of the nation's five largest banks indicated in an interview that his institution was "not aware" of the impending freeze, but that top management had known that Federal Reserve lawyers were making inquiries of the bank's legal staff concerning "[account] blocking techniques." The chief financial officer at yet another of the nation's five largest banks strongly hinted that his institution had been involved in information exchanges with the government before the freeze. (He added, however: "The phrase that 'the thing was put together by the banks and the government' is absolute sheer nonsense.") Interviews with senior officials of two major U.S. commercial banks, New York City, November 29, 1982.

33. Surprisingly, even during the highly charged atmosphere that prevailed in international financial markets during much of the second half of 1982, U.S. regional and smaller banks continued to expand their international lending, although the focus

money center banks still conducted the remaining 58 percent of U.S. commercial bank lending abroad, even these nine banks' headquarters are spread among New York, Chicago, and San Francisco.[34] Although New York will probably always remain the international financial hub of the United States, a dialogue between U.S. foreign policy officials and a select group of New York bankers, to the extent that even this has irregularly occurred, may no longer be sufficient.

There has also been a frequent absence of coordination among the federal offices and agencies concerned with one aspect or another of American international banking. As noted in a 1979 congressional study:

Just as the supervision of domestic banks is divided [at the federal level] among the three financial regulatory agencies, the supervision and examination of the foreign operations of U.S. banks also is decentralized. The Federal Reserve, for example, is responsible for the supervision of the overseas branches and banking subsidiaries of state member banks, the Edge Act investments of all member banks, and the foreign activities of bank holding companies. The Comptroller of the Currency is responsible for the supervision of the branches and banking subsidiaries of national banks while the Federal Deposit Insurance Corporation is responsible for the foreign operations of insured state nonmember banks. . . . The supervision of the foreign operations of U.S. banks tends to be as fragmented as it is domestically. . . .[35]

Only in 1979, and after considerable congressional pressure, did the three occasionally rivalrous supervisory agencies finally implement a uniform examination procedure for evaluating and commenting on "country risk" factors associated with overseas lending.[36] Other prob-

---

of that activity changed. While these banks shifted loans out of problem countries, particularly in Latin America, they increased their cross-border lending to other industrialized countries by nearly 9 percent and to the non-oil-exporting developing countries of Asia by more than 14 percent during this six-month period. Federal Financial Institutions Examination Council, "Statistical Release: Country Exposure Lending Survey, December 1982" (FFIEC, June 1, 1983), and FFIEC, "Statistical Release: Country Exposure Lending Survey, June 1982" (FFIEC, December 6, 1982). Based on amounts owed U.S. banks by foreign borrowers after adjustments for guarantees and external borrowing. The data cover only cross-border and nonlocal currency spending. Loan percentages for year-end 1977 based on data provided by International Research Department, Federal Reserve Bank of New York.

34. As of December 1982, the nine largest U.S. banks (as opposed to bank holding companies) were: (a) in New York: Citibank, Chase Manhattan Bank, Manufacturers Hanover Trust Co., Morgan Guaranty Trust Co., Chemical Bank, and Bankers Trust Co.; (b) in Chicago: Continental Illinois National Bank and Trust Co. and First National Bank of Chicago; and (c) in San Francisco: Bank of America.

35. *The Operations of U.S. Banks in the International Capital Markets,* House Committee Print, pp. 28–30.

36. Ibid. Announcement of the new procedure occurred on November 8, 1978.

lems of intragovernmental coordination go well beyond issues of banking supervision, however. At least some federal agencies have appeared to believe that they could successfully dissociate themselves from one another's actions to influence the international activities of banks. For instance, one senior Federal Reserve official, acknowledging that the U.S. government's approach to international banking problems has been "decentralized," suggested that the State Department has been able and willing to "urge" banks to lend to selected countries (Zaire, for example) because desk officers and others at State could explain the relevant foreign policy considerations to bankers and simultaneously avoid the "commitments" that bank supervisory officials would be undertaking if they made the same statements.[37] The Federal Reserve official, opining that the State Department and less frequently the Treasury may have "gone too far" in the direction of "arm twisting" banks in recent years, went on to point out the potential for conflict among federal agencies if the banks responded to such pressure by making loans that later became problematic. (A complicated and closely related dilemma has to do with what obligations the U.S. government implicitly assumes when the regulators themselves urge American banks to make certain international loans.)[38]

Some U.S. banks can distinguish among the federal government's many voices on international banking issues, in the view of the same Federal Reserve official. The most sophisticated banks, in effect, know to weigh the State Department's counsel on desired international lending patterns differently from the Federal Reserve's counsel. Yet if some banks do know how to pick and choose among the multiple signals emanating from Washington, other large and internationally active U.S.

37. Interview with a senior staff official, Board of Governors of the Federal Reserve System, Washington, D.C., December 23, 1982.

38. Top officials of the Federal Reserve Board, for example, reportedly urged U.S. banks to expand their loans to financially troubled developing countries in late 1982 and early 1983. The Fed officials' action came at a time of growing concern that an upsurge in developing country defaults could trigger a major international financial crisis. According to one published account, the Fed informed commercial banks during this period that they would not be criticized if they renewed their loans to Mexico or, in fact, if they increased them by 7 percent. Conversely, Fed officials apparently indicated that banks failing to go along with such increases would find their Mexican loans coming under closer scrutiny by bank examiners. To some experienced observers, the Fed was implicitly assuming part of the banks' credit risk. Critics of the Fed's approach argued that it could encourage still riskier international lending in the future. See H. Erich Heinemann, "A Fed Push on Foreign Loans Seen," *New York Times,* January 15, 1983.

banks almost certainly do not. Moreover, such a "decentralized" governmental approach to international banking issues fails (in fact, does not even attempt) to establish coherent U.S. policies.

Further evidence of the difficulty of achieving U.S. interagency coordination in the face of international banking problems can be found in the government's handling of the Polish debt crisis of early 1982, when some U.S. officials wanted to press U.S. commercial banks into declaring Poland in default. In late March, many weeks into the crisis, confusion still existed on both Capitol Hill (for example, among key members and staff of the House Foreign Affairs Subcommittee on Europe and the Middle East) and within at least some major American banks as to which offices in the executive branch could even provide accurate information on U.S. policy.[39]

The fact that U.S. foreign policy, including international financial policy, is rarely enunciated with one voice poses special problems for U.S. bank-government relations. In the early 1980s, one could hear different, and at times conflicting, policy positions on various international banking issues expressed by the under secretary of the treasury for monetary affairs, the chairman of the Federal Reserve Board, the under secretary of state for political affairs, senior staff members of the National Security Council, and a host of congressmen, among other Washington policymakers. As the vice-chairman of one large New York bank commented diplomatically, "[Our] government is the reconciliation of conflicting points of view, and Washington speaks with many voices." An official of the New York Federal Reserve Bank phrased the problem more pointedly: "In a system where so many [government officials] feel they can sound off in public, bankers would be scared to death to act."[40]

If some bankers have become frustrated in their efforts to determine what "U.S. policy" is at a given point in time, many bankers have become equally confused and inhibited in their dealings with the government by the fluctuating nature of U.S. policies over time. (This quality stands in noticeable contrast to the long-term consistency evident in

39. Discussion with member and staff of House Subcommittee on Europe and the Middle East, Washington, D.C., March 24, 1982; phone discussion with senior vice-president responsible for Polish debt problems at a major U.S. commercial bank, Chicago, March 22, 1982.

40. Interview with vice-chairman of a major U.S. commercial bank, New York City, November 29, 1982; interview with senior official of the Federal Reserve Bank of New York, New York City, November 29, 1982.

both German and Japanese foreign policies.) One example of the problems that this lack of policy continuity can pose for U.S. bank-government relations concerns U.S. bank lending to Yugoslavia in the wake of growing financial difficulties there during 1982. The State Department, weighing foreign policy considerations, encouraged large U.S. banks to continue to lend to Yugoslavia at least once and possibly several times during the year.[41] Yet, as the senior official responsible for European lending at one large New York bank observed, his institution could be "responsive to pressure only to the extent it made sense from [the viewpoint of] the economic interests of the bank." Furthermore, his bank had sensed little support from the State Department three years earlier on the issue of commercial lending to Yugoslavia, and whether the U.S. government would offer continued support for the Belgrade regime three years hence was "hard to tell."[42] At least this one major New York bank appears to have found potentially transitory U.S. foreign policy positions a difficult basis for long-term lending. U.S. banks, knowing they cannot count on consistent U.S. policies toward at least some strategic but potentially volatile regions of the world, are likely to pursue their commercial lending programs accordingly.

Still another factor compounding U.S. bank-government communication problems on matters of international policy has been a pervasive lack of firsthand knowledge of international banking within the U.S. government. As described by one State Department official responsible for monitoring global financial developments:

Washington, D.C., as a place is extremely ignorant of banking per se. . . . Banking is viewed as very esoteric. The State Department doesn't really know what [bankers] do in terms of foreign policy implications. . . . The senior levels within the government are very concerned, but they don't understand the systemic ramifications. . . . [When you] talk about international banking here in the State Department, eyes glaze over.[43]

Along similar lines, an influential and highly regarded New York banker observed in late 1982, "People in the State Department and Congress talk about the Eurodollar market and don't know what it is."[44] Another

41. Clyde H. Farnsworth, "Washington Watch: Infighting on Europe Loans," *New York Times*, May 10, 1982; S. Karene Witcher, "U.S. Preparing Rescue Package for Yugoslavia," *Wall Street Journal*, December 7, 1982.
42. Interview with senior official of a major U.S. commercial bank, New York City, November 30, 1982.
43. Interview, Department of State, Washington, D.C., November 22, 1982.
44. Interview with senior official of a major U.S. commercial bank, New York City, November 29, 1982.

senior official at one of New York's most internationally active banks added, "Many of the agencies [in the U.S. government] don't have a glimmer of what we're doing. On the recent issue of [establishing special problem-loan] reserves for sovereign risk lending, the regulators' comments reflected their experience: [domestic] commercial and corporate lending and Chapter 11 bankruptcy issues," but not knowledge of international banking.[45]

Important exceptions do exist to these general observations. During late 1982, a number of bankers and government officials consistently identified the same few individuals in the State Department, the Federal Reserve Bank of New York, and the Treasury as highly competent on international banking issues. At the same time, many senior American bankers seemed to hold especially high hopes for Secretary of State George P. Shultz as a government official capable of bridging the gulf between the country's international financial community and foreign policy bureaucracy. But the available evidence still supports the assertion that communication between the U.S. private banking community and the foreign policy machinery of government is hampered by a severe shortage of "hands-on" international banking expertise in the official bureaucracy.

U.S. government agencies rarely, if ever, appear to convey outright instructions to American banks on how to behave internationally. The conspicuous exceptions to this generalization, combined with the intensely negative reactions of many senior American bankers at the very suggestion of government guidance, go far to prove the rule. For example, when a number of American bankers felt that the State Department was attempting to prod their institutions into lending more money to Yugoslavia late in the spring of 1982, the openly critical reactions of certain U.S. Treasury officials as well as of some of the banks involved suggest that the episode was highly unusual. Federal Reserve pressure on banks to continue lending to developing countries during late 1982 and 1983 also appears to constitute an unusual, partial exception to the rule.

45. This banker gave the further impression that his own institution was not especially concerned about most Washington officials' limited familiarity with international banking matters. "Not only do they not look to us; we don't look to them when we get into a jam. . . . We develop our own processes. We [look after] our own interests." The official did suggest, however, that a greater understanding of international finance in Washington might lead to more informed, or simply less, international banking legislation. Interview with senior official of a major U.S. commercial bank, New York City, November 30, 1982.

During interviews conducted in late 1982, senior executives at several of the nation's largest banks indicated a general unwillingness to cooperate with *any* attempt by the U.S. government to instruct them on where and when to lend internationally. For instance, a high-ranking official at one of the nation's very largest banks stated, "If any senior officer of [our bank] got a call from a U.S. government official [urging us to make a loan], we would almost certainly do exactly the opposite." Averred a high official at another of the country's largest banks, "I don't know of any [U.S. commercial bank] lending that was done [explicitly] in support of U.S. foreign policy, and [if we were asked to do so], we wouldn't have lent."[46]

Still, the most experienced international banks in the United States do exhibit a sensitivity to U.S. foreign policy, albeit primarily for commercial reasons, and primarily from a distance. American bankers regularly seem to try to guess which foreign countries carry an official "U.S. umbrella," that is, which countries are a better commercial risk than they might otherwise appear because the U.S. government is willing to ensure their continued economic and financial health. One commercial banker, speaking in late 1982, cited Egypt as an example of a country that some American banks, including his own, were considerably more inclined to lend to because of the magnitude of U.S. government support that it had received over a period of years.[47] A top official at another bank stated that its management had proceeded with enormous loans to Mexico in part because of "the U.S.'s particular interest" in maintaining a secure southern border and in obtaining Mexican oil; this bank, widely regarded as one of New York's best managed, had "weighed the U.S. consideration there all along." From the vantage point of the New York Fed, American banks seem to "make assumptions, including false assumptions, all the time about the [U.S.] political umbrella." Significantly, a senior official at one of New York's three largest banks described his own institution's knowledge of U.S. foreign policy as that of "the prudent man reading the tea leaves." He elaborated that the

46. The Yugoslavian incident is discussed in Farnsworth, "Washington Watch: Infighting on Europe Loans"; quotations are from interviews with senior officials of two major U.S. commercial banks, New York City, November 29–30, 1982.

47. Conversely, the same banker identified Angola as a country "where we'd be much more cautious" because of its strained relations with Washington; he added, however, that his bank would exercise some degree of caution there anyway because it is "relatively unstable." Interview with senior official of a major U.S. commercial bank, New York City, November 30, 1982.

bank's principal source of information on U.S. foreign policy was newspapers.[48]

Recently, some American banks have also sought to divine U.S. foreign policy trends out of fear of being affected by distinctions that foreign governments may increasingly make between loans from friendly countries and loans from unfriendly ones. This concern was fueled, in particular, by the compromised position in which U.S. banks found themselves during the Iranian hostage crisis of 1979–81, and by the special problems that British banks incurred as a result of the Argentine-British conflict over the Falkland Islands in 1982.[49] In addition, officials of some American banks believe that Poland may have singled them out for discriminatory treatment in early 1982 by rolling U.S. commercial loans into reschedulings while repaying certain German credits upon maturity.[50]

In conclusion, occasional interchanges between prominent American bankers and the country's leading foreign policy makers have rarely produced bank-government coordination similar to that found in Germany or Japan in terms of breadth, depth, or sophistication. The bank-government dialogue in the United States on international policy issues has necessarily taken place within a broader context of adversarial bank-government relations. While the dialogue has episodically involved a small number of American international bankers and U.S. foreign policy officials, there is little evidence to suggest that there are frequent, ongoing exchanges. Nor has the dialogue included all major American banks actively engaged in international finance. Banks in both Germany and Japan, in contrast, have appeared more responsive to incentives, signals, and other deliberate official actions intended to influence their international behavior. *Overt* bank-government coordination, combined with coordination among the banks themselves, has also been more common in Germany and Japan, on international as well as domestic matters. In both Germany and Japan, but not in the United States, the

48. Interviews with senior official of a major U.S. commercial bank, New York City, November 29, 1982; senior official of the Federal Reserve Bank of New York, New York City, November 29, 1982; and senior official of a major U.S. commercial bank, New York City, November 30, 1982.

49. With regard to the Falklands conflict, see, for example, Robert A. Bennett, "U.S. Bankers Fear Slow Repayments," *New York Times*, May 1, 1982.

50. Interview with senior official of a major U.S. commercial bank, New York City, November 30, 1982.

executive has effectively maintained an ongoing dialogue with a national banking cartel.

Implications for U.S. Foreign Policy and Bank-Government Relations

If American international bankers as well as foreign policy officials are to comprehend adequately the international environment in which they must function, an improved awareness of other industrial countries' bank-government relations in the international sphere is essential. This does not imply, however, that the United States should or even could attempt to copy them. The complex patterns of interaction that tend to evolve between foreign policy and commercial banking are indigenous to each country, reflecting its underlying political and economic structures, financial customs, degree of reliance on trade, and relative position in the world, among other considerations. By the same token, the U.S. emphasis on distance between banks and government has deep roots in American economic and political traditions. If even marginal changes in the links between American commercial banking and foreign policy are to succeed, they must accommodate existing American values and institutional relationships.

Although it would be dangerous, even futile, to try to graft German or Japanese bank-government institutional arrangements onto the U.S. political economy, the coordination between commercial banking and foreign policy in these two other countries does carry several broad implications for the United States.

Benefits and Drawbacks of the Current Dialogue

First, that coordination exposes a fundamental and enduring feature of the U.S. system. The fragmented arm's-length quality of the dialogue between the U.S. international financial community and foreign policy apparatus poses a minimal hindrance for both U.S. bankers and foreign policy officials during normal times; maintenance of the distance between the two groups may, in fact, offer distinct advantages to both. The arrangement leaves American commercial bankers free to pursue international business based on entrepreneurial assessments, while government officials are not obliged to assume responsibility for the international actions of banks or to accommodate explicitly the banks' overseas interests when making U.S. foreign policy. There is a principle involved, and it was put simply by an official of the New York Fed: "The [U.S.] government shouldn't be telling banks where to lend money, and banks shouldn't be telling the government where to send troops. . . . The distinction that 'we [in the government] have our job, you [in the banks] have your job' serves well."[51] The alternatives to this arm's-length arrangement, furthermore, are decidedly impractical, given the independence of U.S. private enterprise in general from the U.S. public sector: if the government were to make a practice of telling banks where to lend, it would almost certainly be obligated to indemnify them against any resulting losses.

Nevertheless, during periods when the affairs of foreign policy and international banking become snarled, there may be pragmatic reasons for seeking concerted action from U.S. foreign policy officials and bankers. Such a period surely existed, for example, during late 1982 and early 1983, when U.S. foreign policy officials became seriously concerned with maintaining the continued "stability of funding sources for countries friendly to the United States."[52] Concurrently, American and other banks confronted a lengthening list of requests for sovereign debt reschedulings of unprecedented magnitude. These and similar circumstances may require that U.S. officials and bankers attempt to put institutional barriers and even principles aside to devise solutions to shared problems. During such uncommon times, bank-government institutional relationships along German or Japanese lines may be better able to produce quick, synchronized responses to international problems possessing political and financial dimensions.

As issues of foreign policy and international banking become increasingly intermeshed in the 1980s, predicaments demanding concerted action by U.S. commercial bankers and foreign policy officials are likely to occur more frequently; in a sense, they may become increasingly normal. Given these changing circumstances, one must wonder whether it would be possible (and desirable) to develop a system of U.S. bank-government coordination that could be activated only during periods of international financial-political crisis. In any event, U.S. foreign policy

51. Interview with senior official of the Federal Reserve Bank of New York, New York City, November 29, 1982.
52. Interview with senior staff member, National Security Council, Washington, D.C., December 2, 1982.

officials and bankers face challenging work if they are to develop an effective understanding of what aspects of U.S. bank-government relations impede or facilitate cooperation and information exchange during times of peril.

Implications of Unwitting Coordination

Second, American foreign policy officials must ponder the implications of the "unwitting coordination" that may bring U.S. international banking patterns progressively more in line with U.S. foreign policy over the coming years. For commercial reasons alone, U.S. bankers are likely to show special interest in countries outside the industrialized West where they surmise a "U.S. political umbrella" exists. (Examples of such countries during the early 1980s probably included South Korea, Mexico, and Egypt.) Regardless of the ethic of separateness in U.S. bank-government relations, U.S. banks will logically lend internationally where they believe U.S. foreign policy objectives enhance the likelihood of repayment. Yet, as already suggested, many U.S. international bankers may know little more about U.S. foreign policy than what they learn from the media.

In some cases, bankers may calculate accurately the long-term designs of U.S. foreign policy; in other cases, however, they may guess wrong. In either event, U.S. banks may commit financial resources in selected countries to such an extent that their actions end up shifting the course of U.S. foreign policy. Because this de facto coordination of commercial banking activities and foreign policy objectives hinges on bankers' *perceptions* of those objectives, U.S. officials should be aware of the hazards they incur by sending signals that are open to inaccurate interpretation in the marketplace. This unwitting coordination will probably occur more frequently in the future, regardless of the extent of any overt bank-government dialogue or of the intentions of U.S. officials. At minimum, U.S. officials should be alert to this likelihood and its potential for enormously complicating U.S. foreign policy.

Protecting Foreign Policy from Banking Commitments

A third and corollary point is that U.S. officials should actively consider ways in which they can buffer U.S. foreign policy interests from the international activities of American banks. Recent experience suggests that the new global dimensions of U.S.-sourced international banking may both limit and define the foreign policy options available to the U.S. government in an increasing number of instances. American commercial banking abroad can create a tangible American financial stake in another country, in addition to a commercial commitment to the survival of the regime in power there, which U.S. foreign policy may eventually be forced to acknowledge. American foreign policy officials may be increasingly drawn into crises at the eleventh hour, without their prior endorsement or even prior knowledge of the banks' activities.

When Indonesia's Pertamina nearly went bankrupt during 1975–76, for example, some American banks apparently looked naturally (and successfully) to their government for support in obtaining restructuring of billions of dollars of loans, even though American officials had been previously unaware of the full extent of the banks' financial involvement in Indonesia.[53] More recently, massive U.S. bank lending to Mexico helped precipitate that country's 1982 financial crisis, which in turn created a foreign policy imbroglio of major proportions for the Reagan administration. In retrospect, it seems clear that U.S. foreign policy officials (and even bankers) were surprised at how rapidly Mexico had been accumulating commercial bank debt; it is similarly apparent that some major U.S. banks, and possibly banks from other industrial countries as well, had lent to Mexico in part because of their belief that the U.S. government would always ensure its southern neighbor's solvency. In sum, U.S. commercial banking commitments abroad can alter the stakes of U.S. foreign policy and frame the circumstances in which officials must take action.

Need for Greater Governmental Expertise

A fourth point, following from both of the last two, is that the U.S. government must develop expanded international banking expertise within its ranks. A greater official understanding of the operations of international financial markets, combined with more detailed information on commercial bank decisionmaking and attitudes, would constitute an important first step toward shielding U.S. foreign policy objectives from commercial banking pursuits. More extensive bank-government contacts would be an indispensable aid to U.S. officials in their efforts

---

53. See "The Pertamina Affair" (editorial), *Euromoney* (June 1975), p. 3.

to achieve this end; indeed, U.S. commercial bankers should want such contact themselves as a means of acquiring a better grasp of U.S. foreign policy processes and of protecting themselves from misperceptions of official intentions.

A further reason for the U.S. government to develop greater international banking expertise is its record to date of intervening in banking affairs for foreign policy reasons. Fundamentally, that record could be better. For example, when the U.S. government froze Iranian assets on deposit with U.S. banks in November 1979, it did so without knowing the exact quantity of assets affected, and almost certainly without understanding the complex ramifications of the move in international financial markets. With hindsight, some well-placed observers within the U.S. government argue that the apparent success of the freeze was as much a result of luck as of any calculated designs by U.S. officials.[54] Even three years after the freeze was lifted, its long-term effects on foreign investors' willingness to place funds with U.S. banks remained difficult to assess. Government intervention was again considered as early as four days after the imposition of martial law in Poland in December 1981, when Reagan administration officials debated whether to employ U.S. bank loans as a lever to exert pressure on the Polish government.[55] Some insightful observations written in light of commercial lending to Poland during the summer of 1980 seem appropriate:

Banks are political instruments. They always have been. To use that influence wisely and effectively, however, is a complicated and fraught process and the degree of public intervention must depend on each situation. There can be no simple rule of thumb.[56]

Successive U.S. administrations, regardless of ideological bent, are likely to continue to contemplate using the U.S. banking system as a foreign policy lever under extraordinary circumstances. Given the financial magnitude of U.S. banks' far-flung international relationships, a potent political instrument indeed exists here. Yet the possibility of its misuse is both real and immediate, and the consequences for the international financial system could be disastrous. Improved interna-

54. To one experienced onlooker within the German financial community, this "typically American" move displayed the finesse of "an elephant in a china shop." Interview with official of the Federation of German Banks, Cologne, July 2, 1980.

55. Seth Lipsky, "Officials Argue U.S. Role on Polish Debt," *Wall Street Journal*, January 7, 1982.

56. Jonathan Power, "Banks as Political Instruments," *International Herald Tribune*, September 11, 1980.

tional banking expertise within the U.S. government could at least help reduce this risk of misuse and lessen official reliance on luck.

German and Japanese Advantages

Fifth, as Western European and Japanese banks have also become more aggressively involved in international finance, the overlap has increased between their own commercial pursuits abroad and their home governments' foreign policies. In Germany and Japan, this growing overlap has proved unavoidable, not only because of the expanding international roles that their banks began to assume in the 1970s, but also because of the increasingly active, global orientation of both countries' foreign policies (for example, in shaping common strategies among the major industrial countries, pursuing improved relations with various Communist countries, and advancing relations with the developing world). This coincidence of banking and foreign policy activities has been further strengthened by the economic focus of both countries' foreign policies. With mechanisms already in place in Germany and Japan to effect coordination between commercial banking and foreign policy, however, an increase in their convergence will produce consequences for these two countries decidedly different from (and less problematic than) those likely to emerge in the United States.

A Cohesive Foreign Policy

Sixth, the differences that exist among American, German, and Japanese bank-government relations in the international sphere necessarily raise important and difficult questions about the cohesiveness of U.S. policies abroad. The occasional synchronization of commercial banking and foreign policy pursuits in Germany and Japan may give those countries a more broad-based, coherent foreign policy than that of the United States. In both Germany and Japan, banks and government appear less likely to work at cross-purposes abroad and more likely to be informed of each other's international interests and objectives. In addition, both the German and Japanese governments appear more able and willing to use their countries' internationally active banks as positive tools of foreign policy.

If U.S. foreign policy interests were invariably the same as those of Germany and Japan, their greater ability to achieve bank-government coordination would logically be either a matter of indifference to U.S. officials or a cause for minor celebration. But Germany and Japan have assumed increased responsibility for charting their own courses in international political waters over the last decade. Although the foreign policy objectives of the three countries have remained similar on many "high" political issues, their interests in the international economic sphere (for example, regarding OPEC, East-West trade, and the expansion of economic and financial relations with the developing world) have frequently been at odds and actually competitive. Especially in this international economic and trade sphere, bank-government coordination may strengthen German and Japanese foreign policy capabilities. The United States, lacking as sophisticated a capacity for bank-government accommodation, has probably forgone a measure of effectiveness in advancing its own economic interests. Germany's and Japan's gains in this area may be the United States' loss.

At least since the end of World War II, strategic military issues have dominated the official international concerns of the United States. Of the many forces that have shaped U.S. foreign policy throughout the postwar era, none have exerted a greater impact than the fear of Soviet hegemony and the need to maintain the strength and unity of the Western alliance. During the 1970s, however, while U.S. foreign policy continued to be preoccupied with high political and military concerns, economic pressures began to assume rapidly increasing weight in international relations. Among the major Western industrial countries, none has placed less *relative* importance on the economic dimensions of its foreign policy than the United States. At the same time, Germany and Japan have enjoyed remarkable freedom to pursue economically oriented foreign policies by virtue of the military umbrella that the United States has held over them since the end of World War II.[57] In tackling a new generation of international trade and financial problems, Germany and Japan may therefore possess certain comparative advantages.

The significance of economic issues in world politics is likely to

57. Disparities in the three countries' defense spending (as a percentage of GNP) provide one imperfect measure of the greater emphasis that U.S. foreign policy has continued to devote to military issues. In 1982, for example, the United States spent about 7.0 percent of its GNP on defense, compared with Germany's 2.8 percent and Japan's 0.9 percent. For defense spending figures, see International Institute for Strategic Studies, *Military Balance, 1982–1983* (London: IISS, 1982), pp. 4, 36, 87. For GNP figures, see International Monetary Fund, *International Financial Statistics—1983 Yearbook* (Washington, D.C.: IMF, 1983), pp. 237, 311, 525.

continue to expand over the coming years. For the foreseeable future, and for the benefit of Germany and Japan as well as the United States, American foreign policy will probably remain preoccupied with strategic military issues. But this fact need not preclude development of an improved official U.S. capability to respond to international economic problems. Nor does it preclude development of a comprehensive official U.S. policy, from a broad-based foreign policy perspective, toward American international banking.

Can U.S. Banks Compete?

Finally, the differences in bank-government relations in the United States, Germany, and Japan raise questions about the ability of U.S. banks to compete abroad. Even today, the largest American banks as a group retain a decided competitive advantage in many areas of international finance, reflecting, among other factors, their more established positions in a number of world markets, the depth and advanced state of their management expertise, and their generally greater technological sophistication relative to European and Japanese banks.[58] In comparison to U.S. banks' unrivaled status in the mid-1970s, however, that advantage has diminished, and it may well erode further as competition among U.S. and foreign banks intensifies in international markets during the 1980s. Much of the increased pressure that the largest American banks began to face abroad during the late 1970s and early 1980s was a function of the relatively faster growth rates of many foreign institutions. As a 1981 study commissioned by the American Bankers Association noted:

The largest U.S. banks are clearly losing ground to their foreign counterparts in size, as measured by deposits. As foreign banks grow in size, their ability and rationale for more active participation in foreign banking markets will increase, as defined by a diminution of size constraints.[59]

But in addition, foreign banks have often seemed to benefit from stronger home government advocacy of their foreign interests in recent years, including strong support in gaining access to foreign markets. In this regard, the same study made the following observations based on

58. See Peter Merrill Associates for the American Bankers Association, *The Future Development of U.S. Banking Organizations Abroad* (Washington, D.C.: ABA, 1981), pp. 17, 26.
59. Ibid., p. 17.

interviews of senior U.S. bankers located in nine major foreign financial centers:

> It was pointed out repeatedly in the interviews that the U.S. authorities are almost unique among regulators in major banking markets in not effectively supporting U.S. banks overseas in their effort to obtain less discriminatory treatment. However, in instances where U.S. diplomatic and other official bodies have agreed that a discriminatory practice exists and representations are made to local authorities, the general perception of U.S. bankers abroad is that such official representations have not been particularly effective. The lack of effectiveness is attributable by the bankers to a lack of negotiation commitment and toughness on the part of the [U.S.] authorities involved as well as a related realization by their foreign counterparts that the U.S. is not prepared to maintain a strong negotiating position.[60]

The international competitiveness of American banks has also been hurt by the U.S. government's comparatively circumscribed use of export-financing programs. In Germany and Japan, banks have benefited from massive official guarantee or financing schemes that have enhanced the attractiveness of commercial or partly commercial export financing available from those countries. While the U.S. government operates analogous credit support programs through such agencies as its Export-Import Bank and Commodity Credit Corporation, U.S. programs have tended to be more limited in scope, less imaginative, and more subject to fluctuation in response to the vagaries of domestic politics.[61] Moreover, U.S. programs, unlike those of Germany and especially Japan, have been geared primarily to react to foreign governments' initiatives rather than to promote specific national economic objectives in an active, positive way.[62]

60. Ibid., p. 35.
61. During 1978–80, for example, the Export-Import Bank experienced considerable difficulty in obtaining even necessary legal authority for its operations from Congress; similarly, shortly after President Reagan assumed office in January 1981, the bank was constrained by a five-month moratorium on approvals of new long-term loans and guarantees. A problem of fundamental importance in this context has been the U.S. government's continued failure to develop a consistent export policy, even within individual administrations.
62. For an excellent and more detailed analysis of the major issues involved in government financing of exports, see Penelope Hartland-Thunberg and Morris H. Crawford, *Government Support for Exports: A Second-Best Alternative* (Lexington Books for the Georgetown University Center for Strategic and International Studies, 1982), pp. 63–82. The authors argue, in part, that a U.S. shortage of official finance at competitive rates has resulted from "limited authorizations of funds for Eximbank's discount-loan and direct-loan programs and [from] congressional resistance to increasing the contingent liability of the United States (for example, through the use of government

Current official U.S. export-financing programs are of limited usefulness to major American banks seeking to structure internationally
competitive export financing packages. In fact, a growing number of
American bankers have privately come to view the U.S. Export-Import
Bank as neither a help nor a hindrance to their international business;
they are indifferent to the bank's existence in present form. Frustrated
with the scope of official U.S. programs, many American banks have
begun to offer joint export financing with European governments. (A
senior officer of one of the largest U.S. commercial banks indicated in
late 1982, in fact, that his institution has made more money under
France's COFACE export finance programs than from financings undertaken jointly with the U.S. Export-Import Bank.)[63] Because the
involvement of an official European export-support program can prove
instrumental in making an export-financing package competitive, more
and more American multinational corporations, occasionally with U.S.
bank encouragement, are choosing to make international tender offers
through European subsidiaries.[64] An American failure to maintain a
competitive export-financing capability over the coming years is almost
certain to have an adverse impact on the continued growth of U.S.
exports, the number of American jobs in export-related industries, the
U.S. trade balance, and the country's commercial position in overseas
markets. In many cases, a loss of American export sales further implies

---

guarantees)." The subsidy involved in the direct loan program has been limited primarily
by an Eximbank tradition, not congressionally mandated, of being a self-supporting
institution. "As long as U.S. market interest rates were relatively low, this tradition
was not a constraint, but it became a serious one in the late 1970s when U.S. market
rates soared." In the authors' view, the U.S. Congress should remove this constraint
"by confirming that Eximbank's mission is to provide export finance at competitive
rates (which existing legislation does), not to make a profit." A number of observers
concur that these two goals are mutually exclusive. The U.S. Eximbank, in fact, is the
only such institution using its own resources to support current operations. See ibid.,
pp. 70–71.

63. Interview with senior official of a major U.S. commercial bank, New York City,
November 29, 1982. COFACE is an acronym for Compagnie Francaise d'Assurance
pour le Commerce Exterieur, a state institution that provides credit insurance and
guarantees for commercial and political risks in conjunction with the financing of French
exports.

64. During 1981, for example, at least one major U.S. bank ran advertisements
describing its ability to provide joint financing with several European governments'
export support programs. The advertisements appeared in a number of American as
well as overseas business and financial publications.

a loss of international business (and market position) by American banks
to foreign banks.

Conclusion

A number of questions are raised by these comparisons. Can large
American banks develop a closer rapport with the foreign policy apparatus of the U.S. government and still retain their independence to make
international business decisions based on commercial criteria? Would
closer rapport assist the U.S. government in pursuing important foreign
policy objectives? Can measures be taken to promote greater coordination during periods of crisis that would leave unaltered the basic arm's-
length nature of U.S. bank-government relations at other times? Can the
government do more to defend U.S. foreign policy interests from the
entangling, often unpredictable consequences of U.S. (and other) commercial banks' international pursuits? Concurrently, can or should the
government do more to advance the international interests of U.S.
commercial banks? This study, while seeking to define a number of
complex policy questions resulting from the interaction of commercial
banking and foreign policy, does not claim to resolve them. The issues
involved deserve a thorough public debate in the United States, in which
easy answers will prove elusive.

A continued American failure to grasp more fully the public policy
implications of international banking is no longer affordable. A major
education process lies ahead, and it would be aided critically by a better
understanding of the patterns of coordination that exist between internationally active banks and government in other industrial countries.
The United States cannot and should not attempt to copy those patterns,
but it could learn much from them—even about its own institutions and
customs. In addition, the development of a greater awareness within the
U.S. financial community of the goals and objectives of U.S. foreign
policy would seem not only feasible but desirable. So would a deeper
understanding among U.S. foreign policy officials of American banks'
international operations, their significance in extending U.S. influence
abroad and in advancing U.S. foreign economic goals, and their potential
for complicating the execution of U.S. foreign policy.

Index

Abs, Hermann, 26, 36, 51n, 77
Ackley, Gardner, 104n
Adenauer administration, 31
Amakudari, 106
American Bankers Association, 210
Anti-Monopoly Act, *1977,* Japan, 112
Argentina, Japanese syndicated credit to, 142, 144
Association of Southeast Asian Nations (ASEAN), 127, 128, 138

Bahrain, 150–51
Balance of payments, 129, 133; and bank-government relations, 152
Bank-government relations, Japan: compared with United States and West Germany, 8–9, 93–94, 135, 181–83, 192, 193; and current-account disequilibria, 145–62; factors influencing, 104–08, 121–33, 181–82; and foreign policy, 93–96, 114–17, 135–36, 175–76, 182–83; government coordination of, 94, 95, 96, 101, 102, 103–10, 116, 129–34, 181–83; and overseas lending by Bank of Tokyo, 136–44; and overseas resources development, 162–75. *See also* Banking system, Japan; Foreign policy, Japan
Bank-government relations, United States: and balance of payments, 152; compared with Japan and West Germany, 8–9, 93–94, 183, 185, 192, 193; factors influencing, 188–92; and foreign policy, 193–210, 213; and international competitiveness of banks, 210–12; nature of, 190, 194, 203–04. *See also* Banking system, United States; Foreign policy, United States
Bank-government relations, West Ger-

many: and balance of payments, 152; Big Three banks and, 23–25, 27–28, 36, 180; compared with Japan and United States, 8–9, 93–94, 183, 192, 193; factors influencing, 13–14; and foreign policy, 13–15, 31–34, 62–63, 66, 74, 88, 135, 179–80, 182–83; government coordination of, 14–15, 27–28, 30–34, 37–41, 62–63, 88–89, 180–83; history of, 34–37. *See also* Banking system, West Germany; Foreign policy, West Germany
Banking Law, Japan, 102, 103, 104, 105
Banking system, Japan: categories in, 96–98; compared with United States and West Germany, 96–97, 100, 102, 185; concentration in, 96, 100–02, 181; criteria for overseas lending, 136, 142–43; domestic assets, 185; functional specialization, 102, 132; government supervision of, 95, 96, 102, 103–08, 109–10, 129–32, 145–56, 182; interaction with corporate sector, 94, 96, 110–14; international capabilities, 93, 94, 119–21, 137, 139; licensing of banks, 103, 105; response to current-account changes, 145–52; share of international market, 5, 6. *See also* Bank-government relations, Japan; Foreign policy, Japan
Banking system, United States: compared with Japan and West Germany, 96–97, 100, 185; concentration in, 96, 100, 185, 186; domestic assets, 185; international capability, 5–6, 186–88, 210–13; government supervision of, 19n, 191, 193, 196–98, 200–01, 204; regional dispersion of, 188–90, 195–96. *See also* Bank-government relations, United States; Foreign policy, United States